DATE DUE

NEW FORMS OF SECURITY

To our children

New Forms of Security

Views from Central, Eastern and Western Europe

Edited by
PÁL DUNAY, GÁBOR KARDOS
Eötvös Loránd University, Budapest
and
ANDREW J. WILLIAMS
University of Kent at Canterbury

Dartmouth

Aldershot • Brookfield USA • Singapore • Sydney

Published by
Dartmouth Publishing Company Limited
Gower House
Croft Road
Aldershot
Hants GU11 3HR
England

Dartmouth Publishing Company
Old Post Road
Brookfield
Vermont 05036
USA

British Library Cataloguing in Publication Data
New Forms of Security: Views from Central, Eastern
   and Western Europe
   I. Dunay, Pál
   327.116094

Library of Congress Cataloging-in-Publication Data
New forms of security : views from Central, Eastern and Western Europe
/ edited by Pál Dunay, Gábor Kardos and Andrew J. Williams.
      p.   cm.
   Includes bibliographical references.
   ISBN 1-85521-621-3
   1. Security, International. 2. Europe–Foreign relations.
3. Europe–Military policy. 4. Europe–Economic policy.   I. Dunay,
Pál. II. Kardos, Gábor. III. Williams, Andrew J., 1951-
JX1961.E8N49   1995
327.4–dc20
                                                                95-13056
                                                                    CIP

ISBN 1 85521 621 3

Printed and bound in Great Britain by
Ipswich Book Co. Ltd., Ipswich, Suffolk

Contents

Acknowledgements

The chapters that make up this book were originally presented to a workshop at the University of Kent at Canterbury in May 1994. We would like to thank the Faculty of Social Sciences and the Department of Politics and International Relations at the University for their financial and other support of this event. We would also like to thank the Department for its sponsoring of Professor Khroustalev's stay in Britain, and the British Council for its long-standing support of the link between the University of Kent and that of the Eötvös Loránd University in Budapest. Many people who do not figure in this book contributed to the discussion and their views have been taken into account. In particular we would like to acknowledge the contribution of Professors Clive Church and John Groom, Sir John Robson, formerly of the Foreign and Commonwealth Office, excellent graduate students too numerous to name and others who cannot be named. We would also like to thank Irene Knell for her excellent organization of the workshop and Gill Hogarth, Bob Eager and the staff of Darwin College who provided us with a room for our deliberations and made us very welcome.

The editors would like to say a particular thank you to Jane Williams who edited the final manuscript and prepared it as camera-ready copy and to the copy-editors and others at Dartmouth who did their usual thorough job.

Introduction

It has become a truism to say that the security agenda for the 1990s cannot be the same as that which prevailed during the 'Long Peace' of the period 1945 - 1990.[1] It might also be argued that we do not need another book to add to the other premature assessments of the changed security situation in Europe. We do not believe that this is the case, but rather that what is lacking is, firstly, an inability on the part of Western political scientists to actually listen to what our Central and East European colleagues are saying about their security situation, and take on board their perspectives and concerns. Secondly, we are convinced that there are wider theoretical conclusions that need to be drawn from such an exchange, in all the areas covered in this book - military, economic and humanitarian security, as well as the wider concerns of international relations in the broad sense.

This book could equally well have been entitled 'New Forms of Insecurity', especially when seen from a Central or East European perspective. They have had to change their view of the world in all areas of human experience far faster and more radically than we have in the West. There is a danger that in focusing on Western European security needs, such as the (real) need to limit migration flows, nuclear proliferation and 'spillover' from conflicts such as those in the former Yugoslavia we will ignore the needs of those who are direct victims of instability in the area. We can have no complacency about the security problems facing the whole of Europe today. Any recent discussion with an ex-Soviet citizen will reveal a depth of dangerous despair about what they have lost that must temper our glee about having 'won' the Cold War. There are practical security problems on virtually every frontier where civilizations and mentalities meet. There may not be the 'civilisational divide' posited by Samuel Huntington, but we do not harbour any romantic notions of a European race that essentially shares all its norms and can easily live in peace. The European psyche still harbours far too many contradictory urges for it to be at peace with itself. This book is an attempt to elucidate what it means to be a 'European' by focusing on our fears for our collective future and our proposals to improve it.

It is nonetheless probably true that too many academics have rushed into print too fast declaring the changed situation and coming up with such proposals.[2] It is understandable that we should have done so, as the normative and practical implications of the changes in Europe have seemingly opened up vast new vistas of theoretical musing, most of which seems to confirm broadly Western views of ideal governance.[3] In so doing we have undoubtedly prematurely written off much that was useful, for example in the realist tradition.[4] There is however a great temptation to do so given the proliferation of inter-community strife across the globe, and the seeming lack of good old-fashioned inter-state conflict. In this volume Jaap de Wilde and Mark Khroustalev show that this chorus can be heard from different ends of Europe. There is a clear need to think more about the links between domestic and inter-national 'societal' security concerns and not be overly-obsessed with traditional inter-state security concerns, even if they have not by any means entirely disappeared. This book reflects the paradigm shift that can be said to be occurring in security studies, one which brings it into close contact with an equally shifting theoretical debate in international relations.

The problem is that what seems an interesting if bewildering theoretical shift for most academics in Britain and, especially, the United States, has immense day-to-day implications for the peoples of much of Central and Eastern Europe. Their threat perceptions may have changed from worrying about a superpower confrontation, but they have reverted to fear of each other, both internally (as with aggressive 'minorities' or 'majorities') or externally, as with the expressed expansionist aims of Serbia or the fear of a Russian irredentism. This is the pure raw material of the 'Eastern Question' come back to haunt the corridors of power. There have also been useful warning, if perhaps misdirected, notes of caution sounded by writers about the supposed stability of the European Union, like John Mearsheimer who has famously pointed to the dangers inherent in an American pull-out from Europe.[5] This book's main aim is to demonstrate that it is not only Western European political scientists that are concerned to define what the practical results of the changes that are taking place should be for their ongoing and far more troubled security debate.

The chapters of this book demonstrate that a European-wide consensus is emerging that needs to be fully absorbed by the institutional structures that attempt to direct security matters on the continent. The word 'emerging' is carefully chosen, because the authors in this book are modest enough to admit that we are as yet far too close to the dawn of our new era to be able to fully perceive what its full implications will be. We are also too diverse (and stubborn!) in our methodological and empirical foci to be able to yet change course towards each other to find a clear consensus that we could yet fully recommend to policy makers.

One initial common question - what is security? - has directed the planning of this book. There is an awareness now that the Cold War may have provided order and thus security, an absence of violence, but not a 'positive' security, a feeling of being safe. The ever-present dangers of nuclear war, which provided a kind of order have now been replaced by a seemingly more unstable balance of power, because there are a) far more actors on the stage (a multilateral imbalance) and b) far more issues that might `provoke a threat. The first of these factors initially exercised Mearsheimer and others. Among the new issues we can enumerate the obvious ones of hyper-nationalism and its more vague but potent idea of identity, and economic insecurity and its corollary of relative deprivation (where different sections of the continent recognize their relative lack of access to collective and individual goods widely available elsewhere). From these flow concerns about military security and the fear of widespread abuse of human rights, as well as a vague but undifferentiated feeling of being threatened by everything and nothing at the same time. Europe has become prey to its old demons and new phantoms.

Another question that has resurfaced with the growing attempts at the integration of Western Europe is that of what we really now mean by the state. One recent commentator wrote: 'The nation state is weakening, but its weakening is not leading to the political integration of Europe which the idealists of forty years ago hoped for, and which - for economic and security reasons - European governments now need'.[6] Some writers have used this in a wider assault on the whole 'realist' programme in international relations, as does Jaap de Wilde in this collection, and others elsewhere.[7]

One other common question that analysts of many different intellectual persuasions are now beginning to address is that of how new agendas are created and how they are mediated into practical policy decisions and processes. New agendas are created by new circumstances. Over the past forty years or so the dominance of the Superpowers has been one linked mainly, but not exclusively, to their leadership of the great security alliances, notably the North Atlantic Treaty Organization (NATO) and the Warsaw Treaty Organization (WTO). We now need to ask what appropriate level of action (state, international organization etc.) is needed to meet what security needs (national, sub-national, regional), as well as to ask what threats need to be met. The contributors to this book see them as many and varied, but a common approach needs to be found that will deal with them all, or at least make sense of whatever linking factors there are between them.

Hence this book is formally divided up into 'sections', but it nonetheless recognizes links between these sections and the existence within them of quite differing perceptions of where the major threats to security lie. The first group of writers looks at perceptions of the military situation from three perspectives, 'Western', 'Central' and 'Eastern'. This is necessarily the largest single group of chapters in the book because an analysis of these issues is very dependent on a wide range of views, which in turn are dependent on perceptions of where the future military threats will originate, both internally and externally, to states and more widely related to regional perceptions.

Security in Europe has not been regarded as identical with military preparedness for some time now. This awareness has been given a new momentum since the end of the Cold War, especially in Western and Central Europe where the risks are clearly of a non-military nature. Since the end of the Second World War the essential question has been about how security could be provided by military forces and how such forces could contribute to the achievement of the objective of peace. There is a fundamental difference between the assessment of the role of military security during the period of the East-West conflict and during the post-Cold War era. Whereas during the former period the views of both East and West were largely identical there is now a fundamental difference of views in the various countries of the new Europe. As there is such a divergence of view about the assessment of the underlying strategic and political situation there can be no unanimity concerning a plausible military strategy.

Pál Dunay aims to debunk certain myths of military security in the post-Cold War era, starting with the assumption that military activity in Western and Central Europe has become even more difficult to understand than in past decades. One simply cannot know which eventualities are being prepared for by the armed forces of Europe. As the author argues, the declared military doctrines of the Central European states have to grapple with the problem that there can be no clear basis for them. Hence it is only in Russia, and to a certain extent in the countries of the 'near abroad', that we can have an understanding of the role of the military. Dunay also concludes that for the foreseeable future the significant reductions in the military establishments of Western and Central Europe cannot contribute to economic regeneration, even if for substantially different reasons. Finally he deals with the danger of the nationalization of military doctrines and strategies and concludes that this does not *per se* constitute any sizeable military risk and that to understand any possible inherent risks requires a detailed analysis. It is much more the content of the doctrines and strategies that might be perceived as threatening than the mere fact of their national elaboration.

Dan Hiester writes from an American perspective to highlight the changing view that the United States is developing both its commitment to the security structures of Europe and to how Europe should organize these structures. In particular he examines the NATO Partnership for Peace (PfP) initiative from an American and Western European perspective. Monika Wohlfeld looks at some of main supposed beneficiaries of the PfP in Central Europe and asks how their threat perceptions have evolved since the demise of the WTO. She stresses that there are major differences between the main countries of the region and underlines the need to guard against broad generalizations when faced with much ambiguity. But she is quite clear that the threat perceptions of countries in the region are both more diffuse yet more pronounced than ever before.   This has led them to make understandably hasty decisions to reconstruct their military structures at a time of great overall change but with no clear doctrines being enunciated as to what these revamped forces should actually have to do.   The most common ideal is membership of NATO through the PfP, but she also outlines other initiatives.

One of the key questions that is raised by Wohlfeld is that of the threat perceived as coming from Russia, about which she is relatively optimistic. Elaine Holoboff takes a rather less sanguine view.   Russia is now much more aggressive in its demands than even in 1993, and is again aiming to reassert its hegemony over the area, demonstrated by its attitude towards the Ukraine and the CIS in general.   It is also clearly suffering from a political convulsion that has by no means yet been resolved.   Holoboff urges that Western and Central Europe thus must be extremely cautious in its approaches to Russian attempts at peacekeeping in its 'backyard'.   However, she also agrees that any hegemonic desires do not necessarily extend beyond the CIS and that Russia is behaving as great powers always, especially given that there has been very little alternative leadership shown by other Europeans, especially those in NATO.   NATO must therefore develop much more coherent and realistic policies towards Russia and the rest of Europe in general.

Mark Khroustalev takes a perhaps understandably different stance and urges the NATO states to understand the Russian viewpoint.   Moscow sees itself has having made all the changes for the better, and has withdrawn from its former territories, whereas NATO is still in existence,without a corresponding 'enemy'.   If this alliance persists in existence he feels that there will be an inevitable return to confrontational politics and a possible renewal of the Cold War, as the seeming exclusion of Russia from Europe fans the flames of a resentful Russian nationalism.   He therefore echoes other Russians (such as Foreign Minister Andrei Kosyrev)[8] who have urged the abandonment of NATO in favour of a security framework based on the dialogue of the Conference on Security and Cooperation in Europe (CSCE).   The CSCE will act to truly 'integrate' Europe in that it will bring about a fostering of a Europe that is not exclusive.   He also points to the grave dangers of an Eastern Europe excluded from the economic prosperity of the West and the criminalization of Russia if it is not helped along the difficult road to democracy.

John Dunn's discussion of these papers takes up the themes expressed in all of them.   He acknowledges that Russia has genuine security concerns in the CIS and wider region, and that it has especially severe problems with a public opinion alarmed by social dislocation and the loss of so much territory and power.   But he also sounds the alarm as to what might happen if the NATO states persist in a purely reactionary mode of operation, and do not more fully evaluate whether Russian activities are fully consistent with Western (and, it might be added, Central) European concerns and interests.   There are still grounds for believing that the Bear is not as peaceful and well-intentioned as he claims to be.

In the section on economic security issues, Jaap de Wilde has already been cited as believing that there is a need for a totally different view of what security constitutes in a post Cold-War era. His argument concentrates on necessary levels of analysis that need to be examined to make sense of the new situation. He discusses the new idea of 'societal' security at some length. Anna Murphy and Andrew Williams see the threats and the solutions as being in the area of institutional arrangements in the economic sphere. There is a difference of opinion between the two as to what the organizing principle for Europe in this area should be, with Murphy (albeit not with enthusiasm) seeing hope in the development of a pan-European economic and political framework based on the European Union (EU), while Williams puts more faith (albeit hesitantly) in the separate development of strong civil societies in a much looser national framework, within a 'common market'.

Gábor Kardos and Judit Tóth paint a somewhat discouraging picture of a Europe seemingly united in the realization that humanitarian security issues are now at the forefront of the post Cold-War agenda, but seemingly impotent to really resolve how they should be tackled. The area was one where the pre-1990 CSCE could claim a great deal of credit for publicizing abuse of human rights particularly across Central and Eastern Europe. The removal of the Red Army seems, however, to have revitalized old conflicts between 'majority' and 'minority' populations, with the awful results that we have seen in the former Yugoslavia and elsewhere. The member states of the international institutions, including the 'new' CSCE, seem to be unable to assume their responsibilities for these humanitarian problems.

Kardos argues that this is because the nature of the problems in Central and Eastern Europe is not fully understood in the Western part. In particular he stresses that the integration taking place in the West under the auspices of the EU has a foil in the East of a resurgent nationalism, and likewise that the prevailing 'civic' nationalism of Western Europe has as its counterpart an 'ethno' nationalism in the East. He stresses that the causes of conflict in the CEE region are not merely ethnic, as the destabilization of the area has political and economic causes, but that in these circumstances there is little hope of ethnic conflict being reduced. Where the 'majority' feels aggrieved, it is taking its frustrations out on visible 'minorities', frustrations fanned by economic and political uncertainty. Kardos concludes that we must learn from history, even if we must try and repeat its repetition (as has been the case in the former Yugoslavia) and try and help the development of better forms of democracy in the area that will better reflect local particularities and simultaneously protect minorities.

Judit Tóth points to a corollary problem that affects the whole of Europe's security - that of migration. Although the motives for migration can be economic, many are now trying to flee ethnic persecution. The statistics revealed by Tóth are very sobering, but the main thrust of her argument is that the countries of the EU have so far adopted policies to deal with this migration that are less than helpful. She advocates a joint approach by both the EU and the Visegrád countries (Hungary, Poland, and the Czech and Slovak republics) to establish both a better pan-European normative basis and a practical mechanism for dealing with migration, be it forced or voluntary.

The format of this book, and the discussions in Canterbury, England, in May 1994 that are the basis of it, hopefully reflect a useful dialogue that can be read with benefit by anyone concerned with the security debate in Europe over the next ten years.

Andrew J. Williams
Canterbury, December 1994

Notes

1. The expression is of course that popularized by Gaddis: Gaddis, John Lewis (1987), *The Long Peace: Inquiries into the History of the Cold War*, Oxford University Press, New York.
2. This is in part a self-criticism, given Williams, Andrew (ed.) (1994), *Reorganising Eastern Europe: European Institutions and the Refashioning of Europe's Security Architecture*, Dartmouth Publishing Co., Aldershot. Other recent collections on security that we could recommend include Waever, Ole; Buzan, Barry; Kelstrup, Martin and Lemaître, Pierre, (eds) (1993), *Identity, Migration and the New Security Agenda in Europe*, Pinter, London; and Buzan, Barry (1991), *People, States and Fear: An Agenda for Security Studies in the Post-Cold War Era*, Harvester Wheatsheaf, London.
3. For an excellent overview of the normative challenges posed by the changes in Eastern Europe, see Brown, Chris (ed.) (1994), *Political Restructuring in Europe: Ethical Perspectives*, Routledge, London.
4. See for example, Lebow, Ned (1994), 'The long peace, the end of the cold war and the failure of realism', *International Organization*, special issue on 'The End of the Cold War and International Relations', vol. 48, no. 2, Spring 1994, pp. 249-77.
5. Mearsheimer, John (1990), 'Back to the Future', in Lynn-Jones, Sean M. (1991), *The Cold War and After: Prospects for Peace*, M.I.T. Press, Cambridge, Mass.
6. William Wallace (1994), 'Community Integration and the Nation State', *Oxford International Review*, vol. V, no. 3, Summer 1994.
7. One recent and intriguing work attacking realism in an overtly historical-materialist mode uses this attack as a pretext to revitalize Marxism in IR thought; see Rosenberg, Justin (1994), *The Empire of Civil Society: A Critique of the Realist Theory of International Relations*, Verso, London.

8. Kosyrev, Andrei (1994), 'The Lagging Partnership', *Foreign Affairs*, May/June, pp. 59-71.

List of Contributors

Pál Dunay is an Associate Professor in the Department of International Law at the Eötvös Loránd University and Deputy Director of the Hungarian Institute of International Relations in Budapest

John Dunn is a Lecturer at the Conflict Studies Research Centre at the Royal Military Academy, Sandhurst

Daniel Hiester is a Lecturer in International Relations at the University of Kent at Canterbury

Elaine M. Holoboff is the Director of the Programme on Post-Communist Security Studies in the Department of War Studies, King's College, London

Gábor Kardos is an Associate Professor in the Department of International law at the Eötvös Loránd University

Mark Khroustalev is a Professor at the Centre of International Studies at the Moscow State Institute of International Relations (MGIMO)

Anna Murphy is a Lecturer in the Department of Politics at University College Dublin

Judit Tóth is Associate Professor at the Institute of Political Sciences and the Hungarian Academy of Sciences, Budapest

Jaap de Wilde is a Research Associate at the Centre for Peace and Conflict Research in Copenhagen

Andrew Williams is a Senior Lecturer in International Relations and Director of the Graduate School of International Relations at the University of Kent at Canterbury

Monika Wohlfeld is a researcher in the Department of War Studies, King's College, London

Section A:
Rethinking Military Security

1 Debunking Certain Myths of Post-Cold War Military Security in Europe

PÁL DUNAY

Introduction

Europe has never been a united continent. According to historians it has been historically divided into three regions: Western, Central and Eastern Europe.[1] Their frontiers have run through areas which were later identified as the western and eastern perimeters of *Mitteleuropa*. The territory of Prussia, Poland and of the Habsburg Empire belonged to this central area. These three traditionally distinct zones were overshadowed by the East-West division after the end of the Second World War. Even though there were neutral countries in Europe which 'consistently pursue[d] a policy of national interest and not a policy furthering bloc interests...'[2] this did not seriously question the bipolar division of Europe. What one could only suspect during the decades of the East-West conflict has become an undeniable fact thereafter - that some neutral countries (such as Switzerland) were integrated with the West militarily, as well as in other ways. Contingency plans were prepared for their defence, and funds were allocated for this purpose. Thus one can conclude that bipolarity fully dominated the European landscape and, as bipolarity has come to an end in the late 1980s, a broad variety of possibilities has emerged as to what should take its place.

Five years have passed since the fall of the Berlin Wall. Even though a few years is not a long period historically there is no longer reason to doubt that the world has become fundamentally different from that which prevailed during the era of bipolarity. There is now an emerging new international order, even if it is not the object of this chapter to extensively analyze what this new world order might be. It is however relevant for the analysis of post-Cold War military security in Europe that Europe has remained divided and that the bipolar division has been replaced by fragmentation along more than two dividing lines. One may preliminarily conclude that Europe has again been

3

divided into its three historic parts, closely resembling the three main historic regions, even if the frontiers of the three zones are affected by the vanished bipolar order and thus cannot be precisely identified with the three historic regions.

Western Europe, which includes the neutral democracies, is connected by multiple ties that extend to a legally regulated or *de facto* economic, political and military cooperation. The level of integration and the prevalence of democracy provides stability. It is largely impossible to foresee the re-emergence of historic tensions and rivalries in this region, or at least ones that would endanger international security.[3] No state can credibly demonstrate that members of the western security community pose a military threat to any other country in Europe, apart from possibly implementing sanctions against an aggressor. The other region, the former Central European zone, can be characterized as having a certain political and socio-economic instability. It is difficult to list the countries belonging to this group. They are largely identical with the western periphery of the former East, encompassing probably ten countries in all. They are the former non-Soviet Warsaw Treaty member countries, the three Baltic states and Slovenia. Even though the situation of these countries may differ widely in many respects, some common elements have emerged in their international policies. They could all avoid a military escalation of their international conflicts,[4] their political agendas have been dominated by non-military issues and all want to integrate into Western security institutions that have had a significant impact on their international performance. The third group consists of those former republics of the Soviet Union and those former Yugoslav republics which have already been dragged into violent conflicts or could be at any time. The common characteristic feature of these countries is that they fight local wars or have pending conflicts that threaten violent escalation, that military issues play a significant role in their political agenda and given the fact that their integration into Western institutions does not seem realistic in the foreseeable future, that their 'conflict resolution culture' is not affected by western patterns.

If the above presentation of Europe's three regions is correct one can draw the preliminary conclusion that Europe is not aiming at the unification of the old continent but rather the drawing of new borders between East and West[5] or the preservation and maintaince of the current division. The reason for not unifying Europe is not that there are forces which oppose unification, but rather that the developments of the last years that proved that unification is impossible. This chapter on the military aspects of European security will try to demonstrate that it is in the interest of the majority of European countries, as defined by CSCE membership, to militarily integrate those countries which can be integrated as soon as practicable into the western strategic community. There are two reasons for this: Firstly, many of the impediments to integration are based either on western pretexts or misperceptions and; secondly, the integration of those who have demonstrated that their inclusion into the western strategic community would not involve unacceptable security risk can, broadly speaking, contribute to the stabilization of the region neighbouring 'the West'.

Threat perceptions, strategies and doctrines

No credible strategy and military planning are conceiveable without an identification of potential threats and a ranking of them according to their importance. Following the revolutions of 1989, and even more after the termination of massive forward stationing of Soviet forces in Central Europe, the whole strategic landscape changed fundamentally. The previous conflict based on ideological confrontation had a number of important characteristic features that facilitated an understanding of it. First of all, it was a conflict that, regardless of the ups and downs in the process, remained steady during several decades and thus did not require a rapid adaptation to fast changing circumstances. Not even the new rhetoric of the Soviet leadership in the second half of the 1980s made a fundamental conceptual revision necessary. Secondly, it was concentrated in the hands of two blocs and, more importantly, their leaders. It meant the major players had sufficient time to learn what each other's reactions to a given course of action might be and thus to develop a kind of 'intimately adversarial' relationship. Apart from a few exceptions they proved to be rational international actors. Thirdly, though the conflict had a systemic nature, and thus an all-embracing character, it had a separable military component. In sum, it was comparatively easy to conceptualize such a conflict, and thus to develop concepts to deter its military escalation and elaborate the necessary strategic plans.

In sharp contrast with this the situation has changed constantly since the end of the East-West conflict. Henceforth, adaptation will be a permanent feature of European security. Its formation is no longer concentrated in the hands of a few actors. A bigger number of states play an active role in it and non-state actors (e.g. ethnic groups and their organizations) also have their input into the process. Not all of them are influenced by rational considerations. Finally, the sources of conflict are diverse and even though some, most frequently ethnic, rivalries and territorial claims, are made responsible for many of them it is unlikely one could give an exhaustive catalogue of those potential threats to European security in the long run. These difficulties have been reflected in the ambiguous analysis and the partially inadequate conclusions of the post-East-West conflictual European environment.

NATO

The North Atlantic Alliance (NATO) adopted a new strategic concept in

November 1991. Participants at the meeting, having taken into consideration the 'radically improved strategic environment', concluded that:

> '[r]isks to Allied security are less likely to result from calculated aggression against the territory of the Allies, but rather from the adverse consequences of instabilities that may arise from the serious economic, social and political difficulties, including ethnic rivalries and territorial disputes, which are faced by many countries in Central and Eastern Europe. The tensions that may result, as long as they remain limited, should not directly threaten the security and the territorial integrity of members of the Alliance. They could, however, lead to crises inimical to European stability and even to armed conflicts, which could involve outside powers or spill over into NATO countries, having a direct effect on the security of the Alliance'.[6]

Two conflicting interpretations of the statement seem equally convincing. On the one hand, the Alliance correctly observed that either the potential sources of threat or their origin cannot be easily identified. On the other, however, the rather vague language about possible threats reflects that the sixteen had no clear idea about what realistic scenarios could threaten the security of the member states. Neither was it entirely clear who the authors had in mind when they referred to the role of 'outside powers' which could get involved in armed conflicts. The only potential threat might have been the then still existent Soviet Union. On logical grounds one should exclude such an interpretation as the strategic concept dealt with that country explicitly in a separate paragraph, which stated that 'its conventional forces are significantly larger than those of any other European State and its large nuclear arsenal comparable only with that of the United States'.[7] One may suspect that the drafting of the strategic concept was not dominated by logical considerations, but rather by bureaucratic and inter-governmental compromise. Thus, one can imagine the Soviet Union was mentioned both as an outside power likely to get involved in armed conflicts and as a source of concrete military concerns. One could conclude that the only identifiable, though remote, threat could emerge from the Soviet Union. It is clear from the statement that the Alliance did not deem any common action necessary if tensions in Central and Eastern Europe 'remain limited', i.e. do not spill over onto the territory of NATO members. Since the latter was rather unlikely, one can read into the document that the function of the Alliance was to remain unchanged, one of only defending the security of the member states. Such an isolationist approach carried two dangers. Firstly, as a direct threat against the territory of the sixteen members of the Atlantic Alliance seemed highly unlikely the new situation could result in its marginalization and secondly, and more importantly, the unwillingness of NATO to get involved in out of area conflicts in Europe could give a misleading signal to the new democracies. They could see it as implying that if they were to face strategic intimidation then they would have to rely on their own means of defence. Fortunately for them, it was also clear from other NATO documents that the organization was aware that it had to cooperate with its democratizing former adversaries even if it wanted to avoid being drawn into the conflicts of the 'East'.

The new NATO strategy seems to have misunderstood the post-Cold War European environment. The Alliance made a false assessment of the potential threats. As a German analyst wrote: 'NATO analysed the sources of crises in Central and South Eastern Europe and on the periphery of the CIS as potential threats of a classic type ... the same type as those in Northern Africa and Western Asia'.[8] According to Borinski the threat assessment was unrealistic, since it was highly unlikely that the crises in the above areas would spill over into any member state of NATO. The war in former Yugoslavia, for example, has continued for more than three years. None of the neighbouring countries have got involved in this conflict and there has been no sign whatsoever that the conflicts might pose a direct threat to any West European state. 'Nothing was more alien to third parties, including all major European powers or security organizations, than to let themselves ... get involved in these conflicts militarily, apart from a great deal of rhetorical threats and planning'.[9] Even though this prediction did not prove entirely correct - international institutions, including NATO acting as a subcontractor of the United Nations, could not escape a certain, limited involvement in the Yugoslav conflict - the horizontal escalation of the war has been prevented. There was no reason that the limited conflicts in former Yugoslavia or in the CIS would basically affect NATO's threat perception.

In sum, if NATO interprets its security interests narrowly, limiting them to the territory of the member states and to traditional military threats it can observe that it is surrounded by friendly countries that lack both the capability and the intention to pose any risk to itself. It has to contemplate only the long range power projection capacity of Russia which does not seem threatening now but can be regarded as dangerous *in abstracto*. In the light of the absence of a credible military threat it is fairly difficult to conceive what kind of eventuality NATO military planners might prepare for. There is a danger that under such conditions the legitimacy of the organization will diminish.

Central Europe

Military planners in Central Europe, in contrast to their western counterparts, do not have to worry about the absence of a credible threat perception. Their problem is a different one of how to cope with new challenges. There are a number of paradoxical features in the military security situation of Central Europe.[10] It is frequently emphasized that security has diminished in the region and this may be regarded as a correct assessment in the sense that during the East-West conflict under the 'protective umbrella' of the Soviet

Union there was no risk (or desire) to challenge the Central European countries militarily. Paradoxically it was the Soviet Union that posed the biggest threat to the security of the region by imposing a régime on these nations which was not of their own choosing. All international military conflicts in Central Europe between 1953 and 1968 occurred with the involvement of the Soviet Union. Countries of the region have presumed having to face up to two sources of military risk since the end of the East-West conflict. One of them has been the reemergence of revanchism in the Soviet Union and later Russia, the other has been the military escalation of low intensity political conflicts present in the region. The intensity of the former concern has changed several times. It reached its peak during the August 1991 Moscow coup. The dissolution of the Soviet Union put the Central Europeans at ease temporarily, as Russia, the 'core' of the power of the Soviet Union, was detached from most Central European countries. Later, when Russia started to pursue a neo-imperialist policy, and to forcefully implement it in the 'near abroad', the fear of Russia's desire to be recognized as a great power among others in its former sphere of influence, that is in Central and Eastern Europe, has increased. In most cases Russia was not regarded as a concrete military threat, but rather as an abstract danger with a military component. The fears were largely due to the West's propensity to recognize certain special Russian 'rights' in European affairs. This is certainly contrary to the interests of those states which all want to find their place in the future as close to the West, and as far as possible from the East.

The threat perception does not even seem consistent in the individual countries of the region. As one Western analyst stated:

'it is easy to get the impression that different threats are presented to different audiences, depending on the circumstances. One day the audience is confronted with a vision of domestic anarchy and foreign aggression. Another day the same politicians describe their country as exceptionally stable and surrounded by peaceful neighbours ... the latter vision is usually presented to Western bankers and investors; the former to security experts'.[11]

This presentation has contributed to the impression prevalent in western thinking that the region East of the Elbe is to a large extent unstable as a whole. It seems obvious that the primary purpose of presenting such a gloomy picture of the security situation of the region served to attract the attention of the West, to get support for the modernization of the defence sector of the Central European countries and to obtain security guarantees from western security institutions via an early integration. This attempt has failed since it confirmed western suspicions about instability in the region.

The emphasis on the existence of a security vacuum in Central Europe had similarly damaging consequences. If it is assumed that the collapse of the

Warsaw Treaty Organization (WTO) resulted in a security vacuum that had not previously existed, this also implies that the Eastern bloc provided security for its members. Such an assumption is certainly a false one since, as was mentioned above, for most members of the Warsaw Treaty it meant they were deprived of their right to self-determination. The oft-quoted argument, according to which the security vacuum is a temporary phenomenom and that sooner or later something will take its place, most probably some great power, can seem seductive.[12] Rather than there being a security vacuum, something similar does exist, namely an 'adaptation' or 'decision-making' vacuum: an 'adaptation vacuum' in the sense that it is difficult to adapt to the new security constellation in Europe; a 'decision-making vacuum' because most states of the region were deprived of the ability to formulate independent security and defence policies for decades. Consequently, the difficulty of adapting to post-Cold War circumstances generally has been further aggravated specifically by the lack of knowledge in the military-security field. The difficulty caused by the shortage of modern, adequate military equipment has thus been exacerbated by the fact that no state of the former WTO had experience in national strategic-military planning. The Soviet Union/Russia and Romania can be regarded as exceptions since they already had national defence planning during the years of East-West confrontation.

Whereas the West faced one difficulty that it was largely unprepared for, the fundamental change in the European security landscape, the Central Europeans had multiple military-security problems. The politico-military change was accompanied by the apparent inadequacy of military means and the absence of relevant military knowledge. They correctly assumed that under the new conditions there would be very little chance of solving the multitude of problems with which they are faced without external support. This would require integration, or at least close cooperation, with those states and institutions that possess the necessary equipment and knowledge to facilitate the solution of some of them. The new Central European establishments that came to power following the revolutions of 1989 have not recognized the paradox in which they find themselves. This is, that the more instability is present in and around a country, and hence the greater its need to integrate with security institutions in order to get guarantees, the less likely it is that the integration effort will be successful. Hence, it is a precondition of integration that the given country demonstrate that it has made a genuine contribution to stability in its own surroundings.

As the threat perception of the countries of Central Europe is largely similar it is not surprising that their defence policies have some common features, as reflected in their defence doctrines and official pronouncements. They all declare that no country is regarded as their enemy and that their military preparations are not directed against any country. Consequently, they are committed to the idea of a *tout azimuth* defence posture that would allow them to counter aggression from any direction. At least this is the conclusion that can be drawn from the documents publicly available. This is in spite of the fact that it is well known that *tout azimuth* is regarded as a weak form of defence. It is probable, however, that in the confidential part of the defence doctrines and strategic plans the origin of eventual military risks are formulated more specifically, including the identification of countries and sources of priority concern. They all declare that they will continue to respect their obligations not to possess weapons of mass destruction. They are committed to decreasing the size of their armed forces, while improving their effectiveness by increasing mobility. The procurement of defensive weaponry, such as air defence, takes priority.

The area of the former Soviet Union

The third region, the area of the former Soviet Union, differs significantly from Central Europe. Whereas in the former non-Soviet Warsaw Treaty countries military threats have remained abstract and remote, in the Commonwealth of Independent States they are real. Many former Soviet republics are fighting inter-state wars without much chance for a peaceful resolution of the conflicts. The decisive power of the region, Russia, which can be regarded as the country that suffered the biggest loss in the process of the rearrangement of international power relations, acts as a centre of gravity for those twelve countries which belonged to the Soviet Union when it was dissolved. Three years after the dissolution of the USSR many analysts tend to conclude that Russia is attempting to reintegrate the former Soviet Union, or more precisely put the so-called 'new abroad'.[13] This is somewhat of a misconception, in that there is no reason to reintegrate a region that has not disintegrated, except in the formal sense as reflected in the symbols of state sovereignty. It is better to speak about the more visible signs of the efforts of an assertive Russia to tighten the community of the twelve former Soviet republics than about reintegration.

Since the dissolution of the Soviet Union, the development of post-Soviet military cooperation, which has significantly affected national military thinking, can be divided into five distinct phases. Between December 1991 and February 1992, attempts were made to maintain the unity of the former Soviet Union in a military sense. They failed, according to Russian analysts, because of the decision of Ukraine to put forces on its territory under national control. In the second phase, between February and May 1992, a differentiation was made between strategic and general purpose forces, retaining the former under joint command while 'nationalizing' the latter. The third phase, between May 1992 and June 1993, saw the coexistence of two tendencies. On the one hand, nationalization got a new impetus, and on the other, a collective security arrangement under the CIS umbrella was adopted, although without the accession of each CIS state to it.[14] The fourth phase that began following the abolition of the CIS joint military command on 15 June 1993 is the nationalization of defence in the former Soviet area. It will be supplemented by agreements on bilateral cooperation, among other things, on military affairs. A fifth phase of post-Soviet military cooperation began in October-December 1993, for two reasons. One of them was the events of early-October in Moscow when President Yeltsin had to rely heavily on the military in order to consolidate his power and get rid of his political rivals. The other was the result of the December 1993 elections to the Duma. The fact that the new parliament, which held a good portion of extremists and communists, did not mean a disaster for the President could be attributed to two factors - to his powerful constitutional position, but even more to his political wisdom in putting into place a nationalist great power agenda very much in line with the position of many representatives in parliament. Surprising as it may seem, the very same political figures who were celebrated democrats not long ago will try to implement this policy.

It is a matter of taste whether one regards the phase following the completion of Russian troop withdrawals from Germany and the Baltic countries (August 1994) as separate from the ones outlined above. Even though it did not result in a significant change of military thinking from that time on the Russian military has been able to focus its activity exclusively on the twelve former Soviet republics.

Many one-sided analyses have been presented about Russia's role in the region. It is necessary to present both sides of the coin. On the one hand, official statements, among others the military doctrine of the Russian Federation adopted in late 1993, recognized that the danger of aggression against the country had decreased.[15] A fairly peaceful military posture could be developed from this. In fact, under the official military doctrine one could give credit that Russia has no imperialist intentions and prefers stability in the region. Given the fact that the drafters of the document under such conditions faced great difficulties to present a credible description of the military threat, they listed many potential dangers that might lead to military conflict. The document approved by President Yeltsin on 2 November 1993 contained specific references to, for example, the protection of the Russian minority in other countries as one of the directions that would guarantee the military security of the Russian Federation. One has to understand that Russia can hardly remain neutral if the rights of ethnic Russians are massively violated. It is doubtful, however, whether military means are the most effective way of enforcing minority rights.

On the other hand, there is the practice followed by Russia. According to some analysts the elements of 'a new Russian foreign policy have begun to emerge' since mid-1992.[16] If this is correct, one has reason to believe that after recovering from the shock of the dissolution of the Soviet Union the elements of a new Russian foreign and security policy might assume a less pro-western orientation, an insistence upon a recognition of the special interests of Russia in the former USSR, and the right to protect the Russian minority living outside Russia, by force if necessary.

The image of a threatening West is difficult to maintain in the light of the western powers' extensive cooperation with Russia in many fields, including military security and regional conflict resolution. '[T]he enlargement of military blocs and alliances to the detriment of the military security of the Russian Federation' is the only adverse step that seems to refer specifically to an specifically western provocation.[17]   This ambiguous formulation may serve a deterrent purpose, one of preventing the West from considering the enlargement of NATO with the countries of Central Europe.

The 'southern threat', which joins the spread of Islamic fundamentalism, and the possible horizontal escalation of conflicts in former Soviet republics to the territory of Russia is more credible.   As wars continue in the vicinity of Russia the country does not have to make special efforts to depict the situation as highly unstable.   Russia now claims exclusive rights in the management of crises in the former Soviet area.   This is similar to the Monroe Doctrine, declared by the then US President in 1823.   One can regard Moscow's stance as imperialist only in that Russia has engaged selectively in the management of conflicts from Moldova to Tajikistan through Georgia and Azerbaijan. Regardless of concerns that Russia is abusing its power, peacemaking has become an integral part of its military strategy.   It has to be taken into consideration that on the one hand, Russia is very much willing to participate in conflict resolution in the 'near abroad', while on the other, no one else is ready to enter the post-Soviet quagmire to attempt a solution of the violent conflicts in the South of the former USSR.   Either Russia intervenes, under the CIS umbrella, or no one else will.   Russia may be well aware of this.   Before the 1992 Helsinki CSCE Summit the Russian military somewhat anxiously expressed the position of the country by warning that it hoped and expected that 'NATO "blue helmets" w[ould] not participate in the resolution of conflicts between Armenia and Azerbaijan, and Moldova and the Dniester region'.[18] A year later the Russian delegate, well aware of the West's reluctance to get involved in peacekeeping in the CIS was able to express 'the readiness of his country to welcome peacekeeping troops from NATO countries to the former Soviet Union on a case-by-case basis, should the CSCE mandate the operation'.[19] The message was clear - either the West was prepared to tolerate endless killing, or it had to support Russian efforts to keep the peace. Questions remained as to under what conditions and with what types of guarantees such action could be sanctioned.   The most important element is to monitor conflict management in the former Soviet area in order to avoid it taking an aggressive form.

It is not the purpose of this chapter to analyze the threat perceptions and strategies of each European country extensively.   It has to be stated briefly that some other countries of the CIS have either had no time to develop a consistent security concept, by being kept busy fighting civil or inter-state wars or having opted for cooperation with Russia in order to appease it.   One has reason to assume that some of the latter have also perceived the threats to their security as originating in Moscow but have had no alternative to cooperation with Russia, both for military and non-military reasons. The Ukraine has been the only state in the region to give priority in its strategic planning to averting the domination of Russia. The official military doctrine of the Ukraine is understandably laconic in this respect as to declare any country as an adversary in an official document could easily prove to be a self-fulfilling prophecy. The tension between the two has remained the decisive conflict of the region. However, even though Kiev and Moscow have been at loggerheads from time to time on different issues they have nonetheless succeeded in preventing an open military conflict. It is fortunate that after two years of hesitation the world at large seems to have understood that a nearly exclusive focus on Moscow's interests may be to the detriment of long-term stability in the former Soviet Union. Hence since 1993 the West has paid increasing attention to the security interests of Kiev.

It seems one cannot understand the post-Cold War European landscape of military security by exclusively analyzing official concepts and declared threat perceptions. Their analysis is necessary, however, to learn how countries of the three major regions of Europe evaluate their own security situation. In order to get closer to the real problems it may be necessary to focus on those problems which threaten security in different parts of Europe according to countries belonging to other regions.

Perceived security risks imposed by one region on countries belonging to the others

In order to focus on the real problem areas one has to present a one-sided picture. There is no reason to deal with the integrated western part of Europe[20] at great length. The whole area can be regarded as remarkably stable and posing no military threat to any country either inside or outside the group of states. This observation is certainly correct if one is ready to neglect certain complicating factors. First of all, it is known that two members of NATO, Greece and Turkey, have been involved in a continuing conflict over Cyprus and have some pending territorial and maritime claims as well. There are also some more recent disturbing developments with the involvement of some other western countries, as will be evident if we mention the attitude of Greece to the statehood of Macedonia and Italian pretentions to Slovenia. No one seems particularly worried about them. The market economy is stable in these countries, democratic political institutions have been functioning for quite some time and the countries are integrated into international institutions like NATO and the EU. Their military strategy is not offensive and in the case of many countries integrated into that of an alliance. Not even the coming of neo-fascists to power in the Italian coalition Government could undermine the wide-spread conviction that there is no reason to be concerned about destabilization.

In contrast to Western Europe the region East of the Elbe has been regarded as unstable since the end of bipolarity. Two reasons for instability have been mentioned particularly frequently, those of ethnic conflicts and territorial claims. The observation is correct insofar as the Cold War order suppressed ethnic conflicts in Eastern Europe as ones which were inconsistent with the declared internationalist values of the so-called socialist countries, but did not tackle them. Thus, there was no reason to assume that these conflicts would not reappear on the international scene whenever circumstances permitted, that is when the 'cohesion' of the Eastern bloc weakened. Territorial claims were also unimagineable during the East-West conflict and that resulted in a remarkably stable territorial status quo. The fact that state borders were imposed on many countries of Central and Eastern Europe by outside powers either by redrawing them (as with the borders of Hungary and Poland) or by 'including' nations in bigger entities (as with the constituting entities of the Soviet Union and Yugoslavia) should have given ground for concern, but did not at the time.

Neither is it the purpose of this chapter to analyse in detail either the role of nationalism in the region or the ethnic conflict potential of individual countries.[21] It has to be emphasized, however, that in the revolutions of 1989 nationalism served two purposes in Central Europe.

It was used against foreign political and military domination, virtually against an empire, the Soviet Union, even though by that time the Soviet empire could not resist the striving for independence by the Central European nations. Nationalism can also be regarded as a reaction to the internationalist ideology of the communist movement. If one does not share the internationalist 'values' of the communist movement and the form it was given in Central and Eastern Europe, one can conclude that nationalism served positive aims. It is well-known that nationalism has a mobilizing role that can aid the new leaderships of the region which have begun to build parliamentary democracy under very severe economic conditions. There was a need for an ideology that was easy to understand by broad strata of the populace and around which a consensus could be built. Nationalism and nothing else could meet these requirements. If it is assumed that nationalism served such positive aims in Central Europe the question emerges as to why the world at large has been so concerned about the reemergence of nationalism. Nationalism can take different forms, of course, from benign patriotism to malign chauvinism. The worry of the West stemmed partly from the fact it did not have an extensive knowledge of the political course of each country. It was not clear either what form nationalism would take and the frequently harsh rhetoric of newly elected inexperienced political leaders gave ground for concern. If one intends to acquire a more reliable knowledge about the dangers inherent in ethnic conflicts the following three factors have to be taken into consideration.

Firstly, the nationalism of such ethnic minority groups which also form the majority in another country carries more severe risks than one where such groups cannot count on the effective support of a nation represented by a state. Hence, ethnic conflicts with the involvement of the gypsy population of a country do not pose a direct threat to stability and security and may remain the concern of NGOs, like Amnesty International. They certainly do not go beyond 'traditional' human rights concerns. Ones with, for example, the involvement of Russians in other CIS countries or Hungarians in Transylvania do have security and political relevance and can endanger the fragile stability of the region.

Secondly, there is a significant difference between minorities dispersed over a large geographic area, mixed with (an)other, in most cases majority, group(s), and ones which are settled down in separate entities in the vicinity of the mother nation. Whereas the former settlement is not prone to territorial solution by secession, the latter may be subject to the dreams of nationalist politicians. That is why there is an increasing number of analysts, including the author, who are of the opinion that the risks associated, for example, with the approximately two million Hungarians in Transylvania has been largely overstated.

Thirdly, even though the five years that have passed since the fall of the Berlin wall have clearly been insufficient to draw conclusions of unquestionable lasting validity about the historic development pattern of Europe one can make a few preliminary observations. The former Eastern bloc has not remained united after the end of the East-West conflict and can be divided into two parts as far as conflict potential and the way of their resolution are concerned. What we have experienced since the end of the Cold War is that, although ethnic conflicts both characterize the so-called former non-Soviet Warsaw Treaty area and the former Soviet Union and dominate their security agenda, there is a fundamental difference between their modes of management. Despite the often intolerant rhetoric in Central Europe concerning minorities and ethnic issues conflicts remained exclusively political in the former non-Soviet Warsaw Treaty area and there is no danger of military escalation.[22] In the former Soviet Union, on the other hand, such conflicts have nearly always automatically escalated into military ones.

It has to be taken into account that Hungary, a Central European country, whose statements often gave cause for concern between 1990-94, voted in its second democratic elections for a government that obviously does not want to endanger its most important foreign policy priority, that of western integration, by making destabilizing statements concerning minorities. Hungary was regarded as a source of instability not only because of the statements of some of its high-ranking politicians, but also due to objective conditions. After all, a country where only a small percentage of the population belongs to national minorities and that has more than three million ethnic brethren living as minorities in neighbouring countries, could easily emerge with a strong revisionist agenda. It has to be emphasized that for five years the issue of ethnic rivalry has never even remotely threatened becoming one of military escalation.

In the area of the former Soviet Union the military escalation of ethnic conflicts (as between Azeris and Armenians or different population groups of Georgia) has been a reality or a real danger. It has to be noted, however, that Russia has not used force specifically in order to guarantee the rights of ethnic Russians in other former Soviet republics and that she has other means at her disposal to enforce minority rights on the authorities of neighbouring countries. It is hard to conceive of a scenario where Russia has no other option than to employ military force in order to protect its ethnic brethren.

The other most frequently mentioned reason of instability is the emergence of territorial claims. One has to ask if there are states in Central Europe which manifestly or tacitly seek to annex territory from other states? Should that be the case, the question is would that country consider the use of force to attain such an end or would it rely exclusively on peaceful means? Based on official statements, one would tend to conclude that those states which declare they do not want to revise state borders either by peaceful or non-peaceful means contribute to stability whereas those which intend to change borders undermine it. No state has gone so far in Central Europe as to say that it wants to change borders by force. A certain ambivalence has been noticeable concerning peaceful border revisions. Most countries have declared in their official documents that they have no territorial claims whatsoever. Poland has emphasized that it 'considers its borders to be immutable and has no territorial claims against its neighbours'.23 The Czech Republic has no reason to worry about the revision of its borders. The only issue that gives ground for certain limited concerns from time to time has been the Sudeten German problem. In this respect the Czech leadership makes a distinction between the position of neighbouring countries and non-state actors, that would be one that might well be followed by other countries: '[w]ith regard to the demands of the Sudeten German association, the Czech government will not allow any change in the legally determined frontier for purposes of restitution'.24 The other successor state of Czechoslovakia, the Slovak Republic, has seemed somewhat concerned about possible territorial claims by Hungary but was still ready to proclaim that it 'has no territorial claims on any nation's territory'.25

The Romanian leadership faces a complex situation. On the one hand, it could formulate demands on Bessarabia (Moldova) and some domestic political groupings forces would certainly be willing to do just that. On the other, however, it could be the subject of territorial claims by another country. Romanian leaders have emphasized that Romania and Moldova are two independent states. Their concerns can be felt nevertheless. As State Secretary of the Defence Ministry, Ioan Pascu, emphasized:

'the Helsinki document stipulates that borders are not to be modified through the use of force; such changes are permitted only if the parties involved agree to them. The first such modification, in fact, already took place when Germany was permitted to reunify in October 1990. Other such territorial transformations, however, also took place. Former federal states - particularly the USSR and Czechoslovakia - have disintegrated. These processes were, at first, generally peaceful because existing internal borders were maintained and became, automatically, international borders. ... However, Yugoslavia is a special case. Not only has that country broken down violently; internal warfare, particularly in Bosnia-Herzegovina, has further created a dangerous precedent. With the conflict raging on, an increasing number of voices are advocating territorial changes since no other solutions seem in sight. *Were such territorial shifts completed, a powerful legal precedent contradicting the Helsinki Final Act would be created, by which other (provoked or unprovoked) conflicts could be "solved" in the future.'*[26]

It is worth analyzing the position of this Romanian politician, if only because one can assume that it is a mainstream view in Bucharest. It is to be welcomed that Romania also rejects the revision of borders by threat or use of force as it reduces concerns about an eventual military escalation of territorial disputes. Romania seems ready to accept peaceful border changes if the parties can reach agreement. This reflects the realism of Romanian politics on the issue. Such an approach leaves the door open for an eventual unification of Romania and Moldova if the latter also finds this acceptable without risking a challenge on similar grounds by Hungary.

The activity of the first post-communist government of Hungary on the territorial issue was ambiguous. On the one hand, the Antall government made clear it would not seek to change its borders by non-peaceful means. However, it was not ready to give clear-cut guarantees to each neighbour that it would not seek to revise borders by peaceful means. Its activity was often accompanied by an unfortunate, intolerant rhetoric that alarmed the leaders of Romania, Slovakia and Yugoslavia. On several occasions, the Prime Minister reiterated that he would like to be the premier of fifteen million Hungarians 'in spirit'.[27] On one occasion he specifically mentioned that the Vojvodina belongs to Yugoslavia and not to Serbia; thus if the federation dissolved, the status of Vojvodina could be subject to reconsideration.[28] The concept of security policy adopted by the Hungarian Parliament in early 1993 by consensus of the six parties does not fully exclude territorial revisions, but contains an ambiguous sentence on the topic. After referring to the rights of Hungarian minorities, the text continues: '... we reject both the alteration *by force* of existing borders and artificial alteration of the ethnic consistency of the population by any means, not only in the Carpathian Basin but in the whole Central and Eastern European region'.[29]

Hungary was nevertheless ready to conclude one treaty with a neighbour regulating the border issue in clear terms. The treaty of 6 December 1991, with Ukraine, states that both parties mutually respect each other's borders, and have no territorial claims either at present or in the future, which means borders cannot be revised either by peaceful or non-peaceful means.[30] The treaty was ratified by the Ukrainian Parliament on 1 July 1992. The ratification process in the Hungarian Parliament, postponed until May 1993, was not free of heated debate. Clauses which renounced eventual territorial revisions, even by peaceful means, were generally unacceptable to the extreme right, which was partly represented in the Hungarian Democratic Forum, the biggest party of the governing coalition at that time, and also by independent MPs. The government's explanations were not particularly convincing. The Foreign Minister presented the following argument:

'When we confirm in this treaty that we have no territorial demands against Ukraine ... we shall not only proceed in line with the system of norms of democratic states of law and the Helsinki Final Act, but we are also taking into consideration the particular aspects of the Ukrainian-Hungarian relationship. Rejection of territorial claims is the same as confirming in a specific form the rejection of the threat of the use of force - a move banned by international law. As a consequence, it cannot be interpreted as a renunciation of any legal act as permitted by international law. Over and above this important interpretation of law, the specific treaty expands, rather than narrows our political scope for action'.[31]

Regardless of what the Foreign Minister had to say it is clear from the text of the treaty that in this case Hungary went beyond the renunciation of border revision by force, by giving up the possibility of peaceful border changes as well.

In the disturbingly one-sided debate in the Hungarian Parliament on the Ukrainian-Hungarian treaty it became clear that ultra-conservative forces would not be ready to ratify further treaties renouncing peaceful border revisions. Consequently Prime Minister Antall declared that the treaty concluded with Ukraine was a unique exception to the rule in that Hungary was ready to accept the insertion of the border clause only because it would not have been possible to conclude the treaty without it and also because the border between the two states was not fixed in the Paris Peace Treaty of 1947.[32] Unfortunately, neither does the Prime Minister's position hold water in international law. The Paris Peace Treaty of 1947 clearly determined the borders of Hungary with each of its neighbours.[33] One may put forward more convincing arguments, as have some experts in conservative circles, according to which if Hungary were to reiterate in a legally binding document the same commitment it took earlier, in this case many years ago, on the inviolability of the country's borders and the respect for the territorial integrity of each neighbouring country, it would undermine the credibility of the previous legal régime. Such an approach sounds correct legally. There are important political reasons, however, why priority should not be given to the legal argument in this case. If Hungary were to refuse to confirm its earlier position on borders it would give ground for suspicion that the position of the country had changed and that it would eventually seek to revise its borders.

The government formed following the 1994 parliamentary elections recognized the importance of concluding the two most important pending basic treaties, those with Slovakia and Romania, which included the renunciation of territorial claims and thus contributed to changing the image of the country. This was underlined with a number of high level exchanges between the governments involved during the summer of 1994. Even though it may take much longer than expected before the elections to conclude the two treaties, ranking politicians and official documents have reiterated on a number of occasions Hungary's willingness to conclude the debate on the borders. The Foreign Ministry declared officially that '[a]part from a recognition of existing borders and a mutual renunciation of territorial claims, the basic treaties should contain recognition, guarantees and a political assertion of the rights of national minorities living in each other's countries, in line with the norms of the Council of Europe and of the CSCE'.34

In contrast with Central Europe, it is territorial conflicts and the violation of territorial integrity of states that characterizes the situation in the former Soviet Union. It seems the efforts of the West have had to be limited to damage limitation there. Persistent efforts have been made to stabilize the situation surrounding the Baltic states and to help the three countries 'escape' from the zone of instability. Recently some (so far unsuccessful) attempts have been made to roll back the Russian invaders from Moldova. It seems that no resolution of the conflicts of the former Soviet Union is in sight.

The different cooperation frameworks developed by the West to integrate the former East aim in most cases at developing cooperation between two 'groups', grouping certain countries of the West and those of the East. Examples are the North Atlantic Cooperation Council (NACC) and the associated partner status offered by the WEU, or between a group of western states and individual countries of the East, like Partnership for Peace. No specific programme has yet been developed to tackle conflicts between the countries of Central and Eastern Europe, sources of conflict which have been mentioned as causing the most concern to the West as most severely endangering security in Europe, conflicts involving ethnic rivalries and terrritorial claims that can escalate into military conflicts. The so-called 'Balladur Plan' aimed to fill this gap, an idea that was picked up by the EU. Following the late May 1994 inaugural conference of the Pact on Stability the nine Central European countries (the six former non-Soviet members of the Warsaw Treaty and the three Baltic states) were invited to participate and to conclude within one year bilateral or regional treaties to regulate, *inter alia*, good neighbourly relations, 'including questions related to frontiers and minorities'.[35] The danger of disputes about territorial and minority issues must not be underestimated. It is one of the main arguments of this chapter, however, that such a danger was exclusively political and has remained abstract in the former non-Soviet Warsaw Treaty countries in the years since 1989. It represented and continues to represent a concrete military threat only in the two former federations of Europe, the former Soviet Union and Yugoslavia. That is why, although the initiation of a programme to eliminate such sources of conflict is to be welcomed, it is doubtful whether it was very appropriate to address it only to the nine countries of Central Europe (the six former non-Soviet Warsaw Treaty countries and the three Baltic states). One can conclude, therefore that such a Pact addressing such issues will merely eliminate a military risk that was not present in the region before the initiative was launched.

The dangers of territorial claims and ethnic conflicts have been frequently mentioned as impediments to the security integration of Central Europe with the West. In light of the above, this argument sounds more convincing for Eastern than for Central Europe. There is also a third concern put forward many times, namely that of the danger of nationalization of security and defence policies. (Re)nationalization has been a fact since the dissolution of the WTO, a fact not many deplore, with the exception of hard line communists and Russian great power nationalists. After having got rid of an alliance of subjugation it is understandable that the Central European countries did not want to enter into another integrated alliance structure with a similar pattern. When the failure to introduce an effective collective security system in Europe became evident not much after the end of the East-West conflict the Central European countries had two possibilities. Either they could rely on their own resources in military affairs or try to accede to a western security institution. As the latter attempt has failed for the time being the nationalization of security was unavoidable in Central Europe. Even though nationalization carries certain dangers it depends on two factors as to whether they remain abstract or become real. One relates to the content of each national military concept, and the strategy and transparent nature of the military plans of others. As long as political relations are normal, and military plans are defensive and mutually transparent, there is no reason to be worried about the mere fact of (re)nationalization. One can thus conclude that the danger of nationalization is another myth of European military security. A country with a nationalized defence policy based on peaceful intentions and without offensive military capabilities is certainly preferable to a denationalized offensive military bloc.

Conclusion: the relevance of the debate on military security in the new Europe

This chapter does not want to belittle the importance of military issues in the new Europe. It is a fact that for certain countries on the Eastern perimeter of Europe and for some successor states of the former Yugoslavia, military issues are the decisive ones. But neither for Western, nor for Central, Europe are military questions decisive. The West can feel relieved it does not have to devote too much energy and extensive resources to provide for its own defence. Central Europe faces serious military problems, though not ones stemming from severe imminent military threats.

The countries of Central Europe are unable to defend themselves. The forces available, including their training and command structure, are largely inadequate. To a certain extent they still reflect the characteristic features of the large standing armies of the Second World War with some Soviet 'flavour' inherited from the decades of the WTO. If one assumes that the danger of violent escalation of ethnic conflicts and territorial claims are largely exaggerated or practically non-existent in Central Europe then it could be concluded that this is not much of a problem. It is a fact, however, that these countries do not perceive the situation in such terms.[36]

Given the abstract nature of military risks in Central Europe, on the one hand, and the severe domestic socio-economic problems in most of these countries, including budget deficits and the shortage of capital, on the other, when governments set their priorities the militaries turn out to be the regular losers in budget debates. Even though it may seem to be a simplification to say that Central European governments have to decide whether to meet the expectations of the IMF to reduce budget deficit or to spend more on their armed forces there is an element of truth in it. The modernization of the armed forces has thus become a popular slogan, without any decisive steps being taken to implement it. The West seems to be gradually starting to accept that in the absence of real sources of international instability in the region and the desire of the countries of the region to integrate with western security institutions, primarily NATO, the most important obstacle to integration may be that the armed forces are incompatible with those of the West and require significant restructuring.

However, modernization requires investment in the defence sector and without modernization no resources will be made available for this purpose. States of the region will not allocate significantly bigger resources to this purpose given that nowadays they are of the opinion there are more urgent and important tasks. The break out from this vicious circle seems nearly impossible, though some countries have certainly made bigger efforts than others to modernize. The West can, of course, facilitate the process but there are also limits to western generosity. The Partnership for Peace programme gave a clear message in this respect. It stated that the subscribing states 'will fund their own participation in Partnership activities, and will endeavour otherwise to share the burdens of mounting exercises in which they take part'.[37] Not long after the initiative was launched it turned out that some money has to be allocated to facilitate cooperation if NATO wants to integrate the countries of Central Europe. The US announced on 7 July 1994 the allocation of one hundred million dollars for the implementation of joint military programmes with 'democratic partners', of which twenty-five million will go to the programme with Poland. It has to be considered what further measures might facilitate the process. Cooperation in training and joint exercises are understandably high on the agenda. In the future ways and means have to be found to develop the armaments and the military infrastructure of those countries whose integration is likely in the medium run. These efforts of the West will have to be supplemented by making it clear to those Central Europeans who are considered as the first candidates for integration that the incompatibility of their militaries is now a major impediment to such integration.

The Central Europeans also have much to do. They will have to put their military reforms into practice without significant external financial support. They have to maintain the region as a low risk environment militarily as they have done since the end of the East-West conflict. They also have to consider what type of NATO membership they seek, as this has not yet been clarified.

The integration of Central Europe into western security institutions is part of the broader integration goals of the region. The fact that countries of the region are not threatened militarily and that their stability has been endangered much more by factors other than external ones since the end of the East-West conflict does not mean that their integration is unnecessary. This is first of all because belonging to the 'family of western democracies' in the field of security carries the message to the world at large that economic cooperation with these countries does not carry unacceptable political risk. Now it may be more important than anything else. Secondly, because the integration of a part of the former East bloc in terms of security more narrowly defined is a fair weather policy. Its real value will be proven if things go wrong.

For parts of Central and Eastern Europe which cannot be easily or even at all integrated with western security institutions, at least in the foreseeable future, a differentiated policy has to be developed. For those states that can be integrated later it has to be made clear that it depends on them when they can join. For those whose integration seems impossible a programme has to be developed 'to sweeten the bitter pill'.

Notes

1. Szücs, Jenö (1993), 'Three Historical Regions of Europe: An Outline', in Keane, John (ed.), *Civil Society and the State*, Verso, London and New York, pp. 291-332. Szücs's study was first published in Hungarian in 1981

and in English in 1988.

2. Valki, László (1984), 'Neutrality: A Hungarian View', in Neuhold, Hans-Peter (ed.), *The Laxembug Papers*, Austrian Institute for International Affairs, Laxemburg, p. 106.

3. The relationship of Greece and Turkey located on the periphery of the 'political West' can be regarded an exception.

4. Slovenia can be regarded a special case in this respect as its independent statehood was born in violence. Following the recognition of its independent statehood its situation seems to have stabilized though some limited non-military tension has emerged between the country and Italy.

5. Similarly Bertram, Christoph (1994), 'Let's Be Clear: Not One Europe but a New West and a New East', *International Herald Tribune*, 12 July, p. 6.

6. 'The Alliance's New Strategic Concept', agreed by the Heads of State and Government participating in the meeting of the NAC in Rome, 7-8 November 1991, *NATO Review*, vol. 39, no. 6, p. 26, para. 10.

7. *Ibid.*, para. 11.

8. Borinski, Philipp (1993), 'Die neue NATO-Strategie. Perspektiven militärischer Sicherheitspolitik in Europa', *HSFK Report*, no. 1, 1993, p. 29.

9. *Ibid.*

10. Central Europe, as was demonstrated in the introduction of this chapter, is an ill-defined geographical category. In most cases I identify it with the six former non-Soviet Warsaw Treaty member-states. When a different meaning is attributed to the term it will be indicated.

11. Zielonka, Jan (1992), 'Security in Central Europe', *Adelphi Paper*, 272, Autumn, pp. 33-4.

12. This argument was put forward by László Valki in a paper written in 1990 and published in 1992. Even though I regard the notion of a 'security vacuum' as misleading, I think Valki's observation was fully correct when he said that something will have to happen to those countries which have been left in limbo since the end of the East-West conflict. See Valki, László (1992), 'Vanishing Threat Perceptions and New Uncertainties in Central Europe', in Valki, László (ed.), *Changing Threat Perceptions and Military Doctrines*, Macmillan, Basingstoke, p. 92.

13. The 'new abroad' is not identical with the 'near abroad' as the former does not cover the three Baltic states. This might be a reflection of the recognition of the fact that the West, and in particular the Scandinavian countries, have certain well defined interests in that area and consequently any attempt of virtual reintegration would create certain tensions. This may be the reason that Russia was ready to complete the withdrawal of its ground troops from the area.

14. See Dokuchaev, Anatolii (1992), 'Nas ob'edinaet znachitel'no bol'she chem raz'edinaet [Much more unites than divides us]', *Krasnaia Zvezda*, 24 November, p. 2.

15. For an extensive summary see 'Grundbestimmungen der Militärdoktrin der Russländischen Föderation, am 18. November 1993 veröffentlicht', *Europa Archiv*, vol. 49, no. 1, 10 January 1994, pp. D31-46. For the reference see p. D33.
16. Larabee, F. Stephen (1993), *East-European Security After the Cold War*, Santa Monica, RAND, p. 162.
17. Grundbestimmungen (1994), *op. cit.*, p. D34.
18. Grigor'ev, M. (1992), 'Budet li NATO reshat' za nas nashi problemy? [Will NATO solve our problems behind us?]', *Krasnaia Zvezda*, 5 June, p. 3.
19. Seminar on CSCE peacekeeping 7-9 June 1993, Vienna: Chairman's summary (1993), CSCE, Vienna, 23 June, mimeo., p. 8.
20. For the purposes of this chapter western Europe is identified with countries belonging to the European Economic Area and the member countries of NATO.
21. For my views on these issues see my (1994), 'Adversaries All Around? (Re)nationalization of Security and Defence policies in Central and Eastern Europe', *Clingendael Paper*, January, pp. 7-11 and 29-35.
22. However, it has to be noted that Yugoslavia, a non-aligned country, where we have witnessed the bloodiest ethnic conflict since 1991, never belonged to this group.
23. *Tenets of Polish Security Policy* (1992), Warsaw, 2 November, p. 5.
24. Comments of the Minister for Foreign Affairs, Josef Zieleniec, on the foreign policy of the Czech Republic, at the 8th session of the Chamber of Deputies of the Parliament of the Czech Republic (1993), Prague, 24 June, p. 6 of the English translation of the address.
25. Kuchár, Emil (1994), 'Slovakia: Looking West and East', in Siccama, Jan Geert and van den Doel, Theo (eds), *Restructuring Armed Forces in East and West*, Westview Press, Boulder, p. 104.
26. Pascu, Ioan (1994), 'Romania and the Yugoslav Conflict', *European Security*, vol. 3, no. 1, Spring, p. 156 (emphasis added).
27. The population of the Republic of Hungary is approximately 10.6 million and an additional 3.2-3.5 million ethnic Hungarians live in the neighbouring countries. For more details see Schöpflin, George (1993), 'Hungary and its Neighbours', *Chaillot Papers*, 7, May, p. 37.
28. The statement, according to press reports, was made in the course of a meeting between Prime Minister Antall and Italian President Francesco Cossiga in the summer of 1991. No Hungarian official was ready to deny the statement thereafter.
29. Basic Principles of the Security Policy of the Republic of Hungary (1993), *Fact Sheets on Hungary*, no. 4, para. 8, p. 4 (emphasis added).
30. See Szerződés a jószomszédság és az együttmüködés alapjairól a Magyar Köztársaság és Ukrajna között [Treaty on the foundations of good neighbourliness and cooperation between the Republic of Hungary and

Ukraine], Article 2, para. 2.

31. Jeszenszky, Géza (1993), 'Introductory Statement', *Current Policy*, no. 12, pp. 3-4. (Statement delivered at the debate of the Parliament on the Hungarian-Ukrainian basic treaty on 4 May 1993).

32. Antall, József miniszterelnök felszólalása a Magyar Köztársaság és Ukrajna között a jószomszédság és az együttmüködés alapjairól szóló, Kijevben 1991. december 6-án aláírt szerződés megerösítéröl szóló országgyülési határozati javaslat részletes vitájában 1993. május 11-én [The speech of Prime Minister Antall in the ratification debate of the Parliament on the treaty signed between the Republic of Hungary and Ukraine on the basis of good neighbourliness and cooperation on 11 May 1993], *Országgyülési Napló*, galley 26, 685.

33. Cf. Article 1 of the Paris Peace Treaty of 10 February 1947.

34. Statement by the Spokesman of the Ministry for Foreign Affairs (1994), *Press Release of the Ministry of Foreign Affairs of the Republic of Hungary*, 13 September, p. 1.

35. *Concluding Document of the Inaugural Conference for a Pact on Stability in Europe* (1994), point 1.5.

36. For more details see Monika Wohlfeld's contribution in this volume.

37. Partnership for Peace: Framework Document (1994), *NATO Review*, vol. 42, no. 1, February, p. 30.

2 NATO: Approaching the Millennium

DAN HIESTER

Introduction

When the Cold War ended in 1989-90[1] there was widespread speculation about the future of the North Atlantic Treaty Organization (NATO). With the threat removed that had been the *raison d'être* of its creation, what purpose could a standing military alliance serve? With increasing instability in, and then the demise of, the Soviet Union, this view began to change. While in the West there still remained uncertainty about NATO's future role, for the former non-non-Soviet members of the now defunct Warsaw Treaty Organization (WTO), there seemed to be no such ambiguity as they made clear their desire to join the Alliance as soon as possible. For the last few years, the biggest problem occupying the Alliance had seemed to be how to accommodate these desires without alienating Russia, while at the same time not giving Russia a veto over future NATO membership.[2] The identity crisis seemed to be over and NATO had a new purpose, defined as much by non-members wanting to join as by the Alliance itself. But now, five years after the fall of the Berlin Wall, NATO is divided by a rift so deep some feel it threatens the existence of the Alliance itself. The immediate cause of the crisis is policy towards Bosnia, with the United States and the Europeans seriously split. The 'crisis in the Alliance' literature is a rich seam which has never run out of material in the last forty-five years, but some politicians and analysts are beginning to contemplate the unthinkable, that this is the crisis that in the long-term could break the Alliance. And the differences come from fissures opening up within the Alliance over deep seated problems that previously would have been suppressed by the overall concern with the external threat that provided cohesion. In this sense, the instant pundits of 1990 may have been closer to the mark when they predicted the end of the Alliance than those who pondered its long-term alternative futures.

The NATO alliance is not the only victim of the current disarray in world affairs. Talk of a New World Order, a very dubious concept from its first iteration, has now ceased. The always tenuous cooperation, or at least acquiescence, by the permanent members of the Security Council in some kind of broad approach to regional problems seems to be coming to an end. The use of the UN during the Kuwait invasion crisis and the resulting Gulf War may come to be seen as the high water mark of this cooperation. Together, the Bosnian crisis and the question of the expansion of NATO membership eastward, seems to be ending the post-Cold War honeymoon period of relations between the United States, the West Europeans and Russia. At the December 1994 Budapest Summit of the fifty-three nation Conference for Security and Cooperation in Europe (CSCE), President Boris Yeltsin spoke of a 'Cold Peace' descending on Europe.[3] In the days and weeks preceding the meeting, hopes had been raised that it might succeed in papering over some of the cracks that had begun appearing in the pan-European security arena. Instead, the sense of insecurity and division seemed to be exacerbated. While tentative agreement on sending a CSCE peacekeeping force to Nagorno-Karabakh was cited as an achievement, the reality was that of a complete failure to move forward on the major outstanding issues. The most concrete achievement was to effect a change in the name of the CSCE to the OSCE (Organization for Security and Cooperation in Europe), which was intended to give the impression of weight and permanence to the organization but instead highlighted lack of substantive agreement at the summit.

Are the problems outlined above of a short-term nature that will seem of little consequence when analyzed in a similar chapter in twelve to eighteen months time? Or are they further evidence that the period of post-Cold War optimism concerning the possibility of a pan-European security consensus must now be laid to rest? Any analysis that is to be taken seriously must be cautious about jumping too rapidly from one conclusion to another. Every meeting, every summit must not be seen as marking a new advance, retreat or departure that is likely to determine the future course of events. What is much more likely is that we are living through what may be a fairly lengthy period of transition from the certainties of the Cold War to an as yet uncertain future. No one meeting or event is likely to be the 'big one' that provides the watershed which clarifies the European security situation in a way which we would find analytically satisfying. There is not another 1989 on the way.

Having issued that caution, it is necessary to deal with the widespread perception at the moment that serious rifts have opened up in the NATO Alliance between the United States and its European partners, caused immediately by differences over policy in Bosnia, but which are symptomatic of a more fundamental drifting apart in their international outlook. While the primary purpose of this chapter is to analyze the present and attempt to look forward, a brief review of past assumptions may help us to understand whether a basic shift is under way. Do the Americans and the Europeans need each other any longer?   Does the absence of threat mean the Alliance is redundant?   There have been crises in the Alliance before; is this one any different?

The United States, Europe, NATO, and the Cold War

NATO was created to protect Western Europe from a perceived threat from the Soviet Union.   But it served other purposes as well, which are usually summed up by repeating Lord Ismay's famous dictum of keeping the 'Americans in, the Russians out, and the Germans down'.   NATO formalized the US role as the pre-eminent decision-maker in the West European security structure.   It reassured the states of Europe that the balance of power between them that they had succeeded in destroying, would now be kept by a much more powerful external actor.   It provided them with the security that they were both unable and unwilling to provide for themselves.   And, contrary to some of the more superficial contemporary 'crisis in the alliance' analysis, the relationship was always an uneasy one.   The Europeans regularly sought reassurance when they felt that the United States was less than fully committed because of interests elsewhere.   On the other hand, if the United States acted decisively, but without what they viewed as sufficient consultation, they complained of American high-handedness or insensitivity.   This insecurity-reassurance-resentment syndrome began almost immediately after the formation of the Alliance in 1949 with the outbreak of the Korean War in 1950 and the heavy US involvement on the other side of the world.   It led in the early 1950s to NATO becoming a nuclear alliance and the stationing of US nuclear weapons in Europe.   This caused problems from the very beginning but they became very serious when the Soviet Union achieved strategic nuclear parity in the late 1960s.   The centrality of nuclear weapons to the whole of NATO strategy in the past is frequently overlooked in the current discussions over the future role of NATO.

The launch of Sputnik in 1957 - heralding the beginning of the end of American invulnerability to Soviet attack, the adoption of 'flexible response' by the Kennedy administration in 1962 (five years before it would become NATO doctrine), the Vietnam War, and vastly differing views over the meaning and pursuit of détente created periodic 'crises' in the Alliance.   Once the United States began to pursue a bilateral relationship with the Soviet Union over the heads of the West Europeans in the 1970s, matters became even more serious. Given the reaction to the current transatlantic slanging match over Bosnia it is well to remember these and subsequent events to add some perspective. Next to come were the Reagan 'shocks' of the 1980s.   The announcement by President Reagan in March 1983, of the Strategic Defense Initiative (SDI - popularly known as 'Star Wars') without any prior consultation or notice to the Alliance, created shockwaves, since it undermined nuclear deterrence theory, the bedrock of Western security doctrine.   Whatever the reality or unreality of SDI, even worse was to come in terms of NATO solidarity with the Intermediate Nuclear Forces in Europe (INF) episode.[4] What began as an attempt to respond to West European expressions of insecurity *vis à vis* a class of Soviet weapons wound up as a classic demonstration of the US acting over the heads of the Europeans on a matter central to their security concerns.

The events cited above should be familiar to everyone, but it is well to recall them and the dramatic impact they had on Alliance thinking and solidarity, when we are trying to make judgements about the severity of the current Alliance crisis. The story is also a vastly complicated one. It must not be forgotten that it was during the period of the Reagan 'shocks' that the Western European Union (WEU) was 'rediscovered'. Originally set up to oversee West German rearmament, the WEU had become moribund. Needing a forum away from NATO where they could discuss their security concerns without the presence of the United States, the West Europeans began to use the WEU for this purpose. Today, the WEU provides the most likely focus for a West European security community either in partnership with, or independent of, the United States.[5] Its potential for this role is formally recognized in the Maastricht Treaty. Membership of the WEU is even discussed as a possible way of bringing the states of Central and Eastern Europe into a Western security organization while at the same time avoiding Russian objections to these states joining NATO.

What the above discussion demonstrates is that disagreements and 'crises' in the Alliance over fundamentals are nothing new but have been a part of its history since the beginning. The real question is: is there anything different about the current crisis that sets it apart from the previous ones that might lead us to predict a different outcome from those of the past? Unfortunately (or fortunately, depending on your perspective), the answer is probably 'yes'. Before turning to a discussion and analysis of the current situation, a review of developments in the Alliance and elsewhere between between 1989 and 1994 is necessary.

NATO, the United States and Europe after the Cold War

With the end of the Cold War and the swift demise of the Warsaw Treaty Organization (WTO) and the Soviet Union, the security situation in Europe was transformed beyond all recognition. The world was treated to some strange and colourful language in the period leading up to these events. The Gorbachev 'charm offensive' was followed by the 'Sinatra Doctrine' leading to the deployment of the ultimate secret weapon by the Soviet Union, the threat that 'we will deprive you of the enemy'. This all succeeded beyond most people's wildest dreams and NATO was left in an unprecedented position: the threat and the locus of the threat, the Soviet Union, which NATO had been created to counter, had simply disappeared. What purpose could NATO now possibly serve? Could it re-invent itself? Two answers quickly presented themselves. First, it rapidly became clear that the end of the Cold War was leading to long suppressed conflicts breaking out in Europe, even as the threat of catastrophic global conflict had been lifted. The breakup of, and subsequent conflict in, what had been Yugoslavia provided the most acute example. Outside the NATO area, but involving many of the member states, the Gulf War became the first large-scale post-Cold War conflict. The existence of NATO resources and infrastructure were vital to the war effort there even though NATO had no formal involvement, the Gulf War coalition being led by the United States under the auspices of the United Nations. While the Gulf War provided a variety of signals for the future of international relations, it certainly provided pause for thought for anyone suggesting that NATO should be disbanded now that its former putative enemy had ceased to exist.

The second answer to the question of NATO's future was provided by many former members of the now defunct WTO. They began asking to join NATO and made it clear that full membership was their top foreign and security policy priority. From the start, the dilemma for NATO was obvious, acute, and to some extent, embarrassing. Having rhetorically supported for decades the idea of freedom for these states from the Soviet Union, did they not now have a moral as well political obligation to provide for them the security they so anxiously sought? On the other hand, having declared friendship for the former enemy, which was soon to become the substantially smaller but still formidable Russian Federation, was it really possible to extend the territory of the NATO Alliance to the borders of Russia by incorporating its former allies into what had been the enemy alliance, without undoing all the progress in good relations that had been made with Russia? In time, this dilemma was to become a source of division within the Alliance between the United States and the Europeans, and also between some of the Europeans themselves. Whatever was to be done, a cautious strategy was called for:

'In December, 1991, NATO created the North Atlantic Cooperation Council (NACC), composed of the 16 NATO nations and the countries of Central and Eastern Europe and others which gained independence following the dissolution of the Soviet Union. For their part, Allied leaders committed themselves to support reform in the new and independent states of Central and Eastern Europe; to give practical assistance to them; and to build confidence through increased contacts'.[6]

Two years after the revolutions of 1989 and the fall of the Berlin Wall, and one year after the Paris CSCE conference of November 1990 collectively declared an end to the Cold War, this was NATO's response to the Central and East European clamour for membership. It was a politically delicate time and while NATO wanted to offer these states some sort of reassurance, it was in no position to offer security guarantees let alone a timetable for membership.

President Gorbachev was in an increasingly weak and isolated position domestically and the Alliance did not wish to compound his problems. Within a month, however, the Russian flag was flying over the Kremlin.

NACC proceeded on the basis of joint projects and soon began to evolve an annual Work Plan.[7] Within its own terms of reference, NACC can be considered to have been a success. However, it did not offer what many, especially the Cental European, states wanted: a more organic relationship with NATO that involved them in specific NATO activities and seemed to be leading somewhere, including membership at some future date. The result was the creation of Partnership for Peace (PfP). It was described by NATO's Assistant Secretary General for Political Affairs thus:

'Partnership for Peace, launched at the NATO Summit last January [1994], is a new and ambitious initiative intended to enhance stability and security in the whole of Europe by strengthening the relationships between NATO and the countries of Central and Eastern Europe and other CSCE participating states.

In effect, Partnership for Peace is an invitation to these countries to deepen and intensify their ties with the Alliance through practical cooperation. Much of this will be in the military sphere, and will concentrate on fostering the ability to work together in such fields as peacekeeping and humanitarian assistance. In addition, the Partnership has a wider, more political dimension to it, which is the promotion of, and commitment to, democratic principles, thereby increasing stability and diminishing threats to peace.[8]

There are now twenty-two members of PfP including, interestingly, Finland and Sweden, which shows graphically how much things have changed in the post-Cold War era. On 1 January 1995, these two countries, along with Austria, joined the European Union (EU), completing the shift from the neutral positions they maintained throughout the Cold War. In a sense PfP is an extension of the idea of Confidence Building Measures (CBM) in Europe which grew out of the Helsinki Process into a Confidence Building Process (CBP) which extends a link with NATO to all the states of Europe, not just the former members of the two opposing military alliances of the Cold War. In doing so, it conveniently defines a new role for NATO.

For NATO and PfP, the greatest problem has been Russia. PfP really had two, not necessarily compatible, aims. The first has been described above. The second was to somehow create a link between NATO and Russia which recognized Russia's special status as a former Superpower and still great power. The negotiations leading up to Russia's signature of the outline PfP agreement in June1994, were protracted and difficult for this very reason. PFP works on the basis of creating 'individual, tailored programmes of cooperation between NATO and each of its partners'.[9] In November 1994, NATO foreign ministers and the Russian Foreign Minister met in Brussels to sign just such an agreement. At the last minute, the Russian Foreign Minister walked away from the agreement insisting on further clarifications of NATO's intentions in eastern Europe before it would proceed with the proposed programme.[10] This had followed an attempt by the United States to push its European allies into speeding up the timetable for the admission of Central European States into NATO. An additional statement along these lines by President Clinton at the December 1994 Budapest CSCE Summit, created further problems both within NATO and between NATO and the Russians. Realizing the mistake, the United States subsequently backed away from the policy, but the damage had been done. The episode also highlighted the disarray in US foreign policy-making which is not only worrying the Europeans, but is widening the gap in outlook between them and America.

Problems over what to do about the extension of membership are not the only ones the Alliance faces. The problems of differing perceptions within the Alliance over its future have already been mentioned. The January 1994 Brussels Summit also addressed these issues. Reviewing that meeting, former US Secretary of Defence Les Aspin wrote:

> '... European NATO members have long desired a capacity for collective military action without necessarily having the direct involvement of the United States. The problem has always been how to provide for such a capacity within the NATO framework.
>
> NATO's leaders addressed these challenges by endorsing the Combined Joint Task Forces (CJTF) at the Brussels Summit. Under this plan, NATO-trained and integrated military forces and assets can be assigned to European-only task forces and employed on European-only contingencies in those cases when the full NATO membership chooses not to participate. A task force could even include forces of countries outside NATO - perhaps our Peace Partners, once PfP is up and running.
>
> The CJTF concept is closely linked to the emerging European Security and Defence Identity (ESDI) and gives concrete meaning to the idea of an ESDI that's separable but not separate from NATO. By making available such NATO assets and logistics, and command and control for operations, the CJTF will avoid wasteful duplication of capabilities and prevent competition between NATO and WEU. It will also demonstrate strong US support for the development of an ESDI within the European Union.'[11]

It is hard to imagine a more optimistic statement for the future of the Alliance. Unfortunately, subsequent events have undermined this apparent harmony. Following the transatlantic shouting match that ensued when

President Clinton announced that he was forced by an act of Congress to withdraw U.S. forces from enforcing the arms embargo against the Bosnian Government, it is difficult to believe that any European NATO member state believes they can count on the United States making available 'NATO assets and logistics, and command and control for operations' in which the US chooses not to participate.

The Western European Union is the locus for the ESDI, as set out in the Maastricht Treaty. Given the growing disagreements across the Atlantic, European governments are demonstrating an increasingly serious approach to WEU. In addition, discussion is beginning on whether WEU could offer a security alternative to NATO for the Central and East European states. The logic is that these states wish to join the EU and WEU is the EU forum for discussing collective security concerns. There has even been the suggestion that WEU could create its own fFP called 'associate membership'. All of this begs the question of whether the Europeans have the capabilities needed to build a credible security alliance independent of the United States.

Security in Europe in the 1990s

The discussion so far has concentrated largely on the military aspects of security, understandably so in a chapter that focuses on the future of NATO. However, to understand the security dilemma in Europe today, it is necessary to move beyond the military sphere. In an article written a few years ago for a collection called 'Building the New Europe', I argued that increasingly security is discussed in economic rather than military terms. 'The new emerging global power structure is not just based on, but is primarily concerned with achieving economic security.'[12] This is as true for Europe as anywhere else. To be European should mean not only to be free from fears of coercion, but also free from economic privation. The dominant organization in Europe for dealing with economic issues is the European Union, but many other institutions discuss and deal with economic matters as well. It is interesting to note that Partnership for Peace discussions concentrate on the broad economic aspects of security cooperation as well as more narrowly defined military affairs.

At the military level, there is the need for new approaches as well. The rapid decline of the importance of nuclear weapons, especially in Europe, means that NATO must come to terms structurally with this situation. As discussed earlier, NATO was an alliance that depended ultimately on nuclear weapons for its deterrent effect, and this formed the basis of its military strategy. As this is no longer the case, new strategies, already emerging, must include a re-definition of security and not simply a re-structuring of forces. This was brought home by the recent air action in Bosnia where great play was made of the fact that this was the first time that NATO forces had ever engaged in hostile action.

These developments raise for NATO, and its individual members, the issue of out-of-area action. NATO no longer expects an attack on its members, the reason for its creation, so it must contemplate threats to the peace elsewhere which affect Europe. The crucial difference between the Cold War and the present period is that the new strategy is based on a policy of action rather than deterrence through the threat of the use of nuclear weapons. In no member state has discussion on the issue been more acute than in Germany, where the debate over participation in both peacekeeping and peace-making operations was finally resolved in July 1994.[13]

Whither NATO and security in the new Europe?

By the turn of the century, the European Union may comprise twenty or more member states, covering many old adversarial relationships. It began by ending the rivalry between France and Germany that had plagued the continent for over a hundred years. By the millennium, it may be in the process of healing the rift in Central Europe that is the legacy of the Cold War. Throughout its history, the EU has progressed by deepening integration while at the same time widening membership. As the process of widening continues to eventually include the states of Central and Eastern Europe, the process of deepening is expected to include a security and defence dimension. If this process is successful, it will clearly raise questions about the role of NATO. The Western European Union is intended to be the link between the two. Eventually it will come back to the question of whether NATO has a long-term future. And the subtext of every such question is: does the United States have a continued role to play in European security? Until recently, the answer to both questions has always been yes. Increasing transatlantic disagreements, most crucially over Bosnia, have begun to undermine this consensus on European security.

While there are many, and contradictory, statements coming from all sides, it is almost certain that when the situation is clearer in a few years time, NATO will have been weakened by the Bosnian episode. It will remain in being, however, because Europe cannot offer any credible military alternative. The abolition of NATO would create a climate of uncertainty and increased instability in Europe. There may be the creation of a European pillar, but it will only be a supporting beam. This argument presupposes, however, that the United States will remain a willing participant in European security into the indefinite future. Do the Europeans and the Americans want and need each other? There are many reasons to say the answer should be in the affirmative. Without the participation of the US, a Europe-wide security organization is not credible. From the European perspective, a disaffected United States without a voice in any European institutions would have even less restraint on any tendency to act against European interests in the future. In an era when economic security is becoming the dominant theme, this would be a very worrying development for Europe. And a Europe without NATO and the United States would make the project of bringing all of Europe together an unbalanced and unlikely prospect. Since 1945, trans-atlantic cooperation and solidarity has been the cornerstone of peace and stability in Europe. It would be a sad and ironic twist of fate if a conflict in the Balkans was to be the factor which precipitated the beginning of the end of this historic project.

Notes

1. The end of the Cold War can be seen as a series of related events although there is no agreement on a precise date for its end. The usual ones cited are the fall of the Berlin Wall, the unification of Germany on 3 October 1990, or the CSCE Summit in Paris in November 1990. My own choice is the meeting at Stavropol on 16 July 1990, between President Gorbachev and Chancellor Kohl, when Gorbachev conceded that a united Germany could remain within the NATO Alliance.
2. See Latawski, Paul (1993), 'On Converging Paths? The Visegrád Group and the Atlantic Alliance', *Paradigms*, vol. 7, no. 2, Winter 1993.
3. CSCE Summit, Budapest, 5-6 December 1994.
4. For a detailed discussion of the INF episode, see, Hiester, Dan (1991), 'The United States as a Power in Europe', in Jordan, Robert (ed.), *Europe and the Superpowers: Essays on European International Politics*, Pinter, London, pp. 27-47.
5. See discussion on a European Security and Defence Identity (ESDI) below.
6. Von Moltke, Gebhardt (1994), 'Building a Partnership for Peace', *NATO Review*, no. 3, June 1994, p. 3.
7. See for example, 'The 1994 NACC Work Plan', *NATO Review*, no. 6, December 1993, pp. 30-33.
8. Von Moltke, *op.cit.*, p. 3.
9. *Ibid*, p. 4.
10. *The Guardian*, 3 December 1994.
11. Aspin, Les (1994), 'New Europe, new NATO', *NATO Review*, no. 1, February, pp. 12-14.
12. Hiester, Dan (1991), 'New Definitions of European Security', *Paradigms*, vol. 5, nos. 1/2, p. 61.
13. Kinkel, Dr. Klaus (1994), 'Peacekeeping missions: Germany can now play its part', *NATO Review*, no. 5, October, pp. 3-7.

3 The Former non-Soviet Warsaw Treaty Organization Countries' Security Choices in the Post-Cold War Era

MONIKA WOHLFELD

Introduction

Ever since the collapse of the Warsaw Treaty Organization (WTO) in 1991, its former non-Soviet members (NSWTO)[1] have presented gloomy pictures of their security needs, accompanied by dramatic pleas for western security guarantees. Many, if not most, western analysts perceive these Central European appeals as based on exaggerations of the threats and risks to their security, and often point out that they have already survived some four years without facing any genuine threat to their sovereignty and in spite of not having been granted Western security guarantees. Some suspect that the Central Europeans' desire for North Atlantic Treaty Organization (NATO) membership 'may be motivated more by a yearning to 'belong ' to the best institutions of Western life, of which NATO is a prime example, than by a rational assessment 'of the security blanket it could reasonably provide'[2] or that it is a mere 'lyrical invocation of a better future'.[3]

This chapter concentrates on these problems, focusing on the NSWTO countries' military security after the dissolution of the Eastern block. It provides a discussion of the Central Europeans' perceptions of sources of threats to their security, and the policies - both in the external and domestic realms - pursued by their governments as responses to these.

A discussion of the military security of the former non-Soviet Warsaw Treaty Organization members runs into the danger of generalizing where few common features are to be found except their common post-Communist and post-WTO legacy. Even prior to 1989, the non-Soviet WTO countries' national interests differed, though these differences were more or less kept in check by the bloc.[4] After the collapse of the WTO, the differences have become more pronounced. Today, some observers find it useful to divide the region, one which has been described as 'East of the West and West of the East' into northern and a southern tier, or the 'Visegrád Four', and Bulgaria and Romania.[5] Any division of that kind overlooks the fact that, while there are some similarities, even within these groups the approaches to matters of defence and security vary occasionally. Thus, where necessary, the chapter will make distinctions between individual countries.

Perceived sources of military insecurity

The Central Europeans' present day security threat perceptions are surrounded by ambiguity.[6] Following the collapse of the Eastern bloc, all the former NSWTO countries stated that they did not expect military aggression from any direction. Simultaneously, they stressed that their countries require firm security guarantees. They refrain from presenting specific threat scenarios, and yet continue to emphasize the importance of NATO and its vital role in Eastern and Central Europe, even if we may presume that confidential documents identify potential threats with more frankness.

Despite ambiguous definitions of the region's security problems, one can say that the newly democratic governments associate two kinds of potential sources of security threats, or risks, with the end of the Cold War - 'extraneous and home-made'. Domestic military security challenges, unlike the extraneous ones, are common to nearly all the Central European countries and centre around the reform of the armed forces. In Central Europe (unlike in the former Soviet Union) military transition cannot be seen as a threat to the democratic order. Rather, the region's armed forces, which are all undergoing difficult restructuring processes under tight fiscal requirements are often perceived as not being capable of dealing adequately with potential threats to the countries' security. For this reason, this chapter will address a number of issues relating to military reform.[7] Briefly stated, they include the necessary reduction of funding and size of the armed forces, the lack of military and security specialists and problems relating to civilian-military relations, the reform of stationing patterns, and the creation of new defence doctrines.

Extraneous challenges include the tensions between Central European countries themselves (often as effects of minority disputes), the conflict in the former Yugoslavia, the effects of the disintegration of the former Soviet Union, and to some degree also the German factor in the form of the country's unification. Due to their different geopolitical locations, the countries of the Central European region are coping with varying sets of extraneous security concerns.

Poland: The process of disintegration of the multi-national Soviet Union, and later of the destabilized post-Soviet republics, awakened fears of both a powerful and a weak Russia in Central Europe. Central Europeans do not necessarily see Russia as a potential aggressor - although at least the northern tier states take the possibility of a return to authoritarian rule and neo-imperialism in Russia seriously - but rather as reducing Central Europe to function as a *cordon sanitaire* by objecting to its wish for integration with Western organizations and institutions.[8] In this context, the integrity and sovereignty of former Soviet republics between Russia and Central Europe, such as the Ukraine, is seen by Central Europeans as important for their security.

Currently, Poland's relations with all its remaining neighbours can be described as relatively good. However, Poland, but also Czechoslovakia, initially saw their shared borders with a newly united Germany as a security liability. Even after Poland had settled the border issue with Germany in November 1990, it continued to fear German economic domination, and some policy-makers speculated that this influence could possibly culminate in pressure for the regional autonomy of formerly German areas. Germany's support of Central European aspirations for membership of Western organizations and institutions has had the impact of considerably quelling these fears.

In addition, there are tensions between Poland and Lithuania regarding the situation of the Polish minority in Lithuania. In July 1994 Lithuania remained the last neighbouring country with which Poland had not ratified a treaty of good-neighbourliness. The issues preventing the conclusion of such a treaty have largely been eliminated, but the difficult process necessary to find a formula acceptable to both point to the differences between the two governments.

The Czech Republic: This country is not only ethnically homogenous, it also 'has no reason to assume that any of its neighbours seek a revision of borders.'[9] Despite some initial concerns about the process of German unification, Germany is now its largest economic partner. The Czech Republic is the only Central European country which has no shared borders with the former Soviet Union, or with the Balkans.

Slovakia: In addition to the generally difficult relationship of the northern Central European countries with Russia, Slovakia finds itself potentially drawn eastward due to the fact that it has no borders with Western Europe.[10] Furthermore, Slovakia has difficult relations with its neighbour Hungary. The two countries differ on issues of a joint hydro-electric dam project on the Danube, and on the situation of the large Hungarian minority in Slovakia. The two countries have now submitted the dam dispute for arbitration by the International Court of Justice.

Hungary: The most important threat to Hungarian security stems from the continuing war in the former Yugoslavia.[11] This threat includes actual violations of air space and borders by Serb forces, arrival of waves of refugees, and economic losses due to the embargo imposed by the world community on the rump Yugoslavia. In addition, Hungary perceives border and minority issues as security problems. As Pál Dunay points out, 'Hungary is in a unique position in Central Europe, as it is practically the only country that could claim territories from nearly all of its neighbours, without being subjected to similar claims by other states.'12

Bulgaria: Bulgaria, with its traditionally good ties with Russia, is least worried about 'the Russian threat'. It is, however, affected by the war in the former Yugoslavia both directly (losses due to sanctions, disrupted communications and trade, the impact of refugees, and the possibility of a spill-over effect), and indirectly, by creating the perception of Bulgaria as unstable. In fact, the conflict in the former Yugoslavia constitutes probably the most serious trial for Bulgaria's foreign and security policy. Although relations with Greece and Turkey have improved, Bulgarian policy-makers continue to look at these two neighbours with suspicion.13

Romania: Threats to Romania's security include 'strained relations with Hungary, violence in Moldova that endangers the ethnic Romanian majority of that newly independent country, tension with Bulgaria and concerns regarding the emergence of Greater Serbia'.14 Nevertheless, Bucharest has been successful in distancing itself from tensions and crises in neighbouring areas.15

Given the presence of these problems, why do Central Europeans fail to provide clear definitions of threats to their security? Three factors help to explain this ambiguity. The first is the observation that the process of defining potential security threats in a fluid environment is a complicated one. After all, most of the former NSWTO countries have as their neighbours a number of, or even all, new states. Poland, for example, now has seven neighbours - all of them post-Cold War creations (a united Germany, the Czech and Slovak Republics, Belarus, Ukraine, Lithuania, and the Russian enclave of Kaliningrad). Hungary has acquired five new neighbours (Slovenia, Croatia, Serbia, the Ukraine and Slovakia). The second is that naming threats is seen as potentially hindering Central Europeans' not always successful attempts to create friendly bilateral relations with each other. There is also the constant fear of creating self-fulfilling prophecies. The final point is that the region's policy-makers are aware that most likely no immediate aggression will take place but 'recognize that the momentous changes of recent years should induce caution about attempts to extrapolate too much from the present'.16

Despite the difficulties surrounding the process of defining the directions from which security threats loom, Central Europe's post-Cold War perceptions of insecurity have intensified and simultaneously widened. 'A prevailing climate of mistrust and suspicion exists, denying security to proto-democracies that are extraordinarily in need of safety',17 writes Nelson. 'Most Central and East European states (the Czech Republic excepted) feel more insecure in 1994 than they did in 1989',[18] concludes Simon.

Unlike their neighbours to the south and east, however, the former NSWTO countries have so far succeeded in maintaining peace. Restraining factors may be partly rooted in their lack of capability to launch attacks, but most importantly in the policies pursued as responses to the perceived security threats. These policies, discussed further in the chapter, include the completion of bilateral treaties, regional cooperation and, most importantly, Central Europeans' contacts and links with Western institutions and organizations.

Policy responses

Domestic responses

The Renationalization of Defence: One of the processes that uniformly characterize the post-1989 Central European political landscape are a de-Sovietization and the renationalization of their armed forces.[19] Several types of lustration have been employed in a number of Central European countries in order to depoliticize the armed forces, which under the WTO functioned as tools of the communist regimes. Some countries, for example the former Czechoslovakia, have adopted a severe approach by screening all professional soldiers.[20] Countries which pursued a gradual process of transition, in which the 'post-communist' forces are not entirely discredited, such as Hungary and Poland, have so far avoided purges and conducted a de-Sovietization of the officer corps within the framework of reform of the defence sector. As Zielonka reports, 'even in Hungary and Poland about 75 per cent of high-ranking posts have been filled with new people.'[21] In many cases, retirements due to age take care of the problem. Professional soldiers are now required to remain apolitical. These processes have been relatively successful, although in some countries the debate surrounding the issue of lustration is far from over.

A second vital process was to educate civilian experts and establish civilian control of the military. The collapse of the Warsaw Pact left Central European countries (except maybe Romania) with militaries which had complete - and secretive - control over military issues. Without a body of civilian expertise, the Central European countries were forced to reform defence ministries, create parliamentary commissions, decide upon budgets, and begin a public debate on issues of defence and defence spending.

Today, civilians in the defence ministries and parliaments have assumed control over the military. However, some observers warn that 'few of them have developed any expertise in security matters or have any sympathy for the extensive needs of the defence sector.'[22] The area of security and defence policy-making has become a battlefield for many competing interests and political forces (which have nevertheless remained within the democratic framework).

Often, these power struggles translate into political paralysis.

Not surprisingly, civilian-military relations have been problematic, even though nowhere in Central Europe can military forces be considered a threat to the democratic process. Despite official assurances to the contrary, there is no former NSWTO country that has worked out *all* the issues involved in establishing effective civilian control of the military. All countries are, however, currently attempting to cope with this difficult task. As Tadeusz Mitek argues, 'the ability to formulate and consistently implement a cohesive defence policy is one of the main conditions for the stability of the state.'[23] In this process military doctrine plays an important function because its role is to guide the process of formulation of security and defence policies. In Central Europe, post-WTO security and defense policies have been, often on an *ad hoc* basis, adapted to reflect the new European realities, but their directions have for a long time not been codified in post-Cold War defence doctrines.[24] In addition, the new doctrines fail to specify potential conflict scenarios and thus, as Zielonka argues, fail to provide directions on how to cope with security problems.[25]

The defence doctrines of the former non-Soviet Warsaw Pact countries have three significant common features: in their declarations they profess to adhere to the principles of international law, concepts of limited defence, and circular defence. As such, the new defence doctrines constitute symbolic breaks with the doctrines adopted under the auspices of the WTO.

In addition to the declared adherence to laws of the United Nations (UN), and the Conference on Security and Cooperation in Europe (CSCE), as well as bilateral and multilateral agreements, the Central European defence doctrines profess to adhere to the principle of the inviolability of borders (although Hungary with its minorities abroad does not seem to exclude the possibility of peaceful border adjustments). One of the most important principles presented by the new defence doctrines is the move away from offensive posture, and the creation of principles for territorial defence. The main goals are to decrease the size of their armed forces, while increasing mobility, and to acquire defensive weaponry, such as for example required for air defence.[26] The practical implications of that change are further discussed under the section on reform of the armed forces.

Thirdly, in their new defence doctrines, Central European governments have decided to pursue defence based on a *tout azimuth* principle as a logical consequence of the 'no-enemy' concept. Thus, the idea of ensuring the defence of all borders was put forward as a guiding principle of the military restructuring process. The redistribution of forces allowed the Visegrád countries to deal with potential threats from the East without having to declare the Soviet Union as their main potential enemy. As during the existence of the WTO their forces were concentrated almost exclusively in the western or southern sections of their territories, a redistribution was initiated, but has proved difficult. One exception is Romania which even during the WTO years had a national military doctrine based on the concept of 'homeland defence', one which could remain in place largely unchanged after the collapse of the bloc.[27]

The Bulgarian Defence Minister stated recently that in his country:

> 'the relocation of the army from the southern borders inland across the country's entire territory, envisaged by the new military defensive doctrine, is being delayed indefinitely due to the impossibility of raising the money needed for the development, almost from scratch, of a new military infrastructure of the future corps whose mission is to cover the Serbian and Romanian borders'.[28]

Even the richer northern tier countries can claim only partial success in the relocation of the armed forces across their territories.   Considering the tremendous expense connected with setting up new infrastructures, some of the former NSWTO countries can be expected to tacitly move away from this concept, or at least suspend or postpone its implementation.   Kusin points out that the Czech Republic is the only Central European country which 'can bask in a friendly sun "on all *azimuths*"',[29] as it does not face serious threats to its security.

The practical implications of the principles contained in the new Central European doctrines remain rather vague. Generalizing somewhat, it is possible to say that not all of the new ideas presented by the post-WTO defence doctrines in Central Europe actually guide the making of security and defence policies at the moment. While Central Europeans can be expected to continue to adhere to principles which do not require substantial financial commitments, without external financial support they may slow down or move away from carrying out costly redeployments.

Reform of the Armed Forces

Central European armed forces are undergoing the processes of reform. Some of the changes, particularly cuts in the size of the armed forces, date back to the late 1980s, but most were initiated after the dissolution of the WTO. Voluntary and enforced scaling down of the size of their armed forces and levels of armaments is an important trend, with the northern tier countries taking the lead.   While the impact of the 1990 Conventional Armed Forces in Europe (CFE) treaty and the new emphasis on defensive rather than offensive capabilities, as in the WTO, play a role, one of the causes of that process are financial constraints.   The difficult economic situation of the officer corps resulted in what has been called 'an exodus of career and non-commissioned officers'.[30] The CFE treaty in itself has little impact on most former non-Soviet WTO states' militaries.[31]

Another important principle of reform is inter-operability and compatibility with western standards. This principle was intended to guide the modernization of equipment and arms acquisition, as well as the training of forces, but efforts have been hampered by a number of difficulties, including a shortage of English-speakers, a lack of funds to purchase Western equipment and technology,[32] and social costs created by elimination of jobs in the defence industries. Generally speaking, 'Central European armies are opening themselves to the West, but they are still equipped with Soviet arms and dependent on Soviet/CIS weapons procurement.'[33] In addition to financial problems, reducing dependence on Soviet equipment has been hampered by western export restrictions, imposed both by the now defunct Coordinating Committee for Multilateral Export Controls (COCOM), which regulated western trade with the former East Bloc and by national control systems in individual countries, particularly the United States. In July 1994 the US Congress gave permission to the four Visegrád states to purchase American arms. This decision has not led to a stampede of buying as the four countries do not possess the necessary funds to embark on purchases, but the measure does address some of their concerns regarding arms procurement.[34]

Central European defence planners stress mobility over heavy equipment. They are undertaking the effort of creating lightly-armoured, mobile forces and rapid reaction forces, as well as preparing quick mobilization procedures. However, the costs of such restructuring are forbidding. While some units of that kind have been created, in the immediate and mid-term future they can be expected to remain an exception. In addition, the creation of rapid reaction units carries the danger of creating tensions with neighbouring countries, against which such forces might potentially be used.

A further goal is a professionalization of the armed forces. In most Central European countries, around 50 per cent of the total troop strength is made up of conscripts. Despite announcements of expected changes of the ratio of conscripts to professional soldiers, most Central European countries now recognize that such reforms are costly. Furthermore, they realize that it will be difficult to fill professional positions, as young people are deterred by low wages and the often low prestige of military jobs, and choose to enter the private sector.

The effort to professionalize the armed forces is also aimed at creating peace-keeping capabilities. 'Few experts in eastern and central Europe believe there will be highly effective ways to perform regional peacekeeping or peace-enforcement missions in the coming years',[35] but the Central European countries are prepared to participate in international peace-keeping activities and to cooperate with other countries in training peace-keepers. Central European states view peace-keeping operations as a tool for integration with NATO forces. All Central European countries either actively participate in UN peace-keeping missions, or are preparing for such a task. In addition, an extensive network of exchange and training programmes has been built up with the participation of a number of Western European and North American countries.

Although the process of restructuring of the armed forces has been proceeding, it is severely affected by the phenomenon of budgetary shrinkage.[36] It is apparent that countries facing critical domestic problems and dealing with the impact of economic transition cannot give complete priority to the modernization and reform of their militaries and it is impossible to assess the prospects for implementation of the above discussed principles. In the meantime, the armed forces of the former NSWTO countries cannot provide the capabilities perceived to be necessary to cope with perceived threats. The structural changes are limited by budgetary restrictions, but their direction is clear: they are aimed at achieving NATO membership. As Simon reports, Central European governments portray 'their military restructuring as an instrument for achieving the goal of Western integration rather than as one of meeting immediate defense needs and requirements.'[37]

External responses

For the first time since the end of the Second World War, Central European countries had, at least in theory, a number of foreign policy options open to them. The newly democratic Central European governments have advocated a number of different approaches in order to enhance their security. The description of their responses is not an easy task, as they varied from country to country, and on occasion countries advocated several different options simultaneously.

Some Western observers suggested in 1990 and 1991 that a neutral or non-aligned status for the countries of Central Europe would permit them to free themselves gradually from the Soviet Union's domination.[38] Others argued that although no former NSWTO country would wish to be part of a 'buffer zone', they play that role 'by virtue of geography'.[39] After the collapse of the WTO, the Kremlin pursued a policy attempting to 'Finlandize' the region.[40] While in 1989 some of Hungary's policy-makers considered the prospect of a status similar to Finnish neutrality for their country, none of the former NSWTO seemed to see this option as a possibility by early 1991. The total lack of security and economic guarantees that such status would entail meant that from that moment on, Central Europe began to look to Western institutions and organizations when thinking about the future. Recently, there have been reports of a resurgence of the idea of neutrality among Slovakia's opposition. The upcoming elections will show how strong these forces are, but neutral status would certainly mean stronger ties to Russia.[41]

The second foreign policy option explored was a collective, pan-European security framework.[42] Encouraged by the rapid collapse of the Cold War structures, Central European countries, and especially Czechoslovakia, put their hopes in the CSCE process and its future transformation into a pan-

European collective security framework. This country, on its own and jointly with other states, advocated a number of ambitious schemes, beginning in early 1990. However, Central European attitudes towards security began to change substantially in late 1990, which marked the end of the period of euphoria over the collapse of the Cold War frameworks. In addition, the CSCE Paris Summit in November 1990 provided the sobering insight that the organization would not and could not take on the role envisaged for it by Central Europeans. The concept of collective pan-European security has not been entirely abandoned by the former NSWTO countries, but it is no longer seen by them as a source of security guarantees. It does constitute, however, Russia's preferred choice. Recently, Russia's Defence Minister Pavel Grachev presented at a conference of NATO defence ministers a plan according to which NATO would be subordinated to the CSCE.[43] Such a solution is unacceptable to the Central Europeans.

The foreign policy choice at which all former NSWTO countries eventually arrived was membership of Western organizations and institutions. NATO, the WEU, and occasionally also the post-Maastricht EU, were all seen as potential sources of security guarantees, and Central Europeans pursued a 'catch-all' policy aimed at establishing links with as many of these as possible.

The idea of joining NATO gathered momentum and played early on the foremost role for at least the northern tier countries, as it was seen as the only existent and operational security framework. The Central European states saw NATO and the continued presence of the United States in Europe as a more important element of stability than did many of its member countries whose leaderships wondered if NATO had become obsolete. According to the *Security for Europe Project*:

> 'when asked what the benefits of full membership would be, specialists in the Visegrád countries cite two principal things: (1) a reliable military guarantee against external threats; and (2) a vehicle for promoting internal political and economic stability and democratization'.[44]

At the NATO Rome Summit of November 1991, NATO members agreed to deepen the dialogue with nine countries of the former NSWTO and the Baltic republics. They issued an invitation to all former WTO countries to join them in a North Atlantic Cooperation Council (NACC). The invitation reflected the NATO member countries' desire to preserve their interests while offering cooperation on civil-military relationships, defence policy, defence conversion, and peace-keeping[45] that would not carry a large price tag. Central European states found the NACC to be what Kusin calls a 'meet-and-chat-groove'[46] - a forum for communication, and continued to push for full NATO membership.

The Western alliance responded by introducing the Partnership for Peace (PfP) initiative,[47] an American blueprint first presented at the NATO defence ministers' meeting in Travemunde in October 1993. The January 1994 NATO summit adopted the proposal which was open to all CSCE countries.[48] In principle it agrees to opening NATO to new members without specifying when and how. The initiative met with a mixed reception, with Romania and Bulgaria more enthusiastic than their northern neighbours who were hoping for more.[49]

Another, less attractive, alternative was the Western European Union (WEU). Until June 1992, when the WEU offered the six NSWTO countries and the three Baltic republics (Lithuania, Latvia and Estonia) the status of Consultation Partners, it had only informal contacts with the region's countries. The Forum for Consultation focused on discussions on 'the security architecture and stability in Europe, the future development of the CSCE, arms control and disarmament'.[50] The Forum's task was 'to get to know each other better', rather than to provide any sort of security guarantees.

In May 1994, the WEU offered its consulting partners the status of 'associate partners'.[51] The associate partnership status reflects the Central European countries' Europe Agreements. It has been condoned by all the countries at which it was aimed, but has elicited only sparing comment, and little political attention. Generally speaking, it is accepted in Central Europe that it will have little effect on the NSWTO countries' military security. But Central Europeans continue to press for membership in that organization as well. An advantage of the WEU is the fact that, unlike in NATO, there is no threat of Russia achieving special status within it, and that it is linked to other European and trans-Atlantic institutions and organizations.

The Central Europeans occasionally mention the European Union (EU) as a potential source of security guarantees. The EU does not yet have a security role except for stabilizing economies and political systems. Under the Maastricht Treaty, the EU established links with the WEU and created a Common Foreign and Security Policy (CFSP). The first CFSP action undertaken was the decision to back the Stability Pact initiative (discussed below) which has not met with the full support of the former NSWTO countries. Central Europeans continue to press for EU membership, but they do not treat it foremost as a security framework.

NATO in particular continues for Central Europeans to be the most significant organization in terms of security. In the West, however, the debate over the place of Central Europe within the European security architecture is far from being over.[52] That Western dispute is judged as threatening by Central Europe: 'the intensifying quarrels within the Euro-Atlantic community are one of the chief sources of the security deficit and of tensions in Europe, including Central Europe.'[53] In addition, Central Europeans are concerned that NATO and WEU are not inter-locking, as it is often suggested, but rather competitive or even inter-blocking organizations.[54]

As cooperation initiated by Western security organizations fell short of Central European expectations, the regions' governments established a number of regional and sub-regional groupings. Most of them, however, did not have the potential, nor the aspiration, to develop into security cooperation frameworks.

The most prominent regional organization, the Visegrád Group, consists of Poland, Hungary, and the Czech and Slovak republics and came into being in 1990. There is no Visegrád provision for mutual assistance in cases of aggression, but consultations are foreseen. The Group sees the goal of improving relations with Western organizations as its priority. Member countries consider the Visegrád Group as a step towards NATO and EU membership and not as an alternative to either organization. Although the group facilitates military cooperation between the countries, such as training and exchange of spare parts, it chose not to take on a clear security dimension. The Czech republic is most explicitly opposed to a deepening of that group, and sees its future as a consultative forum. It seems that the initial motives (common interest in overcoming the effects of Soviet domination) which bound these countries together have been exhausted and new ones have not yet been defined.

There are other regional organizations, such as the Central European Initiative, the Black Sea Cooperation Zone, and the Council of Baltic Sea Countries, but none have taken on a security dimension. There have also been some, so far unsuccessful, proposals to create regional security cooperation structures. The Ukraine has suggested the creation of a security zone with the participation of Central European countries (but not Russia). Central European countries have distanced themselves from this initiative.[55] A similar plan, the 'NATO-2' proposal, was suggested by Polish President Lech Walesa in 1992, but was not backed by the country's government, and has withered away as NATO established cooperation schemes with Central European countries. There are no comparable cooperation structures in the Balkans, and Bulgaria and Romania cannot draw any comfort from that sort of grouping.

Lack of security guarantees makes bilateral contacts more significant. Nevertheless, in Central Europe bilateral treaties are seen as 'supplementary measures.' This approach characterizes the former NSWTO countries' attitude to the EU's Stability Pact (also called the 'Balladur Plan' after its creator), an initiative aimed at stabilizing the Central European region by means of backing the conclusion of bilateral treaties between states that are experiencing tensions related to minority or ethnic issues. Because the plan is endorsed by the EU, all the countries have pledged to participate in the conference - but without enthusiasm. Central Europeans criticize the plan because they consider it vague, based on inadequate provisions of international law, and most importantly, because it concentrates solely on Central and Eastern European 'hot-spots', even though numerous Western European countries face similar ethnic and secessionist problems. All Central European governments reason that European integration with a strong Atlantic component is a better answer to the region's problems than the bilateral treaties proposed by the Balladur plan.[56]

Admittedly, bilateral treaties have accomplished little. As Nelson points out:

'some countries have gained a modicum of reassurance about the intentions of their neighbours through negotiations, while most states in post-communist Europe have been busily signing accords with as many near and distant countries as possible, hoping to insulate themselves from a hostile environment'.[57]

Bilateral agreements in Central Europe declare the resolve to cooperate. As such their only contribution to the signatories' security is one of promoting transparency and enhancing mutual confidence and trust. For Central European governments, the reassurance provided by bilateral agreements is a necessary, but not sufficient precondition for security.

The future military security of Central Europe

While many Western observers insinuate that events prove that the former NSWTO countries do not require Western security guarantees, in the opinion of Central European governments the current situation of *de facto* neutrality/non-alignment is a dangerous one. Central Europeans do not extrapolate their security threat perceptions from today's relatively peaceful situation, but they do foresee the possibility of a worsening of their security environment. They are afraid that the security vacuum could encourage neighbouring Russia to expand its influence, or that crises in neighbouring areas could destabilize the region.

The new security and defence policies pursued by the former NSWTO members attempt to cope with the fact that no country in Central Europe can guarantee its security on its own, even if it undertakes all-out militarization, and that no security guarantees will be forthcoming in the foreseeable future. They have not been directed towards coping with the threats directly, but rather towards creating conditions for entering Western organizations and institutions, which could provide security guarantees. In addition to the Western-oriented foreign and security policies, the reforms of the armed forces have also been aimed at membership. Thus, Central European countries have tied their fate to the expected NATO membership in more ways than one.

While NATO has indicated that it is in principle open to new members, Central Europeans miss assurances to that effect, as well as some form of timetable, indicating when that goal could be achieved. Central Europe requires an unequivocal time-frame for such a development. As Simon observes, 'an important concern of the Central European states, one that they feel is little understood and under-appreciated in the West, is that their social-psychological imperative requires short-term goals - three to five years.'[58]

Should admission be delayed or rejected, the Central European defence and security policies could find themselves in a blind alley. Central European governments would be forced to return to 'square one' - with the added disadvantages that scarce resources have been wasted on reform measures which in themselves cannot assure the countries' security, that the newly democratic governments could be undermined at home by their foreign and security policy failure, and that the region could be destabilized by a return to offensive defence postures. While security guarantees are beyond reach, Central Europeans can only build contacts with Western organizations, as well as create regional and bilateral ties, and deal with the most significant problems of their armed forces. They do not consider these measures to be sufficient in themselves. There is a growing feeling of insecurity where security is needed so that resources and attention can be diverted to other issues, and foreign investment attracted.

Do Central European governments have any other options but that of pursuing NATO membership? There is certainly the possibility of creating a framework that resembles the former WTO. As long as there are prospects of integration with Western structures, Central Europeans are not interested in any sort of arrangement which could throw them back into the arms of Russia. Such an option would also not be in the interest of the West. For the former NSWTO countries NATO membership remains the only viable policy option. The problem of conjunction between Central and Western European assessments of the situation after the collapse of the WTO is based on the fact that Western observers do not appear to realize how much the entire process of transition and reform of security and defence policies is geared towards membership in Western organizations, and that Central Europeans fail to communicate what it is exactly that drives them into these structures.

Notes

1. The Pact's non-Soviet members were Albania until 1968, Bulgaria, Czechoslovakia, the German Democratic Republic until October 1990, Hungary, Poland, and Romania which followed a relatively independent policy from 1963 onward. The former NSWTO countries discussed here (Poland, the Czech and Slovak Republics, Hungary, Romania and Bulgaria) will also be referred to as Central Europe.
2. Chipman, John (1992), 'The Future of Strategic Studies: Beyond Even Grand Strategy', *Survival*, Spring, p. 121.
3. Liebich, André (1991), 'Wither Eastern Europe', Behind the Headlines, Autumn, p. 9.
4. On this issue, see Bender, Peter (1972), *East Europe in Search of Security*, London, Chatto and Windus.

5. Kjell Engelbrekt argues that the biggest difference between the Visegrád four and the remaining NSWTO countries is that 'unlike in Central Europe, the post-communist era has not caused dramatic changes in the security arrangement in southeastern Europe.' See Engelbrekt, Kjell (1994),'Southeast European States Seek Equal Treatment', *RFE/RL Research Report*, vol. 3, no. 12, 25 March, p. 42. That may be the case as far as their defence posture is concerned, but the war in the former Yugoslavia, and the tensions and violence accompanying the dissolution of the Soviet Union in its former southern republics caused a relatively radical change in their security environment. Pál Dunay indicates for example that 'the strategic importance of ... [Romania] has significantly increased after the collapse of the bloc system in Europe, as it borders on both major crisis areas of the continent, the Balkans and the [former] Soviet Union.' See Dunay, Pál (1994), 'Adversaries All Around? (Re)Nationalization of Security and Defense Policies in Central and Eastern Europe', *Clingendael Paper*, January, p. 41. The impact of the war in former Yugoslavia would suggest a different division, into Hungary, Bulgaria and Romania which are experiencing the crisis at first hand, and the remaining countries of Central Europe.

6. See for example Zielonka, Jan (1992), 'Security in Central Europe', *Adelphi Paper* 272, Autumn.

7. Other domestic instabilities, although probably considered by the Central European governments to be among the most significant security threats, are beyond the scope of security and defence policy-making. This chapter will leave it up to the economists to deal with that issue.

8. Russia's claims to a 'sphere of influence', and its ideas concerning a Western-Russian patronage or condominium in Central Europe are seen by these countries as potentially threatening their sovereignty. Russian claims to have 'special interests' or a 'special role' in the neighbouring countries are seen as equally dangerous. On that issue see for example Kusin, Vladimir (1993), 'NATO and Central Europe: The Problem of Conjunction', *Notes from the Special Adviser for Central and East European Affairs*, 26 October; 'Statement by Mr. Andrzej Olechowski at the Ost-West Wirtschaftsakademie, Berlin, 9 May, 1994', *Materials and Documents* 3-4/1994, p. 406.

9. Dunay, p. 18.

10. The effect of the Czechoslovak divorce seems to have been further reinforced by Germany's insistence on making the border between the Czech and Slovak Republics less permeable due to concerns over migration. See Kadlec, Ladislav (1993), 'Security Perspectives of Central Europe: A View from Slovakia', in *The Search for Peace in Europe: Perspectives from NATO and Eastern Europe*, Charles L. Barry (ed.). Fort Lesley: National Defense University Press, p. 184.

11. Szabo, Zoltan (1993), 'European Security Challenges: A View from East-Central Europe', in Barry (ed.), p. 149.
12. Dunay, p. 18. The 1920 Treaty of Trianon in which Hungary lost a substantial part of it territory left it with large minorities in Romania, Slovakia and Serbia.
13. See for example Srebrev, Mikhail (1993), 'Southern Europe: Concerns and Implications from a Bulgarian Perspective', in Barry (ed.), p. 226.
14. Nelson, Daniel (1993), 'Creating Security in the Balkans', in *Central and Eastern Europe: The Challenge of Transition*, Regina Cowen Karp (ed.), Oxford, Oxford University Press, p. 168.
15. Dunay, p. 41.
16. *Security for Europe Project: Final Report*, Center for Foreign Policy Development, Brown University, December 1993, p. 36.
17. Nelson, Daniel N. (1993), 'Democracy, Markets and Security in Eastern Europe', *Survival*, vol. 35, no. 2, p. 166.
18. Simon, Jeffrey (1994), 'Central European Security, 1994: Partnership for Peace (PfP)'. *Strategic Forum* 1, p. 1.
19. See for example Gasteyger, Curt (1991), 'The remaking of Eastern Europe's security', *Survival*, vol. 33, no. 2, March/April; Engelbrekt, Kjell (1992), 'Reforms Reach the Bulgarian Armed Forces', *RFE/RL Research Report*, 24 January.
20. In Czechoslovakia some 5,000 high ranking officers, including all generals, deputy ministers of defence, heads of military colleges, district commanders and political officers have been released in the process, Zielonka, p. 47.
21. *Ibid.*, p. 47.
22. *Ibid.*, p. 46.
23. *Polska Zbrojna*, 3 November 1992, trans. in FBIS-EU, 10 November 1992.
24. Romania is the only Central European country with a pre-1989 independent national defence doctrine. Consequently, the military doctrine adopted and implemented during the Warsaw Pact years is still applicable. Other Central European countries had to create them from scratch. Poland has a post-Cold War doctrine since November 1992, Hungary since December 1993 (in force since January 1994), Bulgaria since 1993. Czechoslovakia's strategic planning was made difficult by the 'velvet divorce'. The Czech Republic has not adopted its separate defence doctrine yet, and continues to refer to the common 1992 doctrine. Slovakia has had a new doctrine since June 1994.
25. Zielonka, p. 49.
26. Dunay, pp. 37-38.
27. Dunay provides an apt description of Romania's situation: 'For Romania, the problem of military adaptation seems both less and more complex than for the Central European countries. It is less complex, in that the military doctrine adopted and implemented during the Warsaw Pact years

is still applicable. It is more complex in that the country is surrounded by trouble spots and potential adversaries, which may give the impression that modernization is an urgent matter. Regardless of the challenges and temptations, the conclusion is that the Romanian leadership has not taken radical steps and keeps a low profile in military affairs - Dunay, p. 41.

28. 'Bulgaria's Membership in WEU, NATO: a Matter of the Highest Political Morality and Responsibility. Statements by Dr. Valentin Alexandrov, Minister of Defence of the Republic of Bulgaria - The Geostrategic Situation in Eastern Europe and Bulgaria - Statement at the General Staff Academy of the Bundeswehr in Hamburg, 21 September 1993', p. 29.

29. Kusin, p. 8.

30. Reisch, Alfred A. (1993), 'The Hungarian Army in Transition', *RFE/RL Research Report*, 5 March, p. 38.

31. The only exception might be that CFE limited equipment from other NATO countries flows into Turkey, affecting Bulgarian perceptions of security. See Nelson, 'Creating Security in the Balkans', p. 161.

32. In 1993, Hungary accepted 28 MiG fighters from Russia in partial repayment of trade debts. Shortly after Slovakia accepted a similar settlement. Bulgaria appears to be considering the acquisition of MiGs as well. See Riols, Yves-Michel (1994), 'Hongrie: la recherche de l'autonomie militaire', *Le Monde*, 31 January; Robinson, Anthony (1994), 'Eastern Europe caught in a new arms race', *Financial Times*, 12 January; Plichta, Martin (1994), 'Slovaquie: balbutiements', *Le Monde*, 31 January.

33. Zielonka, p. 46.

34. For the history of COCOM, see Rudka, Andrzej (1991), 'Western Export Controls: An East European View', in Kemme, David M. (ed.), *Technology Markets and Export Controls in the 1990s*, New York, New York University Press, pp. 17-19. On the modification of the COCOM régime see Engelbrekt, Kjell (1993), 'Bulgaria and the Arms Trade', *RFE/RL Research Report*, vol. 2, no. 7, 12 February 1993, p. 45. On the dissolution of COCOM, see Buchan, David (1994), 'World Trade Confusion in Shadowy Paris HQ', *Financial Times*, 31 March 1994.

35. *Security for Europe Project*, p. 41.

36. On Poland, Lys, Grzegorz (1994), 'Cost of Joining NATO', *Polish News Bulletin*, 27 Jan.; on Hungary, 'Budget Allocations for national defense "utterly insufficient", says minister', *BBC SWB EE*, 12 October 1993, on Bulgaria, Simon, Jeffrey (1994), 'Central European Security, 1994: Partnership for Peace (PfP)', *Strategic Forum* 1, p. 4.

37. Simon, p. 2.

38. See, for example, Buzan, Barry et al (1990), *The European Security Order Recast: Scenarios for the Post-Cold War Era* , London, Pinter; Kissinger, Henry (1990), 'A Plan for Europe', *Newsweek*, 18 June; Van Evera, Steven (1990/1991), 'Primed for Peace: Europe After the Cold War', *International Security*, Winter; Bitzinger, Richard A. (1991), 'Neutrality for Eastern

Europe: Problems and Prospects', *Bulletin of Peace Proposals*, vol. 22, no. 3, September.

39. See for example Davis, Paul K. and Howe, Robert D. (1990), *Planning for Long-Term Security in Central Europe: Implications of the New Strategic Environment*, Santa Monica, RAND, August, pp. 4-5.

40. Roucek, Libor (1992), 'After the Bloc: The New International Relations in Eastern Europe', *RIIA Discussion Paper* 40, p. 6. The Soviet Union put forward a set of new bilateral treaties with Central European countries. The Soviet proposal included a clause which stipulated that they could not be part of 'any military alliance which could be directed against the USSR'. The clause was withdrawn after the August 1991 coup. See Zielonka, p. 38; Sharp, Jane M.O. (1992), 'Security Options for Central Europe in the 1990s', in *The Future of European Security*, Beverly Crawford (ed.), Berkeley, University of California.

41. Robejsek, Peter (1994), 'Driften Visegrad-Staaten zu Russland ab? Ostmitteleuropas Annaeherung an westliche Strukturen wird sich verlangsamen', *Die Welt*, 8 July.

42. According to Booth, 'the basic principle of collective security is that an attack upon one state will be regarded as an attack upon all states. In theory, the international community would act as one to deter and, if necessary, to stamp out aggression.' Booth, Ken (1987), 'Alliances', in *Contemporary Strategy I*, John Baylis et al (ed.), New York, Holmes and Meier, p. 302.

43. Pflueger, Friedbert (1994), 'Take PfP one step further', *The Wall Street Journal (Europe)*, 6 July.

44. *Security for Europe Project*, p. 43.

45. Mihalka, Michael (1994), 'Squaring the Circle: NATO's Offer to the East', *RFE/RL Research Report* vol. 3, no. 12, 25 March, p. 2.

46. Kusin, p. 7.

47. For the Text of the Partnership for Peace invitation, see *RFE/RL Research Report*, vol. 3, no. 12, 25 March 1994, p. 22. For the list of NATO Partners up until June 1994, see *NATO Review*, no. 3, June 94, p. 6.

48. It is based on the partners' submitting proposals of cooperation (joint exercises and training, particularly in peacekeeping, search and rescue, disaster relief and crisis management) and developing inter-operability at their own expense. It provides for consultations in the event of a direct threat to the territorial integrity, political independence or security of a partner state, but gives no security guarantees. Partnership for Peace emphasizes cooperation in the area of peacekeeping. Partners are represented at the NATO headquarters in Brussels, and a Cooperation Cell in Mons. Joint exercises and defence planning are part of the initiative.
The PfP can be expected to improve multilateral military cooperation with Western countries. Currently, however, PfP cooperation seems to thrive on bilateral levels rather than on an institutional level, thus not satisfying

Central European hopes. See for example 'Bulgarian-German ties boosted', *The Financial Times*, 29 March 1994; 'Hungary welcomes proposed peace-keeping military exercise with Britain, Germany', *BBC SWB EE*, 30 April 1994; 'Polska-NATO: wspolne cwiczenia', *Rzeczpospolita*, 14-15 May 1994.

49. Engelbrekt, Kjell (1994), 'Southeast European States Seek Equal Treatment', *RFE/RL Research Report*, vol. 3, no. 12, 25 March; Reisch, Alfred A. (1994), 'Central Europeans' Disappointments and Hopes', *RFE/RL Research Report* vol. 3, no. 12, 25 March.

50. *Extraordinary Meeting of the WEU Council of Ministers with States of Central Europe*, Bonn, 19 June 1992. See also van Eekelen, Willem (1993), 'Western European Union - The 'European Security Nucleus', *NATO's Sixteen Nations* , no. 3.

51. The offer provides for the possibility of attending some of the WEU meetings. Partners will have the right to speak but not to veto decisions. The agreement does not provide for partners being able to call emergency meetings. They have the right (but not the duty) to participate in WEU actions, for example peace-keeping operations. The new status does not provide any security guarantees, and does not offer prospects for full membership. See *Declaration* , WEU Council of Ministers, Luxembourg, 22 November 1993.

52. Kusin, p. 1.

53. Szlajfer, Henryk (1993), 'A View of Central and East European Security from Warsaw', in Barry (ed.), p. 171.

54. Simon, p. 2.

55. Reisch, Alfred A. (1993), 'Central and Eastern Europe's Quest for NATO membership', *RFE/RL Research Report*, 9 July 1993.

56. The discussion of the Stability Pact draws on Wohlfeld, Monika (1994), 'Implications of the Yugoslav crisis: the impact on relations between EU-WEU and Central Europe', forthcoming as a *Chaillot Paper*.

57. Nelson, 'Democracy, Markets, and Security ...', p. 166.

58. Simon, p. 2.

4   Security Issues in the Former Soviet Union and the Question of 'Russia Resurgent'

ELAINE HOLOBOFF

Introduction[1]

The disintegration of one of the world's two superpowers brought a series of tremors to the region of the former Soviet Union (FSU), as well as to the international community. In the process, post-communist states have faced a multitude of traumas: fragmentation and coalescence of new state structures; economic transition without precedent; political upheaval and chaos; the legacy of environmental degradation; and cultural shock. Given these various difficulties which face the countries of the FSU it is useful to occasionally step back and take stock of the situation. What are the most serious and pressing security issues? How do they manifest themselves? What should western policy be?

The purpose of this chapter is to discuss two central issues which have been of major concern to both Russia's neighbours and also to the international community. Since 1993 there has been increasing concern about Russia's role as a great regional power, as well as the way in which Moscow deals with her neighbours. Secondly, the emergence of ultra-right nationalists in Russia, and their clear successes in the December 1993 parliamentary elections caused alarm among Russia's friends and neighbours. The way in which these developments proceed will have a profound impact on the security of Russia itself, as well as on that of its neighbours. Many governments in the newly independent states anxiously follow political, economic, and military developments in Moscow in the clear knowledge that their security is integrally tied to that of their largest neighbour. Similarly with western countries, there are increasing concerns about 'Russia resurgent', as well as the political situation within the country. In this sense there can be no regional security in the FSU if Russia itself is unstable within and unpredictable in external affairs. How have developments proceeded in these areas? Is there cause for concern? And what path should western policy follow? These are the questions which are considered below.

Defining a new Russian identity

Russia came late in the day to the realization that it was no longer a superpower, and that in the new Eurasia even its role as a regional power was under threat. Throughout 1992 western policy, and especially American policy, sought to protect Russia's great power sensibilities and to promote the image of a still powerful country. Russia was to be included in all major negotiations, an extra measure of fanfare was to accompany any leadership summit, and promises of brotherly economic aid abounded even if they proved disappointing in their delivery. Much of this reflected benevolence rather than reality. It could not compensate for Russia's loss of superpower status nor the country's apparent lack of policy towards its neighbours. Yet the West could afford to be 'charitable'. With communist ideology having suffered from spontaneous combustion and the Russian economy reeling from the convulsions of transition, few believed that there was any chance that Moscow would set about recreating the now dead Soviet sphere of influence.

However, if it was impossible for Russia to recreate its superpower status and activities, there still existed a pressing necessity for the country to define a new regional role. Throughout 1993 a new Russian assertiveness could be discerned in foreign and defence policy. There was a growing belief that 'liberal internationalism', a holdover from the Gorbachev period, was not in the Russian national interest. In particular, aligning the country's interests too closely with the West could obscure real threats and opportunities. Domestic criticism of Russia's 'special relationship' with America, disillusionment with western aid promises, and growing anti-western attitudes all came to the fore. By April 1993 a rough cross-party consensus on foreign policy priorities arose, as evidenced by the publication of Russia's first official foreign policy concept.[2] Though many would come to differ about the 'means' and methods of carrying out foreign policy, few would disagree with the sentiment that Russia had a right to consider the FSU a sphere of special influence, not least because of the 25 million ethnic Russians residing in the 'near abroad'. Thus defence of the Russian population outside Russia became a major security issue. Finally, following the October 1993 attack on the Russian parliament, the military establishment succeeded in consolidating its power, this as a direct result of their seemingly reluctant support for President Yeltsin's actions during these tense days. By November 1993 the military leadership was in a secure enough position to declare a new military doctrine,[3] and to set a more assertive agenda for the 'near abroad'.

All of these developments contributed to an impetus to create a new identity for Russia as a regional power. Moscow has sought to accomplish this in a number of ways, all of which have made for a new Russian assertiveness (some would say 'aggressiveness') towards regions of the FSU. How has this been done? First, Russia has sought increasingly to dominate the Commonwealth of Independent States (CIS) process. Initially Russia's power within the CIS was constrained by other major actors such as the Ukraine and Kazakhstan. Now however, the modest pretence of egalitarianism seems to have been shed and Russia is playing a clear hegemonic role within the organization. Though not always achieving its goals within the CIS, Russia has nonetheless sought to use this forum to exert pressure on its neighbours. Second, Russia is evidencing a new economic assertiveness, for example by using economic means to influence its neighbours. This has included drawing some countries closer into Russia's sphere of influence by bringing them back into the rouble zone, e.g. Belarus; and using economic leverage to achieve political and military aims, e.g. the use of the Ukraine's energy debt to Russia to achieve concessions on the Black Sea Fleet; and pressure on Azerbaijan to not sign international oil agreements without Russia's agreement. It is clear that Russia seeks to dominate the oil and gas industries in the FSU, with all the consequent advantages inherent in such a monopoly.[4]

In addition to political and economic methods of influence, Moscow has also resorted to the use of military instruments to assert its sphere of influence. Most notably Russia has used the deployment of 18,000 'peacekeeping forces' in the region of the FSU as a rationale for being involved in regions such as Tajikistan, Transdniester in Moldova, North/South Ossetia in Russia and Georgia respectively, and Abkhazia in Georgia. Russia is using 'peacekeeping' as a method of accomplishing both strategic and tactical aims in regions of conflict. Strategic aims include securing border regions; containing instability so that it does not spread into Russia itself; drawing countries back into Russia's sphere of influence; and securing outposts for the Russian military. More limited tactical aims include the protection of ethnic Russians, including those in the armed forces and their families; general humanitarian assistance; and stemming the flow of illegal arms and other contraband material. Russia is planning to train and use rapid deployment forces from the Trans-Volga and Urals military districts as peacekeeping and peace-enforcement units. These will include paratroopers, land, marine, and air forces.

Russia has also begun to offer itself as a third party mediator in various regional conflicts of the FSU, for example, in the Armenian/Azerbaijani conflict over Nagorno-Karabakh when the CSCE negotiations failed; in the Abkhazian conflict in Georgia when UN assistance did not materialize; and in Tajikistan as a sponsor of talks between the communist government and banished opposition members.

At the same time Russia has set about signing a series of bilateral military agreements with its neighbours. It has sought and received basing rights for its armed forces in a number of areas in the FSU (e.g. Georgia, Armenia) and has also made arrangements for military support and training to regions currently functioning without armies (e.g. Tajikistan, Turkmenistan). In 1994 there were approximately 132,000 Russian troops in the 'near abroad', though it has to be said that a good portion of these are in Ukraine.[5] The purpose of these types of agreements are several fold: to legalize and legitimize a military presence in non-Russian regions; to assist countries without armed forces to build these; and to obtain funds for Russian military services rendered (e.g. the provision of training).

Has Russia's push for a new role as a regional power been accompanied by a simultaneous push in the broader international sphere? With the exception of the former Yugoslavia the answer is largely not. Indeed, even Russia's vigorous diplomacy on Bosnia-Herzegovina can probably best be understood as part of its push to demonstrate regional leadership and protect its own domestic interests.[6]   One has seen little Russian interest in extending its involvement to other pressing world affairs, with the possible exception of some limited attempts to contribute to the Middle East peace process. Closer to home, however, there has been deep Russian concern about the evolving relationship between the Central and Eastern European countries and NATO. While Russia put a brave face on the issue of the 'Partnership for Peace' (PfP) there was clear displeasure with this initiative in many quarters in Moscow. Many understood that membership of the PfP was acceptable, but only on the basis of a tacit agreement that this would involve merely a symbolic relationship with NATO and not a substantive one. Any moves to proceed towards deeper collaboration would be viewed by many in Moscow as a direct threat to Russia's security interests. In this sense Central and Eastern Europe remains in Russia's sphere of interest, if not influence.

How is one to understand Russia's new assertiveness in the regions of the FSU? There are several possible interpretations. One is that this is simply great power politics, that is Russia is simply doing what great regional powers do when surrounded by weak states by following policies aimed at optimizing its own interests, with only a modest amount of regard for egalitarian relations with its neighbours. The greatest priorities are the protection of its nationals in the 'near abroad', and promoting an image of Russia as a still strong and potent country.

A second interpretation, increasingly common in the West, is that this is Russian imperialism. Russia is attempting to establish either a new empire, or the old Soviet Union. Russia is using deliberate policies of divide and rule in regions of conflict (e.g. Moldova, Georgia); opportunistically taking advantage of instability by drawing governments such as Georgia back into the arms of Russia; and cynically using the issue of ethnic Russians in the 'near abroad' as a pretext for regaining lost territories.[7]

There is a third interpretation which can be called 'leadership by default', that is Russia is simply providing the leadership which others are unwilling to give. The West cannot and will not intervene in the regional conflicts which plague the FSU, therefore for humanitarian purposes and reasons of regional stability it has been left to Russia to manage the situation. The West has in essence forfeited its right to comment on Russia's policies in the 'near abroad' because of its unwillingness to commit substantive money, manpower or diplomatic efforts towards the region. Russia can safely call for the involvement of international institutions because it knows full well that little other than token measures will materialize.

Unfortunately, for clarity of analysis, it is probably the case that each of these interpretations is in some measure true. This being the case, how is one to think about constructing western policy towards the region? Three broad options can be identified. The first can be called the 'free-hand approach'. The West would explicitly acknowledge that regions of the FSU are Russia's sphere of influence and, other than for purposes of diplomatic nicety, Russia is given a free-hand in the region. Western countries then will turn a blind eye to aggressive Russian activities in the 'near abroad'. The tacit agreement in this scenario is that in exchange for a free-hand in the region, Russia's interests will not extend beyond the FSU. The Baltic states would remain in an ambiguous position, though would generally be understood to be within the western European political sphere. Russia would continue to fulfil its role as 'regional peace keeper' but its activities would not be sanctioned by international bodies such as the UN.

The second approach is one of limited involvement: the West would define the FSU as a region of limited interest and promote the involvement of the UN, CSCE and multilateral diplomacy. Preventative diplomacy in potential regions of conflict would be pursued by western states, in cooperation with Russia; official observer missions (UN, CSCE) to regions of conflict would be increased dramatically; Russia would be encouraged, through widespread joint-peacekeeping exercises, to adhere to internationally acceptable standards of peacekeeping; Russia, other CIS states and the West would cooperate on developing models of peacemaking and peace enforcement. Some symbolic UN peacekeeping forces might be introduced into regions of conflict. However this would specifically not include American troops because of the risk of antagonizing segments of the Russian population.

The third approach can be defined as one of competing interests: the West would define the regions of the FSU as an area of vital significance and decide to play a more active role in the region as a counterweight to Russia. This would be stimulated by fears of 'Russia resurgent' and concern that if Russia were not to be contained now, it might turn its sights on areas further afield in the future. This option would include support for UN peacekeeping troops in regions of conflict and a complete rejection of Russian military involvement in the FSU, other than on a strictly supervised and neutral basis; greater economic and military support to non-Russian regions; a harder line towards Russia and an abandonment of the 'special relationship' with the US; and the development of a new long-term strategy of containment towards Russia. This option would seek to deny Russia a major role as a regional power, primarily because of fears of eventual Russian expansionism beyond the borders of the FSU.

It seems evident that it is the first option which is currently in operation. The West, and the US in particular, appears to have acquiesced (some might even say promoted) Russia's self-defined role as regional 'peace keeper'. Western countries are loath to engage in any activities which could mistakenly be construed as interfering in Russia's sphere of influence. The third option is the least likely: western countries have neither the motivation nor the manpower to seriously consider this. The second option is arguably the most desirable because it holds out the potential for some oversight of Russia's activities without offending its great power sensibilities. It should not alienate the domestic audience in Russia because few if any western (and no American) troops would be introduced onto the territory of the FSU. And finally it would call the Russians on their reported desire to accept international intervention and involvement.

The rise of ultra-nationalism

The December 1993 parliamentary elections in Russia saw Vladimir Zhirinovsky and his Liberal Democratic Party (LDP) come to power with almost precisely the same figures with which Hitler came to power in 1933. Even more worrisome is the fact that Zhirinovsky's popularity appears to have doubled since 1991 when he ran in the presidential election against Yeltsin and came in third.[8] Is Zhirinovsky simply a lucky clown, as many Russian liberals and western media analysts would have one believe? Did he ride to power on a so-called 'protest vote', or is there something more sinister behind his success?

To begin to answer these questions one must have some understanding of who supported Zhirinovsky. There has been speculation that the military, and perhaps the intelligence services, gave strong support to the LDP. Indeed, after the December elections Yeltsin himself suggested that up to one third of those in the military gave their support to the LDP. He also appeared to blame the intelligence forces for either Zhirinovsky's success, or a failure to predict and prevent his majority. Shortly after the December elections the Ministry of Security (the former KGB) was disbanded, and replaced with a Federal Counterintelligence Service directly responsible to Yeltsin.[9] Though it is impossible to determine an exact figure for the LDP's support within the military, the fact that the party has made a policy of cultivating the loyalty of mid-ranking officers, and has sought to organize its own detachments within the armed forces, suggests that such support could be significant.[10]

However the LDP would appear to have a broader base than this. A December poll by the respected All-Russian Center for Public Opinion Research has suggested that Zhirinovsky's supporters consist of two types. Hardcore supporters include males between the ages of 25-40 who are well-educated and previously apolitical, and uncommitted LDP supporters include older males who are less educated, live in small towns, and are of the old Soviet-style working class. Individuals from both groups tended to be employed, but to have worked in regions with high unemployment. Their main concerns are about a breakdown in law and order, and weak government, not the economy as one might expect.[11] It is also noteworthy that the greatest support for the LDP came from villages and small towns, not major cities such as Moscow and St. Petersburg.

Given these factors, and the general economic and social conditions within the country, it is difficult to interpret the December vote as simply a protest vote. This view was promoted by the western press after the election, and also by the failed democrats in Russia. However a protest vote somehow also implies that the vote for the LDP was something of a swing vote which could easily revert to some other candidate in another election. This is clearly not the case and there is every reason to believe that support for the LDP, or perhaps some other ultra-nationalist party or leader, will remain a significant factor for the foreseeable future. More than anything the December vote was a sign of a profound dissatisfaction and demoralization among the electorate. For many the LDP represented a long sought after 'third way', that is, neither democratic, nor communist. (The idea of a 'third way' has been promoted since Gorbachev's time). In this sense the LDP have '...positioned themselves as saviors with no responsibility for past failures or current problems'.[12] The LDP is explicitly anti-communist (Zhirinovsky claims he never belonged to the CP) and ostensibly anti-*nomenklatura*. Zhirinovsky likes to portray himself as one of the people, sharing their everyday trials and tribulations.

What is Zhirinovsky's world view? As a politician Zhirinovsky has gained notoriety for his spontaneous, outrageous and irresponsible statements. But what ideas has he consistently advocated in the international sphere? In his book *The Final Thrust South* his central argument involves the idea that a new balance of power must be established. In this the world will be divided along the following lines: Russia would dominate the FSU, Iran (because it is planning a pan-Islamic state), Turkey (because it is planning a pan-Turkic state), Afghanistan (because it's there), and then extend its reach into the Mediterranean Sea, Pacific and Indian Oceans. He is unspecific about who would rule over the Middle East, but the implication is Russia. Western Europe would rule over Africa; the Chinese would rule over Southeast Asia and Japan; and the US and Canada would dominate the Americas. In this way a new and more stable division of the world would be accomplished. Zhirinovsky claims that it is Russia's historic mission to suppress the spread of Islam. Russian expansionism would also be used as a way of restoring the Russian army, and would 'save' and 'cleanse' all Russians.

Zhirinovsky has frequently voiced anti-Semitic views, and has gone so far as to blame Jews for anti-Semitic provocation, as well having been for some time an advocate of the 'purity of the nation'. He proposes to abolish ethnically-based republics in Russia, and replace these with territorial-administrative provinces. 'State capitalism' would bring a highly controlled 'market' to the country, though at least fifteen years of authoritarian rule would be necessary before democracy could be introduced. This would involve a purge of communists and as well as of his opponents. Zhirinovsky does not appear to be homophobic, and indeed some have implied that he himself is homosexual (something he strongly denies). He preaches sexual liberation for all.

When one attempts to evaluate these views four questions become important: Are his pronouncements serious? If so, could he be elected Russian president? Is there a danger he would bring fascism to Russia? And how should the West react? Concerning the first question, there are clearly two dangerous interpretations of Zhirinovsky's rhetoric, both of which are arguably serious mistakes. The first view dismisses Zhirinovsky as a 'clown'. It is curious that in the western press Zhirinovsky is inevitably portrayed as an outrageous lunatic. Why is this the case? Does the media only cover the sensational items of his career? Does he manipulate the media to gain publicity, even if in rather grotesque ways? The problem with this first view is that Zhirinovsky's media image of a buffoon belies the fact that he is a highly educated, intelligent individual with degrees in languages and international law. There is every likelihood that he deliberately displays outrageous behaviour and rhetoric to gain publicity for his cause and party. Second, there is an equally dangerous view (pronounced by some of Zhirinovsky's supporters) that he is merely being a good politician, a populist, that he will change his rhetoric once in power. Once again this is highly dubious reasoning, especially given his extremist views on many subjects.

It is impossible to say whether or not Zhirinovsky is serious in his pronouncements. However, the danger is that there is just enough in many of his statements for them to have a certain resonance with large segments of the population. For example, the military leadership is sympathetic to concerns about restoring Russia's wounded pride, and containing an Islamic threat. His anti-Semitic views are shared both by those who believe that the long years of communism were brought about by a Zionist plot, and those who blame the 'capitalist Jews' for bringing about the downfall of the Soviet Union. And his astute method of populism promises vodka to downtrodden men, and men for lonely women.

Will Zhirinovsky be elected president? Disgruntled democratic opponents would disagree, but Zhirinovsky was among the most politically adept of all the candidates in the December election. He ran what was probably the first modern and successful political campaign in Russia, skillfully using the media and giving fiery speeches to packed halls. However, whether the LDP is able to maintain a broad-based support until the presidential elections in June 1996 remains to be seen. To some extent Zhirinovsky's support within the Russian parliament has waned since his December successes, but this is no guarantee that the sentiments which brought him to power have disappeared among the population. There is a danger that, in the same way that they failed to predict the disastrous results of the December elections, the remaining democrats in Moscow will miscalculate the LDPs support once again, believing that it has decreased, when it has not. The fact is that there are few leadership alternatives. Yeltsin's popularity has plummeted and in many ways he is a spent force (politically and physically). Prime Minister Chernomydrin has a certain following, as do other 'rogue' elements such as the leader of the Russian 14th Army in Moldova, General Lebed. But whether these individuals or other potential leadership candidates are able to gain a solid constituency by June 1996 is difficult to predict.

If elected, would Zhirinovsky bring fascism to Russia? Zhirinovsky can probably best be described as a 'fascist populist'. The LDP does not as yet appear to have the will or capacity to install a widespread fascist régime, yet many of the components of its activities have fascist characteristics. In the December campaign Zhirinovsky frequently used emotionally charged slogans such as 'Russians, service to Russia is in the hands of each of you', or 'I will bring Russia off its knees'. Whereas many of his opponents presented the public with over-intellectualized plans for improving the economy (the last thing a weary Russian public was interested in hearing), Zhirinovsky appealed to the demoralization of the ordinary person, offering them simplistic promises of order, wealth and Russian power. Zhirinovsky has said that it is now 1935 in Russia.[13] Is he correct? Unfortunately the conditions are ripe for fascism in Russia today. These include: a highly demoralized population; seventy years of authoritarian rule; a previous totalitarian régime under Stalin; a highly militarized society; a great power in decline; a population which mourns the loss of national identity; an extremely unstable economy; and fragile political parties.

But what exactly are the characteristics of fascism? They include: a hostility to democracy and egalitarianism; a nationalistic ideology; anti-liberal tendencies; anti-communist views; anti-Semitic rhetoric and activities; an emphasis on collective organization and symbols; a cult of violence; and a cult of personality.[14] To date Zhirinovsky has given every indication that he would pursue a regime with fascist characteristics, according to the preceding criteria. In the western literature fascism has been described as 'ideology without specific content', and this is sadly probably a perfect fit for a highly demoralized, over-ideologized, post-communist society such as Russia. However, the one weak link in this formula is Zhirinovsky's personality itself. Does he really have a strong and charismatic enough persona to develop a full-fledged cult of personality? Possibly not. There are simply too many suspicions about his past (all of which he denies): his Jewish father, his intelligence connections, his alleged homosexuality.

More importantly, in any analysis of this subject it would be a grave mistake to focus exclusively on Zhirinovsky, rather than the serious phenomena that he represents. One survey of far-right and hardline-communist groups in Russia indicated that there are more than eighty of these functioning throughout Russia.[15] Though many groups would have little more than a few dozen followers, others such as Russian National Unity[16] are more substantial. Some have already been around for four or five years, some have paramilitary forces associated with them, almost all are racist and xenophobic, and many groups have already formed coalitions of one sort or another.[17] In the current economic and political environment Zhirinovsky as a personality, and the LDP as a party, may be unimportant. If not them, then other equally dangerous forces may emerge to harness the profound disillusion of Russian society.

What can or should the West do? The first step is that the Zhirinovsky-phenomenon must be taken seriously. At the same time care must be taken not to grant Zhirinovsky or the LDP legitimacy, for example by allowing meetings with government officials. This may be difficult because Zhirinovsky is a member of parliament, and therefore included in parliamentary delegations, for example to the Council of Europe. At the same time governments must make plain their revulsion of the flagrantly inflammatory statements of Zhirinovsky and the LDP. At a minimum the Russian public must know that this is not acceptable political behaviour.

Beyond this, are there ways in which the West can influence the situation, given the conditions which exist in Russia today? One argument is that there is little the West can do except on the margins. There is doubtless much truth in this, however few would be satisfied with such an answer. In general a three-pronged strategy could be considered. First, western countries must develop much clearer policies towards the FSU, and closer coordination on these policies. The approaches of western countries have thus far differed. The US has followed a Russo-centric approach, initially based especially on concerns about the proliferation of nuclear weapons. In contrast the Germans have focused on economic issues, especially in relation to Russia. However, what is missing is an overall approach to the entire FSU, especially on Europe's part. The US has cultivated a 'special relationship' with Russia.[18] Why has Europe neglected to do the same? It is obviously in Europe's interest to have Russia and other states in the FSU recognized as part of Europe, not only in a symbolic sense but substantively. Inasmuch as it is feasible, the West must seek to 'entangle' Russia in Europe and European institutions. Russia's alienation from Europe is a profound fact and many western policies are currently institutionalizing this gulf.

Secondly, there must be a continued recognition that economic reform is the key to democratic reform. To the extent that the West can successfully deliver significant funds and expertise, the reform process will be supported. On this count, however, much of the West's credibility has been squandered by the failure to deliver funds, and what are perceived to be overly stringent criteria for the release of aid. Further funds must not be promised by the international community simply for publicity or 'feel good' purposes. The Russian government and public are after all astute enough to distinguish symbolic from real aid. On the other hand, western governments cannot tolerate a cynical sapping of western resources. If certain government representatives in Russia continue to criticize the provision of western aid as meaningless and insignificant, aid should be withdrawn and directed to non-governmental bodies.

Thirdly, the West must continue to support democratic political reform. However, in the past two years there has been an over-emphasis on the provision of funds and expertise in the economic sphere, to the detriment of assistance with the political reform process. The implicit assumption was that if the economy improved politics would follow. This has clearly not been the case. Economic transition is a long-term process. Political reform is as well, but along the way there are many ways in which democratic processes can be encouraged. For example, democratic political groups must be encouraged to find a *modus operandi* between themselves. A partial explanation for the success of the LDP was the disorganization, in-fighting, and self-interested pursuits of power that the democrats evidenced. Advice can be given to pro-democratic forces about useful methods for running a political campaign, staying in touch with their constituencies, and so on.

Finally, the West must seriously reconsider their overt and seemingly unconditional support for the Yeltsin government. There is every indication that western governments are making the same mistake that they did with Gorbachev in 1991: they are attempting to shore up an unpopular and weakened leader; they are lending support to undemocratic processes by tacitly agreeing with the Yeltsin government's argument that, if such support is not forthcoming, anti-democratic forces will emerge;[19] and they are assuming that there are no other reasonable contenders for the leadership. All of these arguments were advanced in relation to Gorbachev in the 1990-91 period. The key must be to evaluate Russian government policy by objective criteria that take into account western interests, rather than to support personalities (in this case Yeltsin, in 1991 Gorbachev).

Conclusion

Russia's neighbours cannot achieve security without Russia. Thus the way in which Russia develops internally, and the way in which it manages relations with its neighbours, will have a profound impact of stability in the region. There are many indications that, as Moscow seeks to develop a new regional identity to replace its lost status as a superpower, it wants to carve out a special zone of influence within the FSU. There are several possible interpretations of this behaviour ranging from benign to sinister and much will depend on how strongly, and in what manner, Russia chooses to exert its influence. There is, after all, a wide gap between 'leadership' and 'coercion' in the conduct of relations between states. It may be that Russia will require several years to find a balance between various methods of managing relations with its neighbours. However, should political developments within Russia itself turn bad, these distinctions may be irrelevant. A presidential victory by Zhirinovsky, increasingly broad-based support for the LDP, or the emergence of other strong ultra-nationalist forces would make Russia an unpredictable and unsavoury partner for many of its neighbours. There were clear reasons why the LDP won such strong support in the December 1993 elections, and there are few indications that economic and political conditions have changed much since then. The ground for the success of ultra-nationalists has been tilled in Russia today. And yet it has many times in the past proven to be a surprising and unpredictable country, and thus it may be that by the grace of history Russia will avoid the disastrous course which the ultra-nationalists would seek for it.

Notes

1.   This paper is one part of a King's College London Department of War Studies report submitted to the House of Commons Select Committee on Defence in the autumn of 1994; it was earlier presented to the conference on 'New Forms of Security in Europe', University of Kent at Canterbury, 23-24 May 1994.

2.   The document titled 'Fundamental Positions of the Concept of Foreign Policy of the Russian Federation' was published in *Nezavisimaya Gazeta*, 29 April 1993.

3.   On the military doctrine see the summary in *Summary of World Broadcasts*, special supplement, SU/1858 S1/1-10, 29 November 1993.

4.   For example, on the energy question see Blank, Stephen J. (1994), *Energy and Security in Transcaucasia*, monograph from the Strategic Studies Institute, US Army War College, 7 September.

5.   See a break down in *The Economist*, 21 May 1994, p. 53. Lithuania, Latvia and Estonia are the only countries which have been successful in gaining the withdrawal of all Soviet/Russian troops. Russian troops had also left Azerbaijan; however the country is now under pressure to grant Russia new basing rights.

6.   'Humanitarian' motives aside, one must take account of Russia's self-interest in its diplomacy over Bosnia. Given the ultra-right and communist opposition at home there is no way that any Russian politician can afford to be part of a plan that acquiesces to 'aggression' against the Serbs (e.g. air bombardment).

7.   Some such as Emil Pain (Yeltsin's new advisor on nationality problems, replacing Sergei Shakhrai) and Konstantin Zatulin (head of the parliament's Committee on Relations with the CIS) advocate what is

called 'fragmented imperialism'. Labelled the 'Zatulin doctrine', this involves two main principles: protecting ethnic Russians in the 'near abroad', and helping them achieve regional autonomy. Regions such as Abkhazia and South Ossetia, Transdniester, Crimea and eastern Ukraine, and northern Kazakhstan could all eventually be brought back into Russia. See 'Touchy Bears', *The Economist*, 21 May 1994, p. 53.

8. In December 1993 Zhirinovsky's LDP received 22.79 per cent of votes cast (12 million votes) with a 54.8 per cent voter turnout; in the 1991 presidential elections he came in third with 7.8 per cent of the vote (6 million). In December the Russian Communist Party received 12.35 percent of the vote and Russia's Choice 15.38 per cent (predictions had been of 30 per cent).

9. Anatoly Sobchak (Mayor of St. Petersburg) has said that the LDP was set up by the Communist Party (CP) and KGB in 1990 as an easily controllable opposition party; it was the first political party to be registered (June 1990), even before the CP itself. Gorbachev denied this accusation and it remains unsubstantiated. Zhirinovsky served as a lieutenant in military intelligence (GRU) for several years and had a history of short associations with a number of organizations which were traditionally connected with the KGB (The World Peace Council, the Higher Trade Union School, Mir Publishing House, the USSR Confederation of Jewish Organizations); thus all of these factors have lead to the suspicion that Zhirinovsky has close associations with the intelligence services.

10. See Kipp, Jacob W. (1994),'The Zhirinovsky Threat', *Foreign Affairs*, May/June, pp. 84-85.

11. This poll was reported in *Izvestiya*, 30 December 1993.

12. Kipp, 'The Zhirinovsky Threat', p. 81.

13. Zhirinovsky's statement was made to the Serbs during a visit to Vukovar. Reported in *RFE/RL News Brief*, 31 January-4 February 1994, p. 2.

14. These characteristics are described in Scruton, Roger (1983), *A Dictionary of Political Thought*, Pan Books, London, p. 169.

15. Pribylovsky, Vladimir (1994), 'A Survey of Radical Right-Wing Groups in Russia', *RFE/RL Research Report*, 22 April, pp. 28-37.

16. This is a fascist group which admires Hilter, operates in cell-like structures, and has paramilitary forces associated with it.

17. For a more detailed analysis of extreme right movements in Russia see Laqueur, Walter (1994), *Black Hundred. The Rise of the Extreme Right in Russia*, Harper Perennial, New York.

18. Though for a sceptical view of how this relationship will develop see Garnett, Sherman (1994), 'Russia's Reemergence', *The Christian Science Monitor*, 12 October.

19. For example, western governments do not appear to have noticed that Yeltsin is replacing legally elected regional officials with his own appointees, and that these individuals are in turn pursuing undemocratic

practices such as press censorship.   For this and other examples of undemocratic practices under Yeltsin see, Wishnevsky, Julia (1994), 'Problems of Russian Regional Leadership', *RFE/RL Research Report*, 13 May, pp. 6-13.

5 Some Military and Political Requirements of Collective Security in Europe

MARK KHROUSTALEV

Introduction

The aim of this study is not to describe in detail any ideal version of a possible collective security system for Europe. The task is more frugal, and is rather one of expressing some mainly theoretical considerations about the general conditions for, and foundations of, such a system by taking into account all possible factors and trends as an initial step. Given this framework it seems expedient to begin with a theoretical rethinking of the Cold War's institutional legacy. Without this it would be very difficult to understand what could be taken, and what not, from the near past to elaborate on a possible successor security system.

The Cold War legacy: the contradictory 'couple'

The period of the Cold War must be divided into two essentially distinct periods: before and after the Conference on Security and Cooperation in Europe (the CSCE). The signing of the Helsinki Final Act that created the CSCE can be defined as the watershed in the development of security since 1945. During the period before the signing of the Final Act in 1975 the political and military situation in Europe might be characterized as one of 'confrontative stability', or 'stability without security'. During this period the arms race was really unlimited and unregulated and relations between the main two actors (NATO and the Warsaw Pact) were extremely hostile. The spectre of nuclear war knocked at the European door more than once. Although from time to time attempts to reduce military and political tensions were made, not without some success, nonetheless elements of cooperation appeared and disappeared just as suddenly. Consequently there was no real evidence of progress in their institutionalization.   Theoretically speaking these two military-political actors played a classical zero-sum game in spite of the very serious differences in their natures.

On the one hand, NATO was really a defensive alliance based on voluntary membership and democratic principles of decision making.   Its 'leader', the USA, was only a *primus inter pares* despite its great military superiority.   On the other hand, the Warsaw Pact was offensive and based on forced membership and the dictatorship of the Soviet Union.   Nevertheless, both of these blocs had some very significant common points.   Firstly, they were regional but not pan-European alliances.   Secondly, their military structures were specifically organized and directed only against a single enemy - the other alliance.   This meant that all their military structures were predominantly prepared for a global nuclear war.   In effect both sides prepared for collective suicide.

Although there was a clear common understanding of this inevitable result, the steady military confrontation and the arms race continued.   Only at the beginning of the seventies, when all hopes about the socialist camps' expansion in Europe had disappeared, and they were indeed facing some difficulties both in Eastern Europe and in the wider world communist movement, particularly as a result of the Soviet intervention in Czechoslovakia in 1968, did the Soviet leaders decide to encourage some sort of political 'armistice' in Europe.   Thus the CSCE appeared as a new European institutional reality.   This meant a substantial change in the 'confrontative stability' system, as the new cooperative element was implanted into its structure.   As a result the earlier homogenous system was transformed into a heterogeneous one - the former 'stability without security' was transformed into a new 'stability with limited security'.

This second, and final, period of the Cold War, until its official end in 1990, may be defined as the period of the permanent struggle between the cooperative tendency incarnated by the CSCE, and the confrontative tendency incarnated by the military blocs.   Of course, the CSCE did not win the struggle, but it did a great deal to stimulate the development of the two most important processes in East-West cooperation. The disarmament and the demilitarization of Europe began.   This became possible not least because CSCE activity had a very serious influence on the ideological foundations of Soviet society, and particularly as concerns the human rights problem.

NATO: to be or not to be

After the end of the Cold War and the collapse of the Warsaw Pact and then of the Soviet Union, it might have been expected that NATO's fate would be the same, but NATO remained in existence.   The question is why this was so?   At first glance this decision looks like an absolutely irrational one, as it meant the unchanged maintenance of one of the two confrontational elements as well as the CSCE as the leader of the disarmament and demilitarization processes in Europe. Nonetheless the NATO countries' decision was, perhaps, reasonable and right in the then transitional situation, as a temporary measure against any possible relapses of the ex-Soviet militarism. Indeed, the Soviet Union is politically dead but the Soviet Army (now merely re-called 'Russian') is still alive and hence Soviet militarism was seriously debilitated but not expunged. Of course, the new Russian political leadership tried, and undoubtedly will continue to try, to democratize this army. However, resistance from the top military establishment and the majority of the ex-Soviet officers' corps is still strong and there are no hopes that it will weaken significantly in the near future.

If this decision should prove to be final, then it must be qualified as very dangerous and it will augur very badly for the future of Europe. Among the very thorny problems that might result, the first is maybe the most fundamental. Every military alliance (whether defensive or offensive) is generally speaking 'cooperation against...' and not 'cooperation for...' something. There has never been a military alliance directed against nobody and consequently every military must have a real or imaginary enemy.1 Moreover, this enemy must certainly be not merely powerful but, as a rule, *very* powerful. Otherwise there would be no necessity to possess military forces.

Hence, after making their final decision, NATO members will be obliged to answer the question as to who NATO's enemy is to be after the collapse of the Soviet Union. Only one country in Europe can play this role, and this is Russia, as there are no other credible candidates. Insofar as we can consider the outside world, communist China springs to mind, but the essential usual elements of proximity and motive are so absent as to make China not a real menace.

If the option of maintaining NATO in its present form is taken, this will mean, in a best case scenario, a restoration of the old Versailles Treaty system in slightly modified form in which Russia will replace Germany as the enemy, and in a worst case scenario, a return, sooner or later, to a new version of the Cold War. As for hopes of a happy ending, nobody can be sure of this. It could also be stressed that in reality the distance between these two results is not as great as it may seem.

Incidentally, it has been noted that some of the former Warsaw Pact members and the ex-Soviet republics do, and will do, their best to support this latter option and without any doubt will try to stimulate it by conducting various defiant and provocative actions under the slogan of 'a firm struggle against the new Russian imperialism'. In a final analysis such actions can really only serve to increase the influence of the ex-Soviet military establishment and the positions of Russian nationalists both within the ruling circles and outside them, among Russian public opinion. The first noticeable symptoms of this dangerous development have already appeared with the large vote for the 'Red-Brown alliance' in the December 1993 Russian elections.[2]

The great desire of these former Warsaw Treaty states (perhaps more correctly their ruling élites) to accelerate this option is based as much on the understandable fear of their very powerful and frightening neighbour as on the purely pragmatic considerations of strengthening their positions towards Russia by using NATO as a very suitable 'instrument' of regional and internal politics. These considerations were so clear and so badly disguised that the NATO states have until now been forced to abstain from extending NATO membership. However, this decision has not discouraged them.

But even if the option of Russia as the enemy is not realized and Russia is incorporated into or associated with NATO, nevertheless the same question as to 'who is the enemy?' will remain without a satisfactory answer and therefore the problem will be a permanent point of discussion, and not only at the official level. Sooner or later the answer must be given, because the existence of a military alliance against nobody is a nonsense.[3]

The other serious problem arising from a retention of NATO is what the NATO traditional military structures can do to face up to the new military situation in Europe and consequently its new tasks, such as the current Bosnia crisis. The majority of existing tasks are obviously superfluous and in need of substantial modification. Now it is not simple to predict the final result of such a process of dismantling, but if the disarmament and demilitarization processes in Europe do develop successfully, it cannot be excluded that this will render the further existence of these structures merely irrelevant from the purely military point of view (the well-known phenomenon of the 'tadpole' which loses its tail as it grows into a frog). Other such problems can be easily cited and although they are, perhaps, not so fundamental they are no less difficult. For example, there is a very real possibility of a total or semi-total American withdrawal from Europe; there are doubts as to the future relations of the Western European Union (WEU) and NATO; and so on.

All the above permits us to come to the conclusion that, after a certain transitional period, (which may be quite long), with a possible demilitarization of Russia, including the abolition of compulsory military service, the establishment of a strong civilian control over its military forces and a real rejection of all kinds of military propaganda, NATO's further existence will not be able to play any positive role in European security affairs, because of its central nature as a military alliance. In the new military situation NATO must be replaced by another institution tightly tied to the CSCE. Inside this 'coupled' CSCE might be a legislative body and a new institutional (let us call it a 'pan-European collective security system') executive. Of course, such analogy is an approximation, but one that is clear enough.[4]

'European unification': the beginning of the process

The conflicts in the area of ex-Soviet influence, and particularly in the former Yugoslavia, clearly prove that if stability is lost, it will be extremely difficult to guarantee even limited security. Therefore its restoration demands a continuation of the 'European unification' process on three levels - those of the legal (human rights), the political (democratization) and the economic (a free market economy). This process is now the decisive stabilizing factor and only new achievements on all these levels will create the entirely durable foundations for a western European type stability. For the time being there are some serious constraints on this route.

On the legal level the CSCE did a great deal to encourage the inclusion into socialist legislative theory of the human rights issue, one which, as a real 'ideological bomb', destroyed the legitimacy of the totalitarian order. Now their official recognition as the basic social and political values has become absolutely unquestioned, even the ex-*Nomenklatura*, and frankly ethnocratic, régimes dare not try to oppose or neglect them openly.

However, the problem of their real application was, and remains, unsolved in some eastern European states, especially as concerns minority rights. In spite of this the western states have suddenly begun to demonstrate a clear 'double standard' attitude towards this problem and to divide all minorities into 'bad' and 'good' ones. In particular, the West has exhibited a very strange attitude towards ethnic cleansing. Without any doubt there is a great difference between the barbaric version of ethnic cleansing which has been seen in Bosnia and the soft version observed in Estonia, but nevertheless in both cases it is a real 'ethnic cleansing' and there are no grounds to use the double standard and to qualify only one as violating human rights and another as not so doing. One's attitude towards 'ethnic cleansing', regardless of its form and nature, can only be extremely negative.

On the political level the general situation looks more or less satisfactory. After the totalitarian régimes were overthrown free elections were held in all East-European countries and democratic political systems were installed. Although some of these new democracies are far from perfect and have serious authoritarian remnants within them, such are the usual defects of every young democracy. However, one of the most dangerous threats is, of course, various extremist movements, the criminalization of all political life in several ex-Soviet countries. For example, in Russia the big criminal associations have the real control over governmental structures and political parties with the help of bribes and terror, something similar to the mafia-type rule so well documented in Italy or Latin America. In these cases to talk about any democracy is nonsense, as the 'mafia's' rule was and can only be pure dictatorship and nothing else.

As might be expected all East European countries have not been able to achieve very much on the economic level and it is now more than understood that their way from the centralized economic system to the free-market economy will be neither easy nor short, and in any case possibly politically dangerous. The present East-European situation can be characterized as one of 'deep economic crisis' that is more or less different in various countries and with its inevitable outcome, that of political uncertainty and frequent changes of direction.

In summarizing the results of the process of European unification to date, it must be stressed that this process is even now far from being concluded and that even when it is there are no reasons to consider that after the transitional period of Russian demilitarization, European stability and security will be guaranteed. The present general political situation can be defined as 'limited stability with limited security'. However, the real threats to a future European stability and security will be in principle other than they were during the Cold War. These threats are relatively very new because in all probability there are and will be various kinds of border conflicts between new states, as well as civil wars and a new kind of 'terrorist' war. The PLO tried to organize this latter type of war against the Western countries at the beginning of the 1970s. However, in future this type of war will be more dangerous when we take into account modern trends in military technology development, such as miniaturization, 'individualization' (single person use) and the increasing destructive capability of new weapons systems.

Strategies for collective security: which is optimal?

Faced with these 'new' threats, what strategy might be used by the 'European collective security system' to allay them? The following theoretical model might help to answer this question:

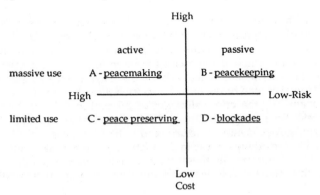

N.B. 'Peace preserving' refers to the use of preventive military measures

An analysis of UN practice shows very clearly that the dominant strategic options types were, and remain, 'B' and 'A' from the above diagram.[5] Although the notion of 'peacemaking' is a relatively recent one, the Korean and Persian Gulf wars can and must be qualified as the results of that 'A' type strategy.   However in Bosnia, the UN is trying to use a mixed 'A + B' strategy, though, if we exclude Bosnia, all UN peacemaking operations have so far been carried out in the Third World.

Now, and how much more so in the near future, we can observe that the European continent is extremely inconvenient for real peacemaking because of its political and social conditions and the existence of many nuclear power stations, chemical plants and other very dangerous installations.   However, even here in some cases the 'C' strategy can be used. A brilliant example of this was demonstrated by Israeli military forces, when only one attack of the Israeli Air Force stopped Saddam Hussein's nuclear weapons programme.   During this attack nobody was killed or wounded and the Iraqi nuclear reactor was not destroyed but only so damaged that it could not be restored. This was really an example of a preventative 'peace preserving' action which avoided a possible nuclear war in the Middle East. Moreover, if this attack had not been launched and Saddam Hussein had got nuclear weapons, what might the result of such massive and active peacemaking operations as 'Desert Storm' have been? Without any doubt the future collective security system must also be able to deploy a wide set of various non-military means and strategies, but their analysis is outside the scope of this paper.

Conclusion

The Cold War stimulated the development of militarism both in the western countries and, particularly, in the former Soviet Union and not only in the form of the various military institutions like the military alliances, but also in the form of specific alarmist mentalities. This mentality is based on two main premises: firstly, that the political environment is hostile in principle and if not now, then potentially will be in future. Secondly, that only weapons of mass destruction (initially nuclear) can firmly guarantee security.

These ideas are still relatively widespread in the certain military and even political and scientific circles.[6]   The creation of any real collective security system on such psychological foundations will be extremely difficult. Therefore maybe now during the past Cold War transitional period one of the most important tasks is the consistent struggle against these ideas, and the struggle for the demilitarization of our continent, because only a demilitarized Europe will be truly secure.

Notes

1. It is very symptomatic that the NATO leadership was forced in the immediate aftermath of losing their old enemy (in November 1991) to begin a search for a new one. Their first reaction was to look to the Mediterranean for threats from Colonel Ghaddafi in Libya and Islamic fundamentalists in Algeria and Egypt. The NATO Defence Planning Committee even decided to create a new naval unit, even though Ghaddafi and the fundamentalists' military assets are negligible. The Bosnian Serbs then assumed the role of 'bad guys', although again only temporarily. See Kaplan, Lawrence S. (1993), 'NATO in the 1990s: An American Perspective', *Paradigms*, vol. 7, no. 2, Winter.

2. The reaction of the ex-Soviet military establishment to the possible extension of NATO was quite traditional. General-Lieutenant L.G. Ivashov (Secretary General of the CIS Defence Ministers) was typical in declaring that: 'during the next two to three years we must create the united military forces of the CIS ... This new alliance will be defensive', *Nevasimenaya Gazeta*, 17 May 1994.

3. A very vivid picture of what this will mean in practice was given in an article by Bracken, P., and Jonson, S. (1993), 'Beyond NATO: Complimentary Militaries' - 'The nature of the enemy was known to a high degree, and the enemy's characteristics and operating patterns drove military planning. In the new European security environment, however, it is not clear what military contingencies will have to be met... Confidence in any one of the scenarios is low, and each scenario involves a set of circumstances so different from the others (such as who the enemy is) that planners cannot use the scenarios to plan. A comprehensive but divergent set of scenarios is just that - divergent.' *Orbis*, vol. 37, no. 2, Spring, p. 206.

    It was not thought necessary by the authors of this quote to explain that any one military policy without military planning is a fiction, and it is not clear how a militray alliance can exist without such a policy.

4. During practically the whole of the Cold War the NATO leadership tried to organize a fusion of the CSCE and NATO. This has so far not happened, see Kay, S. (1993), 'NATO and CSCE: A Partnership for the Future', *Paradigms*, vol. 7, no. 2, Winter.

5. The confidence of UN officials in the future of such stratgeic choices led to the Secretary General proposing in June 1992 a standing UN army, while others have proposed the revival of the UN's stillborn Military Staff Committee, composed of the Chiefs of Staff of the Security Council's Permanent Members: Bennet A. and Lepgold J. (1993), 'Reinvesting Collective Security after the Cold War and Gulf Conflict', *Political Science Quarterly*, vol. 108, no. 2, Summer, p. 234.

6.   At the end of May 1994 the Council for Foreign and Defence Politics in
     Moscow published 'Strategy for Russia-2'. Although the Council is
     officially an NGO its membership leaves no doubt about its real nature
     (which includes twelve political leaders, fifteen top government officials,
     including the President's Secretary responsible for international relations,
     seven top military commanders and the Chief of the federal
     counterespionage service, out of a total membership of 49). This Council is
     therefore representative of the modern Russian ruling élite. However,
     the contents of this document testify to a growing alarmist mentality, and
     its authors affirm that one of the main aims of Russian foreign policy
     must be 'to create in future a real all-European security system into which
     Russia is fully incorporated', *Nevasimenaya Gazeta*, 27 May 1994.
         It should be noted that in the first part of this document the Council
     express their deep satisfaction about the 'practically total' acceptance of
     their recommendations in 'Strategy for Russia - 1' by President Yeltsin, see
     Nevasimenaya Gazeta, 19 August 1992.

6 Russia's Foreign Policy Concerns and the Implications for Western Security

JOHN DUNN

Introduction

During the Cold War the West was faced with a theoretical but specific military threat from the East. The threat was theoretical because its implementation would probably have involved the unthinkable use of unparalleled nuclear firepower, resulting in the certain destruction of much of human civilization. Deterrence theorists, therefore, quickly realized that strategic nuclear weapons, the ultimate means of both attack and retaliation, were useless as military instruments; they were at best political-psychological tools whose use would mean ultimate failure. But, although the threat was theoretical, it was also specific; the West knew from whence the threat came (from Moscow), and that if ever it became more than theoretical, it would affect all the NATO partners equally. This conviction, equally shared among the sixteen, made it easy to identify first the threat, second its relevance and third an adequate collective response. The demise of the theoretical, but specific threat and its replacement with actual but limited and unfocused threats (e.g. Serbian expansionism in the Balkans) have destroyed the certainties on which western defence policy was so long and so successfully based.

Initially, the removal of the theoretical but specific threat to western security blinded the West to the difficulties which, with the benefit of hindsight, were bound to emerge. The old, ideologically motivated Soviet enemy had gone, to be replaced by a newly co-operative Russia, which saw its major foreign policy interests as parallel to, or identical with, those of the West (particularly with those of the other great continental power, the United States). All sides now wanted global stability and an international order in which democracy, market economics and free trade would flourish. Russia agreed to the independence of the other ex-Soviet republics, removed its troops from East Germany and east-central Europe and even co-operated with the West in developing peace plans for former Yugoslavia and in particular Bosnia and Sarajevo. The West returned the compliment. Partly out of force of habit, partly from diplomatic sloth and partly for fear of enraging opposition 'national-patriots' in Russia, the West treated Russia as *primus inter pares* and allowed it to assume primary responsibility for stability on the territory of the former Soviet Union. This western policy of 'Moscow-centricity' was predicated on an initial belief that western and Russian security interests were compatible in the long term.

However, approximately twelve to eighteeen months after the August 1991 coup and the collapse of the Soviet Union, Russia began a serious reappraisal of its accommodation with the West and of its initial 'atlanticist' assumptions. This geopolitical reappraisal was based on the premise that despite the demise of the Soviet Union, Russia had continuing national interests and responsibilities which flowed from its peculiar position and identity. For example, despite its changed borders, Russia still needed access to the sea. It still faced instability on its southern frontiers and thus required sizeable armed forces and a forceful security policy with which to cope with that instability. Also, because of the nature of the economy which it inherited from the Soviet Union, Russia needed to sustain trade and economic links with the other ex-Soviet republics, and thus needed to dismantle the protectionist barriers with which these republics have surrounded themselves immediately after independence. Finally, up to 25 million Russians now lived outside the Russian Federation. Their well-being and security was Russia's special and continuing concern.

All these geo-political concerns are, moreover, linked to a very emotive debate within Russia on the nature and identity of the new Russian state itself. Russia has never before existed within its present borders. It, like the other CIS republics, is trying to define a new identity within new frontiers. In particular the 'loss' of the Ukraine, the common home of the ancient 'Kievan Rus' civilization, is an affront to Russians' understanding of their own identity. Thus, for Russia the loss of empire was much more traumatic than for other imperial powers in Europe, for Russia's colonies, being contiguous with the *Rodina* (motherland), simply became 'Russian' as the empire expanded. To many it seems that Russia cannot be 'Russia' without the territories acquired over centuries to its East and South. Thus, the offended sense of Russian identity, compounded by the realization of continuing interests in the so-called 'near abroad', made Russians of both national-patriotic and liberal persuasions increasingly willing to accept an 'imperial responsibility' for developments in the other ex-Soviet republics.

Furthermore, as the Armed Forces of the Federation were quick to point out, Russia remains a great power despite its reduced circumstances. This means that Russia, like the US, has abiding regional security interests. Thus, although Russian troops have been withdrawn from east-central Europe, the Russian Ministry of Defence has argued strongly that the region remains a 'zone of special interest' because it affects Russia's western security.

Consequently, after some vacillation a consensus emerged that western security organizations should not admit these countries to full membership without compensatory arrangements being made for Russia. East-central European membership of NATO or WEU would, Russians argued, emphasize the vulnerability of the flat open spaces of western Russia, would increase Russia's isolation, and would, incidentally, reinforce Russian feelings of national humiliation, thus giving succour to radical nationalists such as Vladimir Zhirinovsky.[1] Thus, Russia still claimed a *droit de regard* in respect of the security arrangements of central Europe.

In general, the West has shown understanding for Russia's concerns and has appreciated its need to reconsider its long-term interests. Thus the West has accommodated Russia's continuing 'great power status'. A symptom of this accommodation was NATO's 'Partnership for Peace' (PfP) programme which, despite the express desire of the central Europeans denied them full NATO membership in deference to Russian concerns. Also, in dealing with the non-Russian CIS states, the West deferred to Russian concerns by quietly accepting Russian intervention in Trans-Dnestria (Moldova), Abkhazia and Tajikistan. Indeed, many in the West quietly welcomed Russian intervention in these disputes, because no western state or organization has either the ability or the desire to become involved in peacekeeping or peace-making in these remote areas of which it knows little. 'Moscow-centricity' seemed to be in the interest of both Russia and the West.

Recently, however, doubts have increasingly been expressed in western foreign and security policy circles about the wisdom of 'Moscow-centricity' and of allowing Moscow to reassert 'imperial control' in the 'near abroad'. In a seminal article in *Foreign Affairs* the former US National Security Adviser, Zbigniew Brzezinski, argued that the re-assertion of Russian power over the CIS republics would not be compatible with 'geo-political pluralism', that is to say with the establishment of multiple democratic states on the territory of the former USSR which would form a bulwark against resurgent nationalism. Brzezinski further identifies the Ukraine as particularly relevant in this context because it is a test-case for Russia's willingness to set aside its imperial past and to join the community of modern states: 'It cannot be stressed strongly enough that without Ukraine, Russia ceases to be an empire, but with Ukraine suborned and then subordinated, Russia automatically becomes an empire.'[2] Furthermore, Brzezinski insists that Russia can be 'either an empire or a democracy, but it cannot be both.' He argues that '... efforts to recreate and maintain an empire by coercion or economic subsidy would condemn Russia not only to dictatorship but to poverty.'[3]

The question is therefore whether the reimposition of Russian regional control is compatible with either regional stability or long-term western interests. Few analysts expect a Russian attempt to re-occupy ex-Soviet republics (although as a result of historical inheritance or bilateral agreements, Russian troops at present remain in all the ex-Soviet republics, except

Lithuania). More likely is a Russian policy of 'neo-integrationalism' in which Russia exploits the political divisions and economic weakness of its neighbours in order to increase its influence and control. (Many in the West would not object to this scenario; the only condition would be that Russia implements such policies peacefully, with non-military means.) The danger is, however, that in some areas even a non-military expansion of Russian influence may provoke nationalist backlashes.

Further, as Brzezinski points out, it is not clear that Russia can expand its 'imperial' influence and at the same time be rich and democratic. Rather, the alienation of some non-Russian nationalists, particularly in the Ukraine, would increase the likelihood of attacks on Russians and thus increase the need for tough (and expensive) policing actions.[4] This could lead to the radicalization of politics within Russia and a renewed militarization of society. In such conditions the political influence of Russian 'national-patriots', who are inherently sceptical of western motives and interests, would grow.

Already there is concrete evidence that Russia's reevaluation of its security interests and responsibilities may lead to new tensions in its relations with its western partners. For example, Russia is currently establishing a significant military presence in the north Caucasus, one of the most unstable regions of the former Union. This military presence is quite consistent with Russia's November 1993 military doctrine which specifies that its armed forces may be used in support of Interior Ministry (MVD) troops dealing with internal instabilities. The trouble is that the deployment of armour in the region exceeds CFE flanking limits and thus causes tension with NATO, and in particular with Turkey. Tension with NATO was further intensified by Russia's proposal that both NATO and the CIS should be made subordinate to the Conference on Security and Cooperation in Europe (CSCE - a common regional forum) and to the North Atlantic Cooperation Council (NACC - a mechanism for military and political partnership). This was seen as an attempt to emasculate NATO and upgrade the Russian-dominated CIS security system. Moreover, Russia's insistence on a NATO recognition of its special identity as a great power led to repeated postponements of the PfP signing ceremony and to a particularly acrimonious North Atlantic Council (NAC) meeting with the Russians in Istanbul in June 1994.

It is therefore clear that the absence of Soviet ideology and even a continuing common interest in democracy does not mean that Russian and western strategic interests in Europe are necessarily identical or even complementary. Indeed, it is possible that Russia's relations with the West could return to patterns of competition or rivalry established during the 19th century (with the added factor of a much reduced, but still significant, nuclear back-up). Over the past twelve months Russia has reasserted its particular interests in former Yugoslavia and has insisted on consultation over the Middle East and North Korea. In the case of Bosnia, Russia made clear that its cooperation with the West was conditional on the accommodation of its particular interests and concerns.

So far the West's relationship with Russia has not descended into antagonistic rivalry. Such a development is by no means inevitable, nor even necessarily dangerous. Even among traditional partners and allies interests are seldom identical; sometimes they may even be mutually exclusive. The ability to resolve such conflicts, and thus develop a genuine partnership, depends on the ability and will of political leaders to resolve conflicting interests to mutual satisfaction. This in turn depends on a minimum consensus on basic issues of democratic order and law. Given these, even a degree of nineteenth century rivalry, if properly handled, would not exclude cooperation in projects such as PfP and the 'G8'. However, if an increasingly competitive relationship is handled wrongly, either by Russia or the West, the West could again find itself confronted with a new and somewhat amended version of the theoretical, but specific threat which was identified at the start of this chapter.

Notes

1. The reassertion of Russia's national interests was reinforced by the results of the December 1993 parliamentary elections in which Russian nationalists, particularly Vladimir Zhirinovsky's inappropriately named 'Liberal Democratic Party', did unexpectedly well.
2. Brzezinski, Zbigniew (1994), 'The Premature Partnership', *Foreign Affairs*, vol. 73, no. 2, March/April 1994, p. 80.
3. *Op. cit.*, p. 72.
4. *Op. cit.*, p. 72.

Section B:
Rethinking Economic Security

7 Security Levelled Out: the Dominance of the Local and the Regional

JAAP DE WILDE

Introduction[1]

How can we make sense of the post-Cold War security debate? 1989 was supposed to be not just a revolutionary year for practical politics but also for political science. The focus of security analysis in particular was seen as having to change fundamentally, and partly it did indeed change. New debates surfaced, ones that ranged from UN peacekeeping, or 'humanitarian intervention', and ethnic conflicts to questions of how to build a new European security 'architecture' or how to approach the analysis of regional security complexes. However many of the traditional themes also reappeared. Great powers, it appeared, were to continue being backed up by smaller ones and by international organizations as determinants of the dynamics of the international system, and hence the security of it.

Clearly there has been superficial changes in the security agenda. Counting tanks and missiles has become less urgent (except perhaps in the CIS countries, to find out how many of them are missing), conversion has become a popular topic (as with expensive flight simulators finding their way into fun parks), and world military expenditures are falling (except in the South where they are rising). Moreover strategic studies has shifted its emphasis to the needs of 'surgical precision warfare', new variants of the older Rapid Deployment Forces or even to a prolongation of the Strategic Defense Initiative ('Star Wars'), this time not against the Russians but against meteorites.[2] Some other subjects have remained on the agenda: nuclear proliferation still remains topical, with the review of the Non-proliferation Treaty coming up (in 1995) and with Iraq and North Korea testing the nerves of the West (and of themselves); chemical and biological weapons continue to be an issue (if only because destroying stocks is a major environmental problem), as does the arms trade, and some aspects of the old arms control and disarmament agenda are still alive.   But at a deeper level of analysis it is difficult to judge what has changed so far, and what the consequences of these shifts will be. Many studies still concentrate almost entirely on the risks implicit in inter-state wars. Moreover most departments of defence and foreign affairs continue to view this as their major concern and source of legitimization.   Yet inter-state wars have become very rare, and there are few places around the world where governments are fighting governments. Inter-state military conflicts have of course not disappeared entirely.   Recent examples are the wars between Pakistan and India, and between Iraq and Kuwait, and one could argue about the nature of some other armed conflicts.   For example, the fighting in the former Yugoslavia started as sub-state wars, but evolved into inter-state wars once Slovenia, Croatia, Bosnia, and the former Yugoslav Republic of Macedonia were recognized as sovereign states by the bulk of the international community.   Additionally there are of course many states whose relations are mutually tense.   In the Middle East all states live in fear of one another; tensions among the CIS member states are high; the conflict between North Korea, South Korea and the USA may escalate, and so on.

Nevertheless, the overall picture is clearly one of sub-state violence. Almost worldwide, governments are fighting domestic opposition (that travels under such pseudonyms as 'dissident', 'terrorist', 'rebel', 'organized crime', 'guerilla', or 'ethnic minority') and often vice versa. According to the Interdisciplinary Research Programme on Root Causes of Human Rights Violations (PIOOM), in 1993 there were twenty two conflicts in which more than a thousand people were killed.[3] None of these can be called a 'traditional' inter-state war.

The debates about these conflicts and how to solve them are many, even if it is not always clear what they are about.   In the case of peacekeeping and 'humanitarian intervention' (can armies function like police forces, and should they?) there is often a confusing discrepancy between moral norms about human rights and direct national interests in terms of the *raison d'état* Additionally, both aspects are complicated by operational questions.   It is doubtful indeed whether military action is able to end civil wars, and if so at what cost. In Yugoslavia this was not really tried by the United Nations, in Somalia it failed in most respects, even if there have also been (albeit temporary) success stories, like Cambodia.

So what is the goal of all this activity and reflection?   From a traditional military-diplomatic and security perspective, it has to be one that concentrates on the question of national interest and the integrity of the state.   For such 'realists' humanitarian reasoning belongs to another domain of politics and forms an add-on dimension.   But they are far more central to a 'societal' security perspective, one that concentrates on the identity of actors.   The meeting ground of both is the question of the point at which the accumulation of civil wars, low intensity conflicts, local anarchy and organized crime can effectively disrupt the functioning of the international system.

One of the problems of the new debates is that they affect the old division of labour among governmental departments. Security functions in domestic affairs are normally in the realm of (riot) police and the departments of justice, not that of the ministries of defence and foreign affairs. But today these ministers need to know how many unstable governments the state system can endure, globally but foremost regionally. How many holes in a road does it take to slow down or even stop the traffic? At present there is no world war, but civil wars seem to be a structural phenomenon . Over recent decades there have been some twenty to thirty going on simultaneously, albeit in different places.[4] A related question is how many so-called 'weak' states the international system can endure. Weak states[5] are characterized by régimes who have to rely on fierce repression of their inhabitants in order to stay in power. Examples vary from Sri Lanka to Israel, from Turkey to North Korea, from China to Peru, from Uganda to Iran in varying degrees and forms. How do their domestic circumstances affect their international and in particular their regional environments?

When the relations among states are at stake, however, the content of the security debate is still mainly about traditional dichotomies. On the one hand there is the balance of power logic based on the logic of 'immature' anarchy, on the other hand there is security community logic based on the logic of 'mature' anarchy.[6] In a different context the same dichotomy is present in the distinction between 'associative' and 'dissociative' peace. Questions of how to tame aggressive diplomacy and how to prevent unintentional war are the dominant questions in this agenda. This, of course, will remain one of the urgent issues on *any* security agenda. The post-Cold War debates have clearly developed a new focus on them, at least in Europe. The security debates since 1989 in Europe have shifted to attempts at creating a structure of associative peace, mainly by the development of a new European 'security architecture' of international organizations, whereas during the Cold War dissociative peace (or deterrence) was the credo. But this shift of emphasis has left the societal sector and the substate level largely untouched. The debate focusses essentially on who is to be allowed to join the EU and NATO and when.

Naturally everybody is also concerned about the revival of ethnic and nationalist conflict throughout Europe, especially in Central and Eastern Europe (CEE), if not yet about the emergence of states run by crime syndicates. But when it comes to the security debate this is still essentially perceived as a domestic problem for the governments with whom a 'partnership for peace' is now sought in the military-diplomatic sphere. Some organizations, like the European Bank for Reconstruction and Development (EBRD) and the International Monetary Fund (IMF), do concentrate on local societal initiatives, but their effort is as yet too marginal to make a real difference.

This chapter is not so much a plea for more military-diplomatic interference in the domestic affairs of other countries, nor one for a reintroduction of a domestic role for defence ministries, but rather one for a clearer understanding of the international impact of sub-state dynamics. This was precisely one of the lessons of 1989, even if at first in a positive sense, as changes in the Soviet Government and pressure from mass demonstrations brought about largely peaceful revolutions. The face of the international system changed mainly, though not entirely, due to sub-state dynamics. The crucial question is how we are to integrate the sub-state level of analysis into the traditional security debate. To that end, and merely as a starting-point, this chapter offers a general structure for the debate. This structure consists of a matrix combining levels and sectors of politics.

Levels

The simplest and most applied structure in the debate about security is derived from the principle of state sovereignty. Due to the universal acceptance of this legal principle there are three levels of analysis in political science - inter-state, state and sub-state - and to a large extent also three political 'worlds' on the cognitive maps of many people.[7] Sovereignty splits the world into sub-state and inter-state politics, and the state itself is both the river and the bridge between them. To put it slightly differently, sovereignty splits the world into national and international politics, and the national government is both river and bridge. Or again, world politics has a system level, a unit level and a sub-unit level. In other variants 'international' or 'inter-state' are labelled 'global'; and 'national' or 'sub-state' are labelled 'local'. Often an individual level is added as well.

The distinction between sub-state and state levels implies a differentiation between state (also known as 'the authorities', 'the rulers', 'the government') and society (or 'the people', 'the public', 'the ruled', or sometimes 'the nation'), entities which are of themselves a subject of debate in IR theory. In the more 'billiard ball' images of international relations this differentiation loses its meaning, because the state acts on behalf of society by representing its dominant forces and/or suppressing dissenting ones. In the more 'cobweb' images the distinction does matter. Here states are mainly dominant coordinators and arbitrators of international relations and they are seen as having the power to stimulate or discourage specific transactions and interactions. The whole scale of levels can be viewed as a micro/macro axis, but also as systemic layers or tiers.

As a cognitive map this scheme, in all its variants, has clear advantages, and it can serve the purpose of structuring the security debates. But it should be realized that in empirical terms it is largely misleading. Firstly, its very state-centrism might obscure a proper security debate. It might be suggested that perhaps a cultural anthropological approach or a sociological stratification of world politics into élites, classes, or functionally similar groups would lead to a more useful classification of levels than the present one, one which is rooted in international law (itself a product of the dominant European political culture) and diplomatic history. Secondly, if one goes up and down the levels of world politics, the geographical, demographical and economic scales do not follow the same pattern. Because states differ in size, composition, type and level of civilization, location and climate it is strange and misleading to treat them as equal units. Even if they are forced to be part of the same struggle for power and peace, and even if they are equals in international law and diplomatic ceremony, their other characteristics vary widely. The neglect of this reality results in distorted images of political processes.[8]

Transactions on scales that are still local in the USA, China or Brazil, would be part of international relations in Europe. Western Europe began in the 1990s to deal with problems of policy coordination, and divisions of governmental powers which have dominated politics in the USA since 1865, and which are also familiar to huge federations like India or Brazil (if not the late Soviet Union). They involve comparable demographic and economic scales, but they are in different realms of analysis. One improvement in this respect is the growing acknowledgement of a regional level in between the international and the state level - sometimes also called a sub-system level in between the system level and the unit level. At least in terms of geographical scale, and to some extent also in terms of economic and demographic scales, it is more accurate to sub-divide the international system into regional sub-systems. The dominant levels are then global, regional, country and local. Especially in development studies there is a tendency to concentrate on the level of local communities. There is no specific literature about a 'country level', however. It seems to more or less equal the state level, hence reintroducing the problem of disproportionate scales. Not surprisingly, in the literature the term 'region' sometimes refers to sub-state national areas (like Wales in the United Kingdom) or non-state national areas (the territory of the Kurds or the Basques), and sometimes to super-state areas (Sub-Sahara Africa, the Pacific Basin, and so on).

Thirdly, it is unclear how the time dimension influences the nature of the actors and processes at each level. The nature of governments, technology, knowledge, norms, economics, warfare and even of power politics has changed over time[9] - so an important open question is why the essence of the international system and its sub-systems should be constant? These imperfections are listed here to emphasize the need to improve theorizing about levels of analysis in political science. We have to accept the present state of affairs in political science, as it works with several mutually related classifications of world politics, ones in which the principle of sovereignty is central. Moreoover, despite their imperfections, the security debate can be structured along these lines (see Table 1).

Table 1: Related interpretations of levels of analysis in world politics

macro	system	international	interstate	global/world
	subsystem	transnational (regimes, NGOs, MNCs	(IGOs)	region
	unit	nation	state	(country)
	subunit	domestic		
		subnational	substate	local
micro		individual		

Another factor is that these classifications relate to different approaches to the same subject. In principle, it ought to make a big difference whether one thinks in terms of systems and sub-systems, in terms of societies, nations and communities, or in geopolitical categories like regions and countries. But, apart from (strict) IR theorists, in practice most of us use many such categories almost interchangeably, and usually without causing too much confusion. For example, many authors treat the concepts of nation, state and country as synonyms within one and the same text, and typify them as either units or actors depending on the context of the specific sentence rather than due to any fundamental theoretical preference. Likewise, it is common to speak about the international relations of states. Probably implicit axioms are hidden behind this terminology, but for our purposes it is sufficient to present a very liberal and wide interpretation of the levels of analysis in order to create an acceptable axis for structuring the debate on security. Moreover, as long as the empirical inconsistencies of the classifications are not solved in an authoritative manner there is no need to be conceptual puritans.

Sectors

Originally, security debates focussed exclusively on military-diplomatic affairs. The essence of international relations is diplomacy, but it is military (or 'coercive') diplomacy in the sense that the underlying rationale is that if the political power of rulers is ultimately tested, it is by means of war. This was as true for great powers with their imperialistic or hegemonic ambitions, as it was for local rulers faced with attempts to escape from feudal domination, colonization or occupation, if not plunder and genocide. Security debates hence focussed on the stability of the international system (which was supposedly decided by great powers) and the integrity of individual states. Threats to that stability and integrity were perceived in terms of (in)voluntary clashes between state controlled armies, and, in the era before the world came under European domination, the goal of excluding 'barbarians'. Other elements of security politics, like espionage, infiltration, subversive action, alliance politics, arms procurement and trade, domestic tasks for secret services, parts of taxation and government spending policies and so on, were all subordinate to the prevention or preparation of such clashes, and found their final legitimacy in it. Inter-state military and diplomatic relations have been the main focus of the security debate since the seventeenth-century in European politics, up to and including the twentieth-century global Cold War period.

The stability and integrity of the sub-state level could have been an equally important and independent security concern, but was not. Security has always been a foreign policy concern - it is the history of war and diplomacy. The domestic mirror image travelled under the heading 'law and order', and followed a different logic.[10] In the interest of international security concerns domestic security was (and is) often even put at risk by persecuting real or presumed opposition groups, and by impairing individual liberties and human rights. Weak states often legitimize themselves by reference to the pressures the international environment puts upon their behavioural options.

So far the post-Cold War security debate has mainly added to this traditional perspective a discussion about the (neo-colonial) right to interfere in the affairs of one state on behalf of the collective interests of all other states or on behalf of the international system as a whole - when it has been so decided by the Security Council of the United Nations or individual great powers. One of the open questions is how these collective interests should be defined. In cases like Iraq-Kuwait this is clear: one member disobeyed the fundamental rule of the state system, 'thou shalt respect one another's sovereignty', and lacked the military power to get away with it. But in other cases, like the Iraqi régime's persecution of the Kurds, the situation is more confused. Human rights and ideals about freedom and democracy may provide legal and moral justifications for intervention, but in practice these are often either rhetorical flags to dress up national or economic state interests or the intervention does not go beyond powerless resolutions and public speeches of contempt.

The problem here is not whether politicians are cheating and lying about their true motives - they may well believe in what they say. The problem is that it is unclear whether, how and when such issues as human rights put the effective functioning of the international system at risk. The United Nations Organization and its Security Council are a product of the traditional security agenda which concentrates on the avoidance of inter-state warfare, and on guaranteeing the integrity and sovereignty of states. One might call this the basic existential value of states within the military-diplomatic dimension of their existence. Human rights, freedom and democracy are part of another dimension, namely the societal one, which is related to different dominant values, namely the identity of political actors.[11] Moreover, within this sector, actors tend to be perceived in individual and community terms. Hence the legitimacy of a state lies less in its military power and diplomatic skill, and more in its societal, often national, character. This security debate accordingly focusses less on the integrity of the state and more on the living conditions of the people on its territory. Some states may thus disqualify themselves as members of an international societal security order, whereas they may contribute to the international military-diplomatic security order.

In addition to these cross-sector contradictions, there are also inner contradictions when it comes to societal security at the state level. On the one hand the ideal states in societal terms are 'national states' ('societal states' would be a more proper term), meaning that the authorities represent in their composition the composition of the state's permanent inhabitants - the society is itself sovereign. Decolonization obviously fits this logic, as foreign rule is equal to occupation, and therefore deplorable. The extreme variant of this logic asserts that every social group that can claim to form a nationality has the right to govern itself. This is the ideal of the true nation-state, with every nation a state, and every state a nation. Here decolonization is not sufficient so long as colonial borders determine the shape of the national states. On the other hand the ideal states in societal terms are democracies, meaning that the authorities represent in their policies the interests of the state's permanent inhabitants, but additionally requiring that they respect deviating individual and group identities to a maximum. Hence, even if the dominant norm in a society is intolerance against minorities and the authorities act correspondingly (like democratically elected fascist regimes), intervention would be justified. A swift glance through the yearbooks of Amnesty International gives a fair indication of the number of states that should be 'colonized' on behalf of the UN, if the identity of peoples rather than the sovereignty of states were to be taken as the international norm for security.

It is in this societal sector of politics at the sub-unit level that the most violent conflicts and wars take place. This was already the case during the Cold War, but only after it ended did security debates begin to focus on this.[12] Yet these debates have become stuck in the logic that belongs to the military-diplomatic sector, in which states are the dominant units. Because of the violence involved in all the present sub-state conflicts the international community is tempted to perceive these conflicts in terms of traditional security debates. Subsequently, solutions are sought first and foremost in the field of diplomatic relations among states. In Europe this means that security is sought essentially by entangling Central and East European governments in the existing Western networks of international organizations. The populations they rule are expected to somehow follow automatically. But so far the most successful attempt to admit the former 'enemy' countries in the Western world is of quite the opposite nature, as is demonstrated by German reunification. At the price of disappearing from the international system as a state - a complete loss of sovereign integrity and hence of survival in the military-diplomatic sector - the East German population clearly enhanced its societal security, its economic security and its environmental security. It is quite unclear whether membership of the European Union (EU) can do the same for people living in, for example, Hungary, Poland, Slovakia or the Czech Republic. The conclusion should, of course, not be that more states should give up their independence or existence. The recent case of Yemen shows that it is not that simple. The conclusion is rather that there are cross-sectoral conflicting security requirements. For example, when a government's dominant *raison d'être* is the state's sovereignty (if not its own position), foreign interference on behalf of environmental interests is not welcomed or is forced to go through complex government bureaucratic procedures.

One of the results of this is a tendency to deal with domestic conflicts only when they very manifestly threaten the international system. This puts a bonus on violence for oppositional groups in any country. If violence persists long enough, or is brutal enough, and is accompanied by diplomatic efforts abroad, and when it threatens to become a menace for the stability of neighbouring states, the group will finally be invited to the negotiating table, not as an outlaw or a terrorist but as a potential head of state, either replacing the original government or acquiring part of the state's territory (successful examples of this are the ANC and the PLO). In other words, only when the identity concerns of sub-state actors are able to enter the security concerns in the military-diplomatic sector at an inter-state level, will they be taken seriously. This can only be prevented when the stability of the sub-state or local level is given independent priority as a security concern, that is before domestic violence creates international instabilities.

Development aid and investment policies operate within this logic, but they are hardly recognized as security concerns. They are marginal in terms of budget, manpower and policy priority throughout the Western world. Development aid, especially in Africa, suffered even more from the end of the Cold War than it gained. The peace dividend did not flow into development funds; the superpowers could now afford to turn their backs to the non-aligned as well as on former allies that lacked strategically valuable resources. Moreover, arms' producers are desperately looking for new markets in the South.[13] Obviously, there are signs of positive change as well, and some holes in the road are recognized as being potentially dangerous. The EU, followed by the G-7, decided in June/July 1994 to finance the closedown of the remaining nuclear reactors in Chernobyl. In the same months the FBI sought European support for a 'global war against organized crime'; and the IDA decided to give development aid to the inner cities of the United States (albeit at the cost of similar aid to Bangladesh - the shift took place *inter alia* because average living conditions in the inner cities are worse).[14] In other words, there is some practical awareness in politics that the integrity of the sovereign state as the main security concern is undergoing a lot of competition from other existential values. The question is how to first distinguish and then interrelate these different values and the political sectors to which they belong.

There could be endless discussion about how many sectors (or dimensions or issue areas) should be distinguished. So far, the military-diplomatic and the societal ones have been mentioned. An obvious third is the economic sector, in which the welfare and well-being of actors are at stake. Additionally, the environmental sector, centred around the health of actors and living conditions in general, could be added. This division is based on the one proposed by Barry Buzan in *People, States and Fear*.[15] Buzan also distinguishes a separate, political sector but, given his starting point, in fact all sectors are filtered by a political lens. This is especially true for the military sector, which outside the realm of politics is restricted to strategic and tactical operational issues. (To avoid confusion with strategic studies, this sector is labelled here 'military-diplomatic'). Other sectoral classifications could be made as well, and one of the sub-debates ought to focus on which are the most appropriate. Some scholars have argued that environmental issues should not be considered separate from economic ones, because they are at the heart of economic dynamics.[16] It might additionally be argued as to whether demographical issues, like population growth or migration, belong to the societal or the environmental sector or to both in different ways, or whether scarcity of clean water and other natural resources is an environmental or a military-diplomatic issue. But for now the division of world politics into four different sectors will do to structure the post-Cold War security debate.

Security in levels and sectors

Given a sub-division of world politics into four levels and four sectors, the post-Cold War security debate has sixteen boxes to take into account (see Table 2).

Mainstream security analysis has always been close to the Realist line of thought in IR theory. Classical Realism (the Morgenthau School in IR theory, dominant from about 1945-1975) focused mainly on box 3, with a nod towards box 1. States were seen as being caught in the security dilemma and the balance of power logic. Diplomatic history (like the works of Kissinger on von Metternich, and on himself[17]) and foreign policy analysis are central subjects in this tradition. Box 2 only played a role in the European context of the North Atlantic Treaty Organization (NATO) versus the Warsaw Treaty Organization (WTO), accompanying power comparisons, and (relevant during periods of détente) studies on arms control. In the late 1970s neorealism emerged, which in the Waltzian tradition (structural realism) shifted the emphasis to box 1, both by looking for the fundamental causes of insecurity (international anarchy) and by making the security of individual states subordinate to the stability of the international system as a whole.[18] In practice, the continuation

Table 2: A (state-centric) cognitive map of world politics

level of/sector of politics/politics	military-diplomatic	economic	societal	environmental
system [international]	1	5	9	13
subsystem [regional]	2	6	10	14
unit [state]	3	7	11	15
subunit [local]	4	8	12	16
existential values (& dominant norms)	integrity of actors (sovereignty)	welfare and well-being of actors (equity)	identity of actors (human rights)	health and liveability of actors (sustainability)

of bipolarity became the dominant security concern. Neorealism in the Robert Gilpin tradition (one that focusses on political economy) opened the economic sector, in particular box 5: the role of the world economy.[19] Scholars like Immanuel Wallerstein, Paul Kennedy and Joshua Goldstein focussed on both boxes 1 and 5, bringing economic long waves and hegemonic cycles together.[20]

In more marxist oriented studies, like those of Wallerstein, the economic sector is obviously dominant. But though the analyses of Marx and Engels clearly involved the sub-state level (the *Verelendung* leading to world revolution fits in boxes 8 and 12), security studies did not produce much along these lines during the Cold War - were it only because in the West too obvious neomarxist analyses were perceived as security risks in themselves. The *Dependencia* school, for example, did not become part of the debate. There is a lot of literature, on the other hand, related to box 7: studies on the impact of economic warfare, boycotts, sanctions, protectionism, the relation between trade and conflict and so on.[21] But the bulk of these studies look at economic issues with the survival values of the military-diplomatic sector in mind. Only in the literature that compares the fruits and perils of protectionism (the ideal of self-sufficiency, autarky and political independence at the price of welfare) with the fruits and perils of free trade (the ideal of commercial profit and welfare at the price of political dependence or costly hegemonical responsibilities) does the clash of cross-sectoral security interests become obvious.

When pluralist or liberal lines of thought have intruded into the security debate, the focus has been mainly on box 6 (transnationalism and economic interdependence), with some reference to boxes 2 (military alliances) and 10 (security communities). Here it is argued that complex interdependence in boxes 5, 6 and 7 would alter the conditions of boxes 1, 2 and 3, either by making its dominant norm, that of sovereignty, obsolete[22] or by embedding traditional power politics in networks of international organizations and international regimes.[23]

This literature has also opened the debate about the state-centrism of the unit level. Every sector clearly brings in its own units or actors, hence the market is the dominant unit of the economic sector, society dominates the societal sector and perhaps eco-systems or 'habitats' would be the proper units of the environmental sector. Clearly, the state is an actor in all these sectors but for different sub-sets of its overall qualities, and it competes or and cooperates with different sets of actors, such as transnational corporations, labour movements, economic IGOs, non-governmental development agencies and so on in the economic sector; religious organizations, human rights organizations, the media, cultural movements, ethnic groups and so on in the societal sector; grass root movements, industry, development agencies, health care agencies, international organizations and so on in the environmental sector. The problem of this pluralism is that it makes the unit level too complex to handle. It is difficult to define an indisputable unit level for the economic, societal and environmental sectors. Hence, choosing a state-centric point of gravity is very tempting, even though it adds to the shortcomings of the classification at the level of politics. Among the main risks is that security in terms of equity, human rights and sustainability will be perceived as secondary concerns to the main focus of state security, that of preserving its sovereignty.

Earlier explicit studies of the relation between domestic structures and foreign policy making (boxes 4 and 3), especially James Rosenau's concept of linkage politics in the 1970s and 1980s, did not however develop into a separate branch of IR theory.[24] They either ended marrooned in foreign policy analysis or in transnational studies. Clearly such ideas would merit a revival if one wanted to put more emphasis on the local level in IR theory.

The societal and environmental sectors emerged in close relation to liberal thought from the 1970s onward with what can be called the 'global challenges' literature. Boxes 9 and 13 are filled with literature about the 'global village' - which is incidentally a misleading, even romanticizing label.[25] However this literature did not really make much impact on the dominant security debates of the Cold War, and even today much of the literature on environmental security seems to live a life of its own, at any rate divorced from mainstream IR theory.[26]

Though the sectoral approach is only illustrated here with some tentative examples of the literature, the overall characteristic of the Western security debates during the Cold War can now be sketched out (Table 3). The main emphasis during the Cold War was on box 1; boxes 2, 3, 5, 6 and 10 were also part of the debate, while box 4 was at stake in debates about the role of the military industrial complexes (MICs) and about perceived and real attempts to subsidize subversive activities in one another's societies. But it can hypothesized that the local level and the environmental sector were grossly neglected - with an exception to be made for the debates about nuclear testing and the results of nuclear warfare - and the societal sector for the most part.

Table 3:   Dominant focus of the security debate during the Cold War

politics	military-diplomatic sector	economic sector	societal sector	environmental sector
system level	bipolarity Cold War/detente	First, Second & Third World	East-West confrontation (ideological)	(nuclear testing) (nuclear winter)
subsystem level	regional theatres of East-West confrontation			
unit level	foreign policy analysis strategic studies (intelligence offices)			
subunit level	(MIC) (subversion)			

The post-Cold War security debate

Since 1989 much has changed in the boxes of Table 3 - bipolarity has disappeared, the regional theatres of the East-West confrontation have disappeared or at least fundamentally changed their ideological character, especially in Europe. North Korea gives the strongest echo of the old situation; China was and is in a category of its own; the Second World has disappeared, and with it ideological confrontation. It is obvious that many studies concentrate on these changes and the question of what has taken their place. The general tendency seems to be an emphasis that world politics is dominated for the time being by its regional dynamics (at the sub-system level), in which international organizations and regional great powers seem to dominate - if not in practice then at least in the debate.[27]

Meanwhile security problems seem to be located especially in the societal and environmental sectors and at the local level. Today's agenda seems not so much to depend on disruptive or stabilizing dynamics at the international level, but rather on those at the local level and in particular the way these interact with regional dynamics. Hence, the international community can tolerate civil war or other anarchic conditions in some inaccessible countries (as was the case with Afghanistan, Somalia, Angola and Mozambique for more than a decade, as well as parts of the former Yugoslavia, parts of Central Asia, the inner cities and suburbs of most megalopolises, and so on) but there are limits to this tolerance. This limit is felt at the regional level (which in case of huge countries may coincide with the state level) when they create snowball effects, for example caused by massive flows of refugees or the destruction of the infrastructure. But the origin of the disruptive dynamics are local. In the military-diplomatic sector there are increasing micro insecurities, ranging from decreased safety on the streets, at home or in the company (indicated by the increasing investments in so-called 'security' services, tougher policies by insurance companies, and rising extremism), to structural inner city warfare between well-organized and well-armed gangs or 'war-lords'. In the economic sector social security networks are in crisis or absent, while unemployment has become structural, adding to older problems of wide-spread corruption in many states. In the societal sector ethnic conflict, waves of refugees (especially within Africa), ideological and/or religious extremism and organized crime add to the older problems of human rights violations. In the environmental sector the disruption of ecosystems, the exhaustion of natural resources, not least of which is that of drinking and irrigation water, promise a grim future for many. If we are to wait until these issues echo through all levels of world politics, the security debate will come after realities on the ground.

To some extent there has been a growing awareness of these developments. In his *Turbulence in World Politics* James Rosenau is one scholar who has at least offered a starting-point for studying the relation between macro and micro developments.[28]   His thesis is that at present the macro level is relatively stable, while the micro level is in crisis. Wæver, et al. have opened up a debate on security and the societal sector, by discussing societal security in terms of identity values.[29]   Some of the literature on environmental security has been mentioned above. In the economic sector much of value can be found in the development literature, while in the military-diplomatic field studies like that by van Creveld on *The Transformation of War*, and Cox on the social effects of new (arms) production modes, thus opening a novel perspective on security issues.[30]   Taken together, there are insights in all the boxes of the simple model presented in Table 4 below.

The next step must be to examine the interrelationships of these levels of security in such a way that we are able to go beyond doomsday scenarios like the brilliant, but grim, one by Robert Kaplan. His essay has the telling subtitle - 'How scarcity, crime, overpopulation, tribalism, and disease are rapidly destroying the social fabric of our planet'.[31] However, Kaplan neglects the role of international organizations completely, and hence only sees negative accumulations at the regional level of world politics.   One of the major changes of emphasis in the security debate may well be increased direct activity between organizations with a regional mandate and local communities of people - leaving the state apparatus in between the choice of being a bridge or a river.

Obviously, this model is but a first step, and its aim is not to talk down the value of studies that concentrate on only one of the boxes illustrated above. Such studies are crucial, if only because of the complexity of the studies that will be needed. But framing security debates in terms of levels and sectors may be essential to highlight the dilemmas of choosing at times between integrity, welfare, identity and health - as well as choosing between individual, state, regional or global interests.

Table 4: Some dominant issues for the post-Cold War security debate

politics	military-diplomatic sector	economic sector	societal sector	environmental sector
system level	polarity + UNSC? UN peacekeeping? trilateral hegemony?	North-South GATT/IMF/ World Bank/OECD organized crime	global megalopolis cosmopolitanism	disruption of ecosystems food, energy & health problems
subsystem level	security complexes IGO & NGO networks	NAFTA/EEA/APEC Latin American, African and Asian Third Worlds	cultural/religious conflict? security communities?	*ibid.* top box role of IOs? migration problems
unit level	weak/strong states	free traders vs. protectionists corruption	weak/strong states democracy vs. autocracy?	facilitator or obstuctor or adjustment
subunit level	growing anarchy and/or militarization armed societies	unemployment social insecurity corruption organized crime	human rights violations xenophobia political extremism	*ibid.* top blox environmental disasters migration growing anarchy

Notes

1. The author would like to thank Barry Buzan, Lene Hansen, Wojciech Kostecki and Ole Wæver for their comments on an earlier draft of this chapter.
2. See about the latter: *The Economist*, 11-17 September 1993.
3. These were: Angola (over 100,000 casualties in 1993), Burundi (>100,000), Liberia (>50,000), Zaire (>5-20,000), Tajikistan (>10,000), Georgia (>10,000), Azerbaijan/Armenia (>7,000), Somalia (>6,000), Sudan (>6,000), Afghanistan (>5,000), Turkey (>4,000), Bosnia-Herzegovina (>3,500), South Africa (>3,000), Algeria (>3,000), Rwanda (>2,500), Pakistan (>2,000), Guatemala (>2,000), India (Kashmir) (>1,700), Peru (>1,200), Sri Lanka (>1,000), Colombia (>1,000), India (hindus/muslims) (>1,000). Source: PIOOM Newsletter, vol. 6, 1994 no. 1, pp. 20-21.
4. For a survey of the most recent ones see note 3, and also Wallensteen, Peter and Karin, Axel (1993), 'Armed Conflict at the End of the Cold War, 1989-1992', Journal of Peace Research, vol. 30, no. 3, pp. 331-346.
5. A term coined by Barry Buzan. See Buzan, Barry (1991), *People, States and Fear. An Agenda for International Security Studies in the Post-Cold War*

Era, Harvester Wheatsheaf, New York, (first ed. 1983), pp. 96-107.

6. See about immature and mature anarchy, Buzan, (1991), p.175, and on the prevailing dichotomy between balance of power and security community logic, see de Wilde, J.H. and Wiberg, Håkan (eds) (forthcoming): *European Security Exposed. States, IGOs and Peace in Europe*.

7. These three worlds are central in various assessments of the level of analysis problem, though often implicitly. For recent evaluations see Buzan, Barry (1994), 'The Level of Analysis Problem in International Relations Reconsidered', in Booth, Ken and Smith, Steve (eds), *International Political Theory Today*, Polity Press, London, 1994 and Onuf, Nicholas (1994), 'Levels', paper, School of International Services, American University, February, 28 pp.

8. See de Wilde, Jaap H. (1993), 'Peace Research After the Cold War. An Essay on the Micro/Macro-Dimension of Security Issues', in Balázs, Judit and Håkan Wiberg (eds), *Peace Research for the 1990s*, Hungarian Academy of Sciences, Budapest, pp. 41-50.

9. See de Wilde, Jaap H. (1994), 'The Power Politics of Sustainability, Equity and Liveability', in Smith, *et al.*, (1994) pp. 159-176.

10. See for example Hansen, Lene (forthcoming), 'R.B.J. Walker: State Sovereignty and International Relations', in Neumann, Iver B. and Wæver, Ole (eds), *Masters in the Making. International Relations Theorists Assessed*, Routledge, London. On Walker's analysis of a world divided by sovereignty - Walker, R.J.B. (1993), *Inside/Outside: International Relations as Political Theory*, Cambridge University Press, Cambridge.

11. Ole Wæver *et al.* argue convincingly that identity is the main stake in societal security: Wæver, Ole; Buzan, Barry; Kelstrup, Morten and Lemaître, Pierre (1993), *Identity, Migration and the New Security Agenda in Europe*, Pinter, London.

12. See for example, Creveld, Martin van (1991), *The Transformation of War*, Free Press, New York.

13. Hubel, Helmut (1990), 'Neue Waffen in der Dritten Welt und ihre Folgen', *Europa-Archiv*, no. 15, pp. 453-460, and Michaels, Marguerite (1993), 'Retreat from Africa', *Foreign Affairs*, vol. 72, no. 1, pp. 93-108.

14. Reported in the *International Herald Tribune*, of respectively, July 2-3 1994, June 29 1994, and June 27 1994.

15. Buzan, Barry (1991), *op.cit.*

16. MacNeill, Jim; Winsemius, Pieter and Yakushiji, Taizo(1991), *Beyond Interdependence. The Meshing of the World's Economy and the Earth's Ecology*, (A Trilateral Commission book), Oxford University Press, New York/Oxford; Smith, Philip B.; Okoye, S.E. de Wilde, Jaap H., and Deshingkar P. (1994), *The World at the Crossroads. Towards a Sustainable, Liveable and Equitable World*, Earthscan, London.

17. Kissinger, Henry, A. (1964), *A World Restored. Europe After Napoleon: The Politics of Conservatism in a Revolutionary Age*, Grosset and Dunlap, New York (first ed. 1957), and (1994), *Diplomacy*, Simon and Schuster, New York.

18. Waltz, K.N. (1979), *Theory of International Relations*, Addison-Wesley, Reading, Mass.

19. Gilpin, Robert (1987), *The Political Economy of International Relations*, Princeton University Press, Princeton.

20. Wallerstein, Immanuel (1974), *The Modern World System* (vol I), Academic Press, New York. Kennedy, Paul (1989), *The Rise and Fall of the Great Powers. Economic Change and Military Conflict from 1500 to 2000*, Vintage Books, New York (first ed. 1987), and Goldstein, Joshua S. (1988), *Long Cycles. Prosperity and War in the Modern Age*, Yale University Press, New Haven.

21. See for example: Wallensteen, Peter (1968), 'Characteristics of Economic Sanctions', *Journal of Peace Research*, vol. 2, pp. 248-267; Knorr, Klaus and Trager, F.N., (eds) (1977), *Economic Issues and National Security*, Allen Press, Lawrence, Kansas; Goldmann, Kjell and Gunnar Sjöstedt (eds) (1979), *Power, Capabilities, Interdependence: Problems in the Study of International Influence*, Sage Publications, London; Polachek, S.W. (1980), 'Conflict and Trade', *Journal of Conflict Resolution*, vol. 24, pp. 55-78; Bergeijk, Peter A.G. van (1990), *Handel en diplomatie*, dissertation University of Groningen. van Bergeijk, 1990; Ham, Peter van (1992), *Western Doctrines on East-West Trade. Theory, History and Policy*, Macmillan, Basingstoke, London.

22. As with Vernon, Raymond (1971), *Sovereignty at Bay*, Basic Books, New York or Soroos, Marvin S. (1989), *Beyond Sovereignty. The Challenge of Global Policy*, University of South Carolina Press, Columbia, (first ed. 1986).

23. Keohane, Robert O. and Joseph S. Nye (eds) (1972), *Transnational Relations and World Politics*, Harvard University Press, Cambridge, Mass., and (1977), *Power and Interdependence. World Politics in Transition*, Little Brown, Boston.

24. Rosenau, James N. (1969), *Linkage Politics*, Free Press, New York.; Hanreider, Wolfram (1971), 'Compatibility and Consensus: A Proposal for the Conceptual Linkage of External and Internal Dimensions of Foreign Policy', in Hanreider, W. (ed.), *Comparative Foreign Policy: Theoretical Essays*, McKay, New York.

25. In a village people know one another, and take care within their social common culture. This is not a global characteristic. It is more accurate to talk about a 'global megalopolis', in which people hardly know or understand one another, a town complete with violent quarters, neglected suburbs, super rich parts, etc.

26. See for example Sprout, Harold and Margaret Sprout (1968), *An Ecological Paradigm for the Study of International Politics*, Center for International Studies, Princeton; Brown, Neville (1989), 'Climate, Ecology and International Security', *Survival*, vol. 31, no. 6, pp. 519-532; Westing, Arthur H. (ed.) (1990), Environmental Hazards of War. Releasing Dangerous Forces in an Industrialized World, Sage (PRIO, UNEP), London; Homer-Dixon, Thomas (1991), 'On the Threshold: Environmental Changes and Acute Conflict', *International Security*, vol. 16, no. 2, pp. 76-116.

27. Lynn-Jones, (1991), reflects the debates in International Security between, among others, Gaddis, Mearsheimer and Mueller; Keohane, Nye and Hoffmann, 1993, provide an institutional perspective in the European context; Buzan, Barry; Kelstrup, Morten; Lemaitre, Pierre; Tromer, Elzbieta and Wæver, Ole (1990), *The European Security Order Recast. Scenarios for the Post-Cold War Era*, Pinter, London, introduces security complex theory to analyze regional dynamics; see also Gutteridge, William (1989), 'The Case for Regional Security. Avoiding Conflict in the 1990s', *Conflict Studies*, p. 217, and Hettne, Björn and András Inotai (1994), *The New Regionalism. Implications for Global Development and International Security*, UNU/WIDER.

28. Rosenau, James N. (1990), *Turbulence in World Politics. A Theory of Change and Continuity*, Harvester Wheatsheaf, New York.

29. Waever (1993), *op.cit.*

30. Creveld, Martin van, (1991), *The Transformation of War*, Free Press, New York; Cox, Robert W. (1993), 'Production and Security', in Dewitt, D.; Haglund, D. and Kirton, J. (eds), *Building a New Global Order. Emerging Trends in International Security*, Oxford University Press, Oxford, pp. 141-158.

31. Kaplan, Robert D. (1994), 'The Coming Anarchy. How scarcity, crime, overpopulation, tribalism, and disease are rapidly destroying the social fabric of our planet', *The Atlantic Monthly*, February, pp. 44-76.

8 Economic Intervention by International Economic Organizations in Central and Eastern Europe: Will it Lead to More or Less 'Security' for the Region?

ANDREW WILLIAMS

Introduction

As Jaap de Wilde stresses in his chapter the end of the Cold War has led to a radical rethink of the basic concept of security. A new debate has emerged which explores the links between security, economics and 'society'.[1] As a corollary we have to ask how the institutional structures that are supposed to guarantee security in Europe can be adapted. This chapter will address the question as to whether the intervention proposed and so far practised by the economic intergovernmental organizations (IGOs), and particularly the European Union (EU), and the European Bank for Reconstruction and Development (EBRD), has helped and can in the future help in improving the security of the region. In so doing it hopes to ask some basic questions about the desirability and utility of economic intervention and about the nature of European security in the post- Cold War era.

This chapter argues that the record of the IGOs in the region has so far been abysmal and that it is predicated on the same basis of misunderstanding of the nature of the region which plagued Cold War logic and which will lead to yet more mistakes being made. It is suggested that a light-handed, generous and noninterventionist approach with an appreciation of the possibilities and limitations of the region would be much more appropriate than a mere transfer of institutions from 'West' to 'East'.

What is 'security'?

(a) What was security (1957-1989)?

For thirty years, from about 1957 to 1989, security was seen in terms of a policy of 'containment' of the Soviet Union.[2] The debate in what were then purely Western circles was about how to ensure a sufficient and appropriate level of armed response to a state that was assumed to be expansionary in its foreign policy goals and revolutionary in its aims. This revolutionary zeal was seen as being aimed as much against the institutions of liberal capitalism as against the armed forces of the West. Containment was consequently seen in terms of ideology and economics as much as in terms of physical constraint. The military institutional consequences of this were the establishment of the North Atlantic Treaty Organisation (NATO) and a number of analogous institutions and alliance structures around the 'free' world (ASEAN, SEATO, CENTO etc.). The economic consequence was the Coordinating Committee for Export Controls (CoCom), often known as the 'strategic embargo', which aimed to restrict the export of military or 'dual-use' technology (i.e. that was of civilian origin but might have military uses).[3]

(b) *What is security (post 1989)?*

Since 1989 Europe has been widely seen as having been faced with a number of contradictory but simultaneous integrative and disintegrative processes. The most obvious of these have been apparent in the European Community (EC) (since November 1993 the European Union (EU)) with the debates over 'federalism' (or sovereignty), 'subsidiarity' and 'widening' or 'deepening' dividing opinion across the EU. Britain has naturally been blamed for much of this disruption, with bitter discussions about the EU as the norm in the governments of both Margaret Thatcher and that of John Major, although there are clear signs of cracks appearing in the previously monolithic opinions about the desirability of further union in even France and Germany. This debate has yet some way to run.

A second obvious dilemma has been posed by a revival of forms of ethnic rivalry that have led in their most extreme case, in the former Yugoslavia, to civil war, massive loss of life and abuse of human rights (as with mass rapes, 'ethnic cleansing', and the setting up of concentration camps). As will be seen in other chapters in this book, the abuse of human rights for wider political aims has become widespread. We might cite the introduction of language laws that have the laudable aim of restoring sovereignty to previously captive peoples, but that have the result of apparently disenfranchising 'non-native' speakers. This is most obvious in the countries of the former Soviet Union (FSU). Wars or civil unrest have erupted with this as a central issue, as in Moldova, the Baltic states and in some Central Asian republics. Nationalism has replaced both Marx and Islam as the main guiding ideology, and this is of course one that divides as much as it unites.[4]

A third uniting and dividing security issue is that of economic growth. Until 1990 the whole of Central and Eastern Europe existed (or rather stagnated) in the cocoon of a centralized and inefficient economic system, dominated by the Soviet Union, while maintaining a social security system that avoided both extremes of wealth and poverty and too much comparison with the joys of market (or rather social market) capitalism in Western Europe. There has been a simultaneous (if partial in the West) dismantlement of the social state in both halves of Europe since about 1988, with social unrest and a growing disparity of wealth both within and between states a consequence. Lech Walesa put this most poignantly when he spoke of a 'silver curtain' having replaced the iron one. He exaggerated, in that Poland has actually gone a long way to bridging the gap with the West, but he was right in that there is now a 'North-East' divide, with the Balkan and FSU states in a far worse condition than those of the so-called 'Visegrád Quadrangle' (Hungary, Poland, and the Czech and Slovak Republics). Certain FSU states are in a state of quasi-total collapse, such as the Ukraine, and others, including Russia itself, have to put up with catastrophic economic decline.[5]

Economic insecurity

The dangers of waves of emigration to the richer 'North', or of the seizing of resources in sheer desperation, or indeed of civil war are real ones in some obvious cases, like the former Yugoslavia. The anniversary of the fall of the Berlin Wall as this book goes to press (November 1994) has led to a plethora of sober press analyses of the desperate state of many of the losers from the arrival of capitalism - often the old and the disadvantaged.[6] Crime rates are up, expectations for many, but by no means all, have been dashed. The paradox is thus that the full acceptance of capitalism in Europe has led to greater insecurity and division. The debate has particular acuity in the consideration of whether EU membership should be extended to other Central and Eastern European states.

One view is that we have no alternative. Key figures in the EU Commission and the wider political world have staked their reputations on enlarging the EU eastward as rapidly as possible, and to take in the 'Visegrád Four'. As Smith and Wallace put it, '[h]ardly any will explicitly reject the case for an eastern enlargement.' The negotiations for entry have already started in the cases of Hungary and Poland. There is also an evident popular desire among ordinary citizens in Central and Eastern Europe for 'reintegration' into Europe, which for most means membership of the EU.[7] But it has also been pointed out that enlargement would lead, probably as a minimum, to the collapse of the Common Agricultural Policy, major strains on the political unity of the key European powers who had to pick up the bill for enlargement, and the fear that, as Russia and the CIS would have to be initially excluded, that this would actually exacerbate tensions, not reduce them. Might even a 'Visegrád enlargement option' thus bring about a lower 'common denominator', with a corresponding rise in unemployment in the 'dearer' West and perhaps a new,

more virulent, nationalism in these areas as well?   The rise of the extreme
right might be seen as a harbinger of that tendency.

How in these conditions can we define 'security', especially as it relates to
the economic nexus? It is clear that (as with other forms of security, military or
otherwise) we must largely jettison the old Cold War jargon and reasoning. A
number of writers now see security as being 'societal', and they claim that a
'new definition of the relationship between state and society is under way.'[8]
Barry Buzan, drawing on work by Pierre Hassner, points out that both the
benefits and disadvantages of economic integration are creating new tensions -
a dislike of the implied homogeneity (economic and even cultural) that such
integration implies, along with the above-mentioned dangers of economic
migration. These could well in turn lead to crises of identity across Europe.
Buzan and Hassner see this as particularly a problem in the countries of Europe
previously dominated by the Soviet Union, where (they assert) there is also
little experience of either independent statehood or democracy, and no
tradition of 'civil society'. Buzan paints a rather worrying picture of problems
created by an inadequate satisfaction of identity needs, leading to massive
waves of migration and the domination of weaker states by stronger ones, with
the problems of environmental collapse thrown in for good measure.

His latest thinking on the subject indeed seems to render him even more
pessimistic than in 1990, when at least he saw an alternative scenario of an
integrated Europe which 'effectively transformed Europe into a single security
entity, making it an actor in a wider global balance of power rather than a
regional complex.' In the long run, 'the ultimate outcome has to be one or the
other', either the EU absorbing all the new states as an integrated whole, or its
opposite in a truly Hobbesian view of European interdependence turning into
a nightmare of societal 'fragmentation' and collapse. In the short and medium
run, we will get a 'dialectic of fragmentation and integration, where each
drives the other' and an increase of one leads to an increase of the other.[9]

Is this stark view a valid one?   The success or failure of the EU
integrationist drive is clearly central to Buzan's project, even if he does nod in
the direction of other forces at work outside Europe, especially the 'global
networks of trade, finance, production, transportation, information, culture
and R&D ... [which] form a security community in military terms, and ... shares
an economic regime, though it retains immense economic competition
amongst rival economic centres.'[10] The ideal for him is clearly an EU from the
Atlantic to the Urals. In this he is not alone, and there is a widespread
perception that there will be a 'security and economic void' that will prove far
more dangerous than the alternative of a few years of economic adjustment.[11]

What kind of economic Europe?

The clue to whether Buzan and others are correct certainly lies in economic and societal progress or regression. But the underlying assumptions of the emerging collective logic must be questioned. Firstly, is the assertion that civil society is such a novel idea in Central and Eastern Europe correct and, secondly, is 'disintegration' necessarily such a bad thing? The awful nemesis of Yugoslavia hangs as a cautionary tale over all of us. However, a number of Central European commentators have pointed to an alternative vision which sees as necessary a shake out of the imposed 'solutions' for Central and Eastern Europe that have been meted out to the area since at least 1914. Yugoslavia, Czechoslovakia, and Hungary were only a few of the creations of Versailles and Yalta. As László Valki puts it, 'it is misleading to speak about a stable past and an insecure present', and that rather the demise of the Soviet Union has left the area 'fundamentally safer than at any time since the Second World War.' Bipolarity was only 'safer', says Valki, by accident, and it was bought at the cost of societal and economic enslavement of the 'East'. His analogy is of a sarcophagus lid having been placed over Central Europe by the superpowers, stifling initiative and wasting the lives of several generations.[12]

Why, in other words, should the creations of Versailles *not* disintegrate, given their artificiality? Valki also makes the point that it was the EC's hamfisted intervention in Yugoslavia, first recognizing Slovenia, Croatia and Bosnia and then washing their hands of the consequences that made the conflict far worse than it might have been. It might be added, though Valki does not, that where the EU played only a minor role, in Czechoslovakia, the breakup was peaceful and looks set to be perpetuated with reasonably moderate nationalist regimes. The countries of the former Yugoslavia have reason to regret the EC's actions and it must be hoped that the EU has now learned the lesson that it either has to have a coherent foreign policy or not have one at all.

The assumption that the Central and Eastern European states did not generally have a 'civil society' before 1989 is also open to question, or that what there was, in Miklós Molnár's colourful phrase, 'une masse amorphe de millions d'individus fouillant dans les décombres.' If that was the case why do some of the countries of the region seem to have a flourishing civil society? This cannot have grown up since 1989. Molnár has suggested convincingly that in the cases of Poland and Hungary there was a flourishing civil society well before 1989. Russia had a flourishing intelligentsia under the Czars and even in the darkest period of Stalinism, and Molnar quotes Solzhenitzyn as pointing to that basis of a civil society, the family, as the irreducible basis of Russian civil society pre- and post 1917.[13] *All* societies have a civil society, and to claim otherwise about Central and Eastern Europe is to assume that communism was indeed a totally effective and all-embracing system, which it clearly was not, or it would not have failed.

Under the communist system in the whole of the former Soviet Empire a more important element of a civil society continued to exist in the informal economy and among dissident intellectuals, both of which have now emerged as the basis of a crude but lively capitalism and democracy. The societal results of this have evidently been a mixture of good and bad, but they are not self-evidently a total disaster as might be assumed from reading, for example, western reactions to the Russian elections of November 1993. What did we expect would happen once ordinary Russians (or Poles, or Hungarians) got the chance to 'make a fast buck' or create new democratic institutions - a ready-made Wall Street and Capitol Hill replete with high moral standards and checks and balances? To read the fulminations of Harvard's Jeffrey Sachs in late 1993, who left in high dudgeon after the elections, is to be subjected to the full force of those who have written off Russia's three-year experiment in liberal capitalism as a total failure. Should we be so arrogant? It was almost inevitable that Russia and other former East Bloc states would create their own form of institutions (by no means yet fixed in stone).

Buzan's diagnosis might therefore plausibly be criticized as yet another simplistic 'neo' realist (in that he nods in the direction of economic régimes as a possible stabilizing factor) solution to a realist-created problem. The balance of power doctrine that dictated the agreements at Versailles and Yalta cannot now be used to create a new 'sarcophagus' in the guise of the EU. Neither can Western Europe impose its view of what Russian (or other Central and East European) liberal capitalism must look like. To do so would be positively dangerous and merely engender more anti-Western hostility, fuelling the fires of extreme nationalism in Central and Eastern Europe as a natural antidote to our economic and intellectual intervention. A much looser economic and societal framework must be found for Europe that does not replace one homogenous view with another. Civil society never ceased to exist in Central and Eastern Europe, even in Russia, and it can be argued that an encouragement of it is incompatible with centralizing tendencies in the interests of stability within the EU. Surely the EU cannot, and should not, aim to become an 'economic security community' especially given its own growing democratic deficit. In so doing it may indeed run the risk of all Cold War logic and end up in the dustbin of history, ultimately rejected in both Eastern and Western Europe.

Institutional reasoning and economic security

If, however, we allow ourselves to accept that there is a democratic deficit in Central and Eastern Europe, the question is whether any economic IGO could or should try to change this by using the tools of economic statecraft. The suggested tools available are many and varied. The most obvious carrots are the opening up of trade through an extension of Most Favoured Nation (MFN) status or the EU's 'Association Agreements'. They also include export credits, foreign direct investment (FDI) (by companies),[14] loans or grants, 'know how' and technical assistance. Much has been promised in these areas by IGOs, but not much delivered.

Other chapters in this book address the question of whether the EU can (or should) provide for Buzan's ideal of an umbrella military and economic security organization. However, this chapter also wants to address other institutional attempts of a similar nature to attempt a comparison of their utility and desirability. There are many to choose between, including the Organization for Economic Cooperation and Development (OECD), the Bretton Woods organizations (the IMF, the World Bank and the GATT), and various United Nations agencies.[15] All of them have taken as a collective aim the need to promote a certain kind of capitalism in Eastern Europe.

The form of capitalism promoted is essentially one intrinsically modelled on the version advocated in the United States and Britain, one based on free market principles, a progressive and definite reduction in the role of the state (or 'deregulation'), free trade and the reduction of debt. This has led to the advocation of an often draconian pattern of deflation and a reduction of state subsidies, especially by the IMF, and with many parallels to the programmes advocated in developing countries in the 1980s. Arguably the result has been disastrous, especially in fostering the rise of a nationalist right, as in Russia. However, there are still many (not uniquely western) economists who advocate a faster transition.[16] They point to the successes of the Czech Republic, the relative stabilization in Poland as demonstrating the success of a 'fast track', and use the failure of the Ukraine and Russia as showing the failure of a slower transition.

A different model, of 'Rhineland Capitalism', one that is more interventionist may well be preferable, and the election of 'Socialist' (i.e. what used to be called 'Eurocommunist') régimes in Poland, Slovakia and Hungary might be the harbinger of a rejection, or severe modification, of the open market model. More widely (and also in Western Europe), the process of globalization is already provoking a societal backlash that will require cool political heads to avoid a dangerous return to economic nationalism. The economic IGOs must therefore attempt to guide this process with a minimum of coercion and a maximum of disinterested (and untied) help. I do not believe that the EU can provide this, but perhaps a lighter approach might have more success.

The EBRD as case study

The European Bank for Reconstruction and Development (EBRD), founded in 1990, is a key example of western economic intervention in this context, because it is the most 'purpose built' of the economic IGOs, the least likely to have a sclerotic view of the aims and needs of Central and Eastern Europe. It has indeed had a tempestuous start to its life and already had one major reorganization. The EBRD aimed to be an IGO with a major difference, for it was required by its statutes to act as a 'bank', but with an added conditionality, one that was 'political'.[17]

There are of course parallels for these stated intentions. There are a number of regional development banks (the African, Asian and Latin American Development Banks to name but three of the best known). These banks operate generally 'according to sound banking and investment principles'. But other central distinctive features are distinctive indeed. Although the World Bank (IBRD) has had a policy of only funding environmentally sound projects for some years now, a policy that has made it very unpopular with the governments of some developing countries, this is the first Bank that has such an intention built into its 'mission statement'. Equally, the EBRD is the first IO that has explicitly mixed the role of merchant and investment (or 'development' banking), two roles that are often seen as incompatible or even contradictory. As for its commitment to democracy and human rights, this is the first time that any financial IO has explicitly built in such a linkage. The President of the EBRD fully recognizes the inherent difficulty of the task ahead.[18]

The structure of the Bank was initially conceived as correspondingly potentially more complicated in practice than, say, the World Bank or the IMF, because of the conflicting aims that the Bank set itself. The official position on this potential difficulty was glossed over in the bank's literature, by pointing to the use of 'multi-disciplinary' teams from both the two vice-presidencies, respectively merchant and development Banking. The role of merchant Banking was to develop relationships, in particular with corporations in the private sector and to oversee the privatization and restructuring process. The staff of this Vice-Presidency were allocated a particular country and an industry within it so as to develop particular expertise in what must of necessity be a very changing sectoral situation. The Development Vice-Presidency aimed to formulate country strategies and to have relationships with governments, and to concentrate on infrastructural and supply side issues, like training. However, the logic of these two activities is different, and there were reported difficulties of duplication of effort from the outset. The slow rate of lending was at least partly to do with this overlap and confusion of aims.

By the time of the ignominious departure of its first Director General, Jacques Attali, in June 1993 commitments had risen to Ecu 2.6 billion, but it had only actually disbursed Ecu 244 million, less than a fifth of its end-1992 commitments, a figure that had grown by early November 1993 to Ecu 2.8 billion.[19] This discrepancy was the ostensible source of some of the most damning criticism of the EBRD's activity. This relatively low level of activity might be compared with agreement by the 'Paris Club' of official creditors to reschedule $15 billion of Russian debt in April 1993 on the eve of the Clinton-Yeltsin Summit, a move that would clearly have far more impact than anything done by the EBRD. This rescheduling was also linked to the provision of a Group of Seven (G7) aid package to Russia that might be worth up to $2 billion. These sums were widely quoted to the detriment of the

EBRD.[20]   Much of the criticism of both the EBRD and of Attali himself was generated, at least initially, by this discrepancy between grandiose design and paltry reality.[21]

In the EBRD's defence there are several points that need to be made. Firstly, the Bank is not the only institution operating in the area. Secondly, its cautious attitude to giving money might be defended as sensible in such a shifting situation. Thirdly, Attali often warned that the West ran grave risks with its disjointed and ungenerous response to Central and Eastern Europe. The economies of the region it serves have been moribund for many years, afflicted both mentally and economically by years of neglect. But the EBRD might find itself with the problems of the World Bank and the IMF combined, and no clear priorities. Now there is a possibility to define those priorities. Among these problems have to be:

- The increased number and variety of states, all of which have different problems.
- An acceptance that the transition to democracy and capitalism is going to be far more painful than was thought in 1989.
- The need to accept that the private sector cannot absorb money (through the merchant banking vice-presidency) that is given under very cautious conditions, because the nature of the new capitalism in Central and Eastern Europe is that it is of a high-risk variety. Perhaps the suggestion made during the ousting of Attali of actually putting more money into the infrastructure, i.e. through governments and the 'development' arm of the Bank, will be a necessary compromise. It should also be noted that the legal framework in Central and Eastern Europe is often still very primitive.

The decision taken by Attali's successor at the head of the EBRD, Jacques de Larosière gives an answer to some of the criticisms. The two old banking departments, development and merchant banking, were abolished in November 1993 and their mandates absorbed into two new 'banking departments' that cover, respectively, the northern and southern 'tiers' of countries of Central and Eastern Europe. The rationale for this is that the needs of the two tiers of Europe have different needs, with the south requiring more infrastructural help and the north being able to move more quickly through privatization. The most important change is effectively to abolish the merchant banking department, which distinguished the EBRD from all other financial IOs and now makes the EBRD more like, but not identical to, the World Bank. There are still sectoral specialists, but the balance will swing in favour of country specialists. The sectoral specialists, formerly from the merchant banking arm, are now being used by both the new geographical sections, with the aim of thus using them more efficiently.[22]

De Larosière is a great *aficionado* of the EBRD lending as much money as possible (up to the 60 per cent allowed for in the statues of the Bank) to small and medium enterprises, as the G7 originally intended it to do in 1992, and not to become mainly involved in public sector infrastructure projects, as seemed to be the case under Attali's presidency. The problem seems to still be as to how it will do this. These types of enterprise will require more 'soft' loans from other organizations, which the EBRD will have to try and mobilize. It will also have to find more reliable institutions within Central and Eastern Europe to work with. There will be a clash between its role as a solid bank and the desires of its political masters, who will nonetheless not want their hard capital wasted in the present economic climate.[23] There is also a problem, largely unspoken in the corridors of the EBRD, that if it were to succeed in its task of reconstructing Central and Eastern Europe, its very existence would become redundant.[24] However, this is not likely to be the case for some time yet.

The EBRD's political mission - governance

It is the last feature of the Bank's self-stated mission, which pertains to its political mandate, that is the most interesting for the student of politics. The political mandate covers a wide range of factors that encapsulate most of the basic civil and political rights as defined in the UN, European Court and CSCE conventions on human rights. The EBRD thus has a hitherto unheard of conditionality clause for an economic IGO in its Constitution, that of 'governance', a recognition that lending money to any officially recognized régime had to have a proviso that that régime must be democratically elected and genuinely responsive to the political needs of its population. For a state to receive EBRD money is theoretically conditional on its respecting the rules of governance. This was in stark contrast to the often stated requirement that IGOs must not interfere in the 'internal affairs' of a sovereign state.[25] The question was whether the EBRD would be able to, or be allowed to, pursue this vision or have to tone down its demands.

While Attali was in charge, there was no sign that the political mandate of the EBRD would be relaxed. In the 1992 Annual Report, the comments on the political developments in Central and Eastern Europe came before that on economic development. There was much comment in the former about the fragility of democracy and comparisons with the 1920s and 30s. Although no one would disagree that property rights, for example, are as much to be considered a political as an economic matter (indeed the two have always been indissolubly linked in Western political theory since John Locke), the main concern in the Report is about the dangers of authoritarian control. Perhaps the example of China demonstrates that economic democracy need not necessarily be threatened by authoritarian governments, but it could be argued that this is a naive viewpoint given such instances as the Tienanmen massacre. Equally the use of 17th century language (like 'governance') might serve to remind us that democracy is still very fragile in most of Europe and that it must be encouraged with 'sticks' for governments as much as with 'carrots' for businessmen.

The only comprehensive political position to have so far publicly emerged from the EBRD is that of the question of minorities in the area of its mandate. This argues that the Bank should 'be prudent' but 'monitor events concerning the rights of persons belonging to a minority in the countries where the Bank operates', in the light of relevant CSCE and UN agencies that deal with minority and human rights questions. What they would actually do to stop or impede any such abuses has not yet been made clear.[26]

On the effect of the political mandate as an operational feature of the EBRD even before Attali's departure, there is not much clear evidence. It has been suggested to the present writer that the best place to see the application of the governance clauses is in the breach, rather than in the execution, of EBRD lending. So Croatia has not been lent money, for example, as a gross violator of human rights, in spite of being a member of the Bank. However, it might also be argued that Croatia is hardly a good risk at present in purely economic terms. It has also been suggested to me that the political mandate very rarely actually comes up in the deliberations of the governing bodies of the Bank. Most of the members of these are from economic, not political ministries. When a strong political point has to be made therefore it needs to filter through from the political ministry, often a hard process to carry through given the rules of bureaucratic politics.

However, it might be repeated that this is perhaps not the best activity that a bank should be pursuing, at least not in the almost personalized way that it has been pursued up till now. Is not the CSCE or the UN a better forum for such discussions, not a bank? Is there not a danger of the appalling 'politicization' that has so affected the UNCTAD and many other UN bodies, even if they are obviously not exactly the same kind of IO? This is clearly the new President's view. And there are signs that the West is less keen on enforcing norms of human rights than not getting its money back or at least a political stability in return for capital invested.[27] But surely the political information gathering and analysis will need to continue in some form, if only because banks rely on risk analysis to make sure that they do not make wrong or misguided decisions. Perhaps any organization that gets involved in the 'new' Europe will have to be 'politicized' whether it likes it or not.

One argument that has been made in favour of Attali's approach is that it did emphasize the really 'big' issues, like European hypocrisy about trade with Central and Eastern Europe. Attali has been quoted as believing that the EBRD's main job is to 'influence the West' to open up markets for Eastern European products, i.e. to stimulate trade. One question has still to be as to whether the EU or the US are in the mood for the desired boost to trade, especially as most eastern exports would be of food or steel, both delicate problems within the EU. Equally it has been argued that the EU has not the knowledge necessary in the secretariat to understand the problems of even Central, never mind Eastern, Europe. There is no real European foreign policy and the policy towards the East is piecemeal and reactive. Are the carrots and sticks of EBRD promises and threats of credits of any use in the midst of this disarray?

Conclusions

The experience of the EBRD is clearly a telling one, but what exactly does it tell? One argument, as suggested by Buzan, might be that unless the EU takes over the 'rescue effort' for Central and Eastern Europe, everything, at least to the east of the 'Curzon Line' will drift off into destruction, probably bringing down Western Europe with it. In this scenario the EBRD has failed to use its political and economic mandate properly. An alternative view is that the EBRD has pulled back from the brink of an embarrassing attempt at massive social engineering, led by Attali, that was doomed to failure. It was doomed partly because the resources at the disposal of the EBRD were never going to be sufficient to make it a very useful carrot or stick wielder. Only the G7 acting in massive concert could do that, and they evidently have neither the desire nor the means to do so at present. For the EU to do any better it will have to demonstrate a far higher level of political will than it has so far.

Given that the expectations raised in 1989 were dashed on the rocks of economic and political reality a much more honest, and possibly successful, approach might be to be more explicitly modest in promising help to Central and Eastern Europe. The results of over developed expectations have already proved to be the election of increasingly interventionist, anti-'globalist' governments in much of Central and Eastern Europe. If the advocates of security through the extension of the EU are not careful, we might have even more nationalist régimes being elected.

The EU approach outlined by Buzan and others is doomed for the same reasons that the initial course embarked upon by Attali is doomed. This is because Attali's approach seems to have been predicated on a view of liberal capitalism that made the implicit assumptions that the form of capitalism and democracy that Central and Eastern Europe need are better decided by the West than by the local evolving and differentiated forms of civil society. If the EBRD now has a leadership that recognizes that its role can (and should) only be marginal in influencing political and economic change in Central and Eastern Europe, and especially in Russia and the CIS, then it stands a better chance of seeing that influence have some long-term, if unspectacular, effect than all the bluster of Attali's regime could have achieved. If it stays on its new course, the EBRD may thus well prove in the longer run to be a model for western economic intervention in Central and Eastern Europe and not a case history of disaster.

Notes

1. For a brief exploration of these relationships see Buzan, Barry (1994) 'The Interdependence of Security and Economic Issues in the "New World Order"', in Stubbs, Richard and Underhill, Geoffrey R.D., *Political Economy and the Changing Global Order*, London, Macmillan, pp. 89-102.
2. The date of 1957 is chosen because it was the date of the publication of Henry Kissinger's *Nuclear Weapons and Foreign Policy*, New York, Harper and Brothers. This book can be seen as the key publication that led to the adoption of the idea of 'flexible response', including the stationing of American short-range nuclear missiles in Europe. It also led to 'three decades, from the late 1950s to the late 1980s [during which] the theory and pursuit of 'arms control' dominated international relations.' For a succinct account of this see: Isaacson, Walter (1992), *Kissinger: A Biography*, New York, Simon and Schuster.
3. For a useful account of the CoCom see: Mastanduno, Michael (1992), *Economic Containment*, Princeton U.P. For a summary of the CoCom's achievements up to and since 1989, see Williams, Andrew in Williams (ed.) (1994), *Reorganizing Eastern Europe: European Institutions and the Refashioning of Europe's Security Architecture*, Aldershot, Dartmouth Publishing.
4. For Central Asia, see: Hiro, Dilip (1994), *Between Marx and Muhammad: The Changing Face of Central Asia*, London, Harper/Collins. He makes the point that the much-heralded Islamic 'fundamentalist' surge that was expected in 1990 has singularly failed to happen.
5. For example, Russian industrial production in January 1994 was 28 per cent lower than the previous (already disastrous) year. See also accounts of the report by Russian economists to the State Duma in early 1994, which estimated that more than one third of the population was below the poverty line, and painted a terrible picture of rising child mortality and decreased life expectancy, *The Guardian*, 3 February 1994.
6. One particularly good collection of essays was printed by *The Guardian*, 'After the Wall', 3 November 1994.
7. Smith, Alasdair and Wallace, Helen (1994), 'The European Union: Towards a Policy for Europe', *International Affairs*, 70, 3, pp. 429 - 444, page 437. For a typical account of the 'popular view', see Barber, Tony, 'Minority Rule' (from Komarno, Slovakia), *The Independent on Sunday*, 28 November 1993.
8. Buzan, Barry, 'The changing security agenda in Europe' in Waever, Ole, Buzan, Barry, Kelstrup, Morten and Lemaître, Pierre (1993), *Identity, Migration and the New Security Agenda in Europe*, London, Pinter, p. 2.
9. Buzan (1993), *op.cit.*, page 6-7. The 1990 reference can be found in Kelstrup, Morten, Lemaître, Pierre, Romer, Elzbieta and Waever, Ole (1990), *The European Security Order Recast: Scenarios for the Post-Cold War Era*,

London, Pinter.
10. Buzan (1993), *op.cit.*, page 12.
11. See for example an excellent piece by Morris, Bailey, 'Drift to Nowhere in Central Europe', *The Independent on Sunday*, 10 July 1994.
12. Valki, László 'Security Problems and the New Europe: A Central European Viewpoint', in Williams (ed.) (1994), *Reorganising Eastern Europe, op.cit.*, pp. 108-109.
13. Molnár, Miklós, 'Pouvoir et société civile dans les pays de l'Europe de l'Est: concepts et réalités', *Cadmos*, Autumn 1982, pp. 34-53.
14. Although not strictly within the ambit of this paper it might be pointed out that flows of FDI to Central and Eastern Europe have so far been very low, about $5 billion in 1993, with total estimated stocks of FDI at the end of 1993 put at only $13 billion. The UN comments that this latter total is 'about as much as the FDI stock of Thailand' and that Mexico alone received more FDI in 1993. The only silver in this cloud is that 'fears expressed a few years ago that FDI to Central and Eastern Europe would be at the expense of FDI to developing countries do not appear to be justified', *World Investment Report, 1994*, summarized in UNCTAD Bulletin, May - June 1994, p. 3.
15. I talk about all of these in some detail in my chapter in Andrew Williams (ed.) (1994), *Reorganizing Eastern Europe, op.cit.*
16. See for example Uvalic, M., Espa E. and Lorentzen J., (eds) (1993), *Impediments to the Transition in Eastern Europe*, Florence, European University Institute.
17. See: The EBRD, *Organisation of the European Bank*, London, March 1993.
18. Jacques de Larosière, 'La Transition est un art difficile', *Le Monde*, 25 October 1994.
19. EBRD figures, November 1993.
20. *Financial Times*, 3/4 April 1993. The total Russian debt was put at the time at $80 to $87 billion.
21. *Blueprint*, 12 May 1992, p. 5 and the *Financial Times* 14 April 1992. For a recent report on the progress of the internal inquiries, see the *Financial Times*, 25 May 1993.
22. *Ibid.*
23. Confidential interview, EBRD.
24. See 'La BERD réhabilité', *Le Monde*, 25 October 1994.
25. See the chapter by Williams in Williams (ed.) (1994), *Reorganising Eastern Europe, op.cit.*
26. EBRD, *Political aspects of the mandate of the European Bank in relation to ethnic minorities*, London, EBRD, March 1993.
27. I believe that only US Secretary of State Warren Christopher and EU Commissioner Hans Van den Broek made explicit reference to human rights conditionality at the Moscow Human Rights Conference over the summer of 1993.

9 Towards an Eastern Enlargement; Scenarios for the European Union

ANNA MURPHY

Introduction

The European Union (EU) in 1994 faces the prospect of future enlargement to the East even before it has absorbed the candidate EFTA states. The collapse of communism ushered in this eventuality but, since 1991, the European Community (EC) has been under pressure to give a clear commitment to the new democracies of Central Europe. The EC first recognized their membership aspirations in the Association or 'Europe' Agreements concluded in 1991 with Poland, Czechoslovakia and Hungary. Later, in June 1993, EU leaders gave their explicit support for enlargement to the associated states. However, Hungary and Poland submitted formal applications to join the EU, on 1 and 4 April 1994 respectively, amid concerns that relations with the EU had not developed into a real partnership.

This chapter considers possible scenarios for an enlarged Union based on its existing relations with Central and Eastern Europe (CEE). Since 1988, the EC/EU has constructed a web of bilateral and regional agreements across the European continent.[1] These are made up of several strands: aid, trade, political dialogue and association with EU activities. At the apex of these arrangements are the four Visegrád states (Poland, Hungary, and the Czech and Slovak Republics), with whom Association Agreements were negotiated in 1991. This group was joined by Romania and Bulgaria in 1993 and Slovenia is set to join in 1994. In contrast, the EU moved cautiously to develop relations with the Baltic States. In early 1994, it began negotiations on free trade areas (which would align EU trade regime with that of the EFTA states) 'with the understanding that the final objective of Estonia, Latvia and Lithuania is to become members of the Union through European accords'.[2]

The context in which EC/EU policies have evolved has been one of tremendous change, including German reunification, the disintegration of the

Soviet Union and of the institutional arrangements of which it was the core. In 1994, uncertainty of, and about, Russian foreign policy had a defining impact on the foreign policies of the states of Central Europe and the Baltic which sought security guarantees from the West. As a consequence of this, and of the gradual reduction of US involvement in Europe, the Union and its principal members face increased demands to provide security within and beyond their borders, (in spite of their less than impressive record in the former Yugoslavia).[3]

This chapter first looks at the motivations for accession in the applicant states and in the Union. Whilst the Union as a whole gave its support to Eastern enlargement, there is some reticence amongst the member states. This is increased by the fact that the Maastricht Treaty and the accession of the EFTA states takes the Union into a new phase of integration, one whose waters are uncharted. In addition, further enlargement questions the capacity of the Union to act as a unit, its ability to achieve objectives such as the completion of Economic and Monetary Union (EMU), the implementation of the Common Foreign and Security Policy (CFSP) and the achievement of economic and social cohesion. Seen in this light, future enlargement relates directly to the future of the Union. Possible scenarios for the future are sketched in the third section of this chapter. This highlights the need to make an important distinction between actual enlargement, which is a possibility for the medium-to long-term, and preparatory moves in this direction which are possible in the short- to medium-term.

Outsiders looking in

The goal of EC/EU membership has been a central tenet of the foreign policies of the Visegrád states since 1989. The EU forms a central point of reference for their economic and political development: 'it is viewed as a kind of modernisation centre, able to provide impetus and help... and contributions towards consolidating democratic structures'.[4] Additionally, membership of the EU is regarded as a source of security and as being symbolic of belonging to a certain concept of European civilization.[5] President Havel brought together these diverse meanings of membership in his address to the European Parliament in April 1994:

> The Czech lands lie at the very center of Europe and sometimes even think of themselves as its very heart. For this reason, they have always been a particularly exposed place, unable to avoid any European conflict... Like certain other Central European countries, we have always been a dramatic crossroads of all kinds of European spiritual currents and geopolitical interests. This makes us particularly sensitive to the fact that everything that happens in Europe intrinsically concerns us and

that everything that happens to us intrinsically concerns all of Europe. We are the prime witnesses of Europe's interconnectedness. That is why our sense of co-responsibility for what happens in Europe is especially strong, and also why we are intensely aware that the idea of European integration is an enormous historic opportunity for Europe as a whole, and for us.' [6]

That 'historic opportunity' refers to the possibility of integrating Europe through voluntary cooperation, the hallmark of the EU and that which distinguishes it from previous attempts to establish a European political order.

Kolankiewicz[7] argues that membership is an important legitimating factor for the ruling élites in Central Europe. In the late 1980s, the 'push' factors of dismantling the communist system and the 'pull' factors of democracy and market economies in the West combined to provide legitimacy for the policies of the new governing élites. The 'normative straitjacket' of Association Agreements served to anchor the reform process. Eventual EU membership was envisaged as part of the broader move to 'return to Europe' and to implement economic and political reforms. The legitimacy of ruling élites, then, is bound up with successful transition on the one hand, and integration with the EU on the other.[8] Kolankiewicz further observes that policies of macro-economic stabilization and liberalization 'generate groups of winners and losers for whom European membership is an increasingly important part in their calculus of deprivation. To this extent, the manner in which élites respond to the conditionalities of EC membership is also part of the political electoral equation'.[9] The issue of membership may acquire greater saliency in domestic politics when governments begin preparations for it. Until the middle of 1994, the consequences of membership have not been debated in detail in the applicant countries although all mainstream political parties support the general objective.

In April 1994, Hungary and Poland submitted formal applications to join the EU. These followed the completion of EU enlargement negotiations with the EFTA states and the entry into force of the Association Agreements. The timing of the initiative was linked to the (then) forthcoming Hungarian parliamentary elections and German presidency of the EU (as of July 1994). Both states aim to join the EU by the year 2000 and wish to open negotiations in 1996, after the scheduled EU Inter-Governmental Conference has been concluded (see below).

European Union entry requirements

At the Copenhagen Summit of June 1993, EU leaders agreed that 'the associated countries in Central and Eastern Europe that so desire shall become members of the European Union' and that 'accession will take place as soon as an associated country is able to assume the obligations of membership by satisfying the economic and political conditions required'. These conditions were identified in the following statement:

> '[M]embership requires that the candidate has achieved stability of institutions guaranteeing democracy, the rule of law, human rights and respect for and protection of minorities, the existence of a functioning market economy as well as the capacity to cope with competitive pressure and market forces within the Union. Membership presupposes the candidate's ability to take on the obligations of membership including adherence to the aims of political, economic and monetary union.
> The Union's capacity to absorb new members, while maintaining the momentum of European integration, is also an important consideration in the general interest of both the Union and the candidate countries.'[10]

Fulfilment of these criteria demands adjustment on the part of the applicant states and by the EU in that the latter must be able to absorb new members. The EC did not agree to a timetable for accession or to requests from the Visegrád states and the EU Commission is to review relations in 1995/96.[11] Further improvements in market access were agreed, as was greater flexibility under the PHARE assistance programme and further region-to-region cooperation. The offer to enlarge to all Associated states in Central and Eastern Europe (CEE) placed the Visegrád states on a par with the less advanced states of Bulgaria and Romania. This was interpreted by some officials in the Visegrád states as an attempt to delay accession by dealing with the region as a bloc. This was also interpreted as an imposition of regionalism which *inter alia* ignored serious differences in transformation within the group.[12] Doubts about the commitment of all EU member states to enlargement were increased by French attempts, before the Copenhagen Summit, to include references to Gross Domestic Product (GDP) amongst entry requirements: the Polish Government argued that the health rather than the wealth of the economy should be given precedence.

In supporting enlargement, the Copenhagen decision was driven by concerns about security and stability in the region, about which Germany was most sensitive. Chancellor Kohl emphasized his view that enlargement was a priority for German foreign policy. He stated that it was 'unthinkable that Germany's eastern border, the Oder-Neisse border with Poland, should remain the eastern border of the European Union'.[13]

Scenarios for enlargement[14]

The timing of any Eastern enlargement is affected by EU plans for other EU candidates already in the queue, namely Cyprus, Malta and Turkey. In June

1994, EU leaders agreed that the next phase of enlargement would involve the small Mediterranean states. The Turkish application was effectively put on hold. The Presidency and EU Commission were mandated to report on a pre-accession strategy for the CEE states which would focus on full implementation of the Association Agreements and Copenhagen decisions.[15]

An attempt to sketch scenarios for EU enlargement to the East seems foolhardy given the uncertainty about the current round of enlargement to the EFTA states and implementation of the Maastricht Treaty agenda. The timetable for completion of European Monetary Union (EMU) was thrown off course in 1992/93 and public support for integration declined.[16] Representation, accountability and legitimacy were seen to be critical determinants of the future integration process in the debates surrounding the Treaty. One school argued that the Treaty signalled a qualitative shift in integration towards a 'partial polity' or 'an entity that might develop into a form of direct governance in its own right' in which case, Wallace argues, 'the questions of what political identity, loyalty and affiliation are attached to the EC level of governance become crucial. These then require attention to be given to the full range of forms of political representation and legitimacy'.[17]

An alternative line of thought stresses the quality of the EU as a policy framework in which case numbers matter less than ability to generate policy. Future enlargement will test these divergent perspectives on integration. When EU relations with the states of CEE are considered, the stability and security of Europe enter the equation. Should the primary goal of the EU be the successful transition in CEE? Would EU membership best achieve this? Could this lead to paralysis in the EU, which might also obstruct integration of both regions? If the EU is considered to be essentially a framework for action amongst its member states, a Union devised along functional lines of cooperation seems likely to emerge. If it is considered to be a polity-in-the-making, further deepening of the Union can be expected. This would raise the entry threshold. On the other hand, further deepening may not be acceptable to all member states: in which case, one could envisage a smaller, tighter, core around which the CEE and other states would converge.

The CEE states too face a considerable task of adjustment. One entrance requirement concerns the capacity of the applicants to cope with competitive and market forces in the EU. The Association Agreements will create free trade areas with the EU within ten years but not an internal market (with common policies and market regulation). The Polish Government argued in April 1994 that its economy will be capable of meeting the challenge. However, a 'clear perspective in the form of a calendar and convergence programme will be crucial for ensuring stability and creating conditions for further systemic transformation'.[18] It is clear that long transitional arrangements will be required along with the protection of certain industries. Sectoral interest groups, previously poorly organized and unable to exert influence on governments during negotiations on the Association Agreements, may exert pressure for protection or more gradual policies of adjustment in the future. The implementation of the *acquis communautaire* places a considerable burden on the political, legal and adminstrative apparatus of the applicant states. This ranges from policy preparation and participation in decision-making to implementation of EU legislation. Already, many states have introduced measures to effect compatability between national and EU legislation. The Association framework provides scope for cooperation with EU officials in this exercise. At a political level, participation in the CFSP demands policy adjustment and may arouse sensitivities. In addition, public support for enlargement must be assured: perceptions of the benefits of EU membership may be affected by the development of the EU and the course of economic transition.

Status quo

One scenario suggests that the Maastricht Treaty will be implemented without further change to policies or institutions. This seems most unlikely because of the unbearable strain this would place on the institutions, designed for a Community of Six, and the EU budget. Studies of the budgetary impact of enlargement report transfers to the CEE states of between Ecu 8-26 billion per annum in 1999.[19] The application of current principles of cohesion and solidarity in a larger EU would require a major increase in the EU budget and affect the distribution of costs/benefits of membership to current member states. EU *largesse* vis-à-vis Central Europe cannot be expected against a background of tight pressures on public spending at national and EU levels. Accession of the EFTA states will result in an estimated net gain to the EU budget of only Ecu 6.5bn over the period 1995-99. However, it should be recalled that the EC budget remains but a fraction of total EU GDP (less than 1.3 per cent) - in that perspective enlargement is not a costly option.

The policy implications of enlargement can be considered with reference to the Common Agricultural Policy (CAP). It is inconceivable that, in its current form, it could be extended to Central Europe: Gros and Brenton estimate that this could cost Ecu 17bn per annum.[20] The EC refused to countenance major market opening for agricultural imports under the Association Agreements, despite clear evidence of its importance to those states.[21] Radical reform of the CAP seems out of the question given the history of stiff resistance to the MacSharry plans and trade liberalization in the Uruguay Round of the GATT. Failure to achieve radical reform presents a large obstacle to any Eastern enlargement because of the impact of an enlarged CAP on output, spending and competition.

Graduated integration

Graduated integration is taken to mean that all EU members subscribe to common goals/objectives but are not obliged to reach them simultaneously. Some elements of this are present in the EU and suggest a possible scenario for the future. The proposed path towards EMU enables a core group to move ahead of the rest. In the security field, Ireland and Denmark are not members of the WEU but share the common goals of the CFSP. Were this pattern of differentiation to be extended, it could prove difficult to reconcile the goals of cohesion and solidarity in the Union. It could also prejudice the unity (and unifying force) of the legal order of the EC/EU. On the other hand, such a process would not prevent the establishment of a core group of member states ready to 'deepen' integration. This idea could appeal to France and Germany (the axis of the EU in the past), increase the capacity of the EU to act by facilitating decision-making and limiting the potential of blocking minorities to frustrate common action. The membership and size of this core group is difficult to determine.

European areas: political, economic and judicial

Enlargement could be tackled through the gradual involvement of applicants in specific areas of EU activity short of participation in policy formulation. This could lead to partial membership of areas of EU life and eventual full membership. In 1992, the EC Commission suggested the creation of a European Political Area within which 'like-minded countries would engage in intensive political dialogue and through which the countries of Central and Eastern Europe would participate progressively in the political work of the European Union'.[22] The Commission proposed that CEE states could, for example, participate in EU Council meetings on a regular basis in areas of common interest, for example transport, and be associated with specific Community policies. This led to the development of the multilateral dialogue, first with the Visegrád states in 1992, then extended to the six associated states at the Copenhagen Summit in June 1993. This was intended to operate in three areas of activity: EU, Justice and Home Affairs (JHA) and the CFSP. This would involve meetings at ministerial level and joint consultations. The critical difference between this dialogue and earlier Commission proposals is that the latter is clearly a region-to-region dialogue rather than an extension of the EU umbrella (via 'enlarged meetings') to non-members. In practice, only one poorly prepared meeting of Transport Ministers took place on EU activities in November 1993. Discussions about the CFSP were largely organized at the level of the Troika (the three EU states which precede, hold and succeed to the Presidency) which, to the CEE states, underlined the absence of a real partnership. In March 1994, as a result of an

Anglo-Italian initiative, the EU agreed detailed procedures for a multilateral dialogue on foreign policy.[23]   An important advance towards actual participation in the CFSP was the agreement that:

> 'in appropriate cases the associated countries will be invited through an agreed mechanism publicly to align themselves jointly with European Union declarations on a particular subject; when certain demarches are made by the Troika, associated countries could be invited to support them; the associated countries could be invited to associate themselves jointly with the implementation of joint actions'.

It is too early to evaluate the effectiveness of such moves, especially as the CFSP itself is in an embryonic stage. They may encourage alignment of national foreign policies with EU initiatives (for example, some CEE states already participate in the EU observer mission in the former Yugoslavia). But from a CEE perspective, a real voice in EU decision-making is absent. Furthermore, the process entails a considerable administrative burden for both sides: in this regard, the EU Council suggested that the associated countries might be required to nominate a single representative to facilitate contacts and coordination. This created difficulties for the CEE states sensitive to regional cooperation on foreign policy.

Baldwin[24] suggests that Eastern enlargement be approached by first developing a free trade area for industrial products in the wider European region, equipped with a light institutional structure. Next, the most advanced CEE states could in effect create an internal market with the EU. Non-participation in the EU budget, CAP and the free movement of labour[25] would sideline the contentious questions of redistribution, institutional reform and a voice in EU decision-making. The merit of these arrangements, says Baldwin, is that they provide a gradual approach towards the EU and overcome the 'hub and spoke' character of existing trade arrangements.[26] They reflect emerging trade patterns in the wider region which centre upon the EU. They may appeal to EU states opposed to large-scale financial transfers to the East and states, such as Spain, which are concerned that a North-Central tilt of the Union would be to the detriment of the Mediterranean region.

A combination of the Baldwin and European Political Area strategies could theoretically 'buy time' for the EU until it deals with current enlargement and plans to review EU institutions in 1996. However, it could translate into a permanent holding strategy, feared by the CEE states. Moreover, this perspective reflects the view that priority should be given to developing the EU and Maastricht Treaty agenda and/or that political realities dictate only such a strategy will win support of all EU states. Should security concerns prevail, rapid enlargement may be perceived to be a better route towards security/stability in Europe.

Conclusions: getting to yes

Eastern enlargement of the Union questions the design, policy scope and goals of the Union. The very development of the Union is intrinsically bound up with such enlargement. At the Corfu Summit in June 1994, EU leaders decided to establish a 'reflection group' to prepare for the Inter-Governmental Conference to review the Maastricht Treaty in 1996 'with a view to making the European Union better able to confront the challenges of the 21st century, including those arising from enlargement of the Union to the East and to the South'.27 This does not suggest that a 'deeper' Union will result or that the entry threshold will be raised. This would be contrary to the wishes of member states such as the UK which see enlargement as a means of constructing a wider, looser Union. The Foreign Secretary, Douglas Hurd, in supporting their participation in JHA and the CFSP, stated 'there is no reason why Poland and other countries who wish should not join quickly in that work before there is full accession and full membership. This fits our flexible outward-looking concept of how Europe should evolve'.28

A timetable for an Eastern enlargement has not been agreed. Given the adaptation required by both sides and the complexities involved, an entry date of 2000 seems ambitious. Formidable obstacles to enlargement remain in the areas of the CAP and the budget. There is limited scope for further EU generosity (notwithstanding the enlargement to EFTA states). In the trade field, the EU seems to have exhausted the scope for liberalization by bringing forward timetables of scheduled market opening. This is reflected in the shift of attention in the EU in mid-1994 to a discussion of pre-accession strategies, the implementation of which could reassure the CEE states about eventual enlargement. There is considerable scope under the Association Agreements to move beyond trade to a) support the CEE states in efforts to adopt the *acquis communautaire*; b) to permit policy adaptation and c) to tailor EU initiatives towards the individual circumstances and priorities of CEE states. Additional financial assistance could be extended through pre-accession funds. Initiatives in the area of JHA and the CFSP offer possibilities for closer contacts: the Polish Prime Minister Olechowski proposed partial membership of CEE states in these Maastricht Treaty pillars.29 The critical issue remains that of participation in EU policy formulation: many of the member states remain adamant that this privilege is for members only.

Baldwin's proposals offer a means of building upon existing forms of bilateral and multilateral association. Some CEE officials have reservations about an approach which a) may not create clear stages in the progression towards membership and thus may be an alternative to such, and b) may not guarantee the initial downpayment is repaid by membership. The latter refers to concern that the loss of sovereignty entailed in, for example, an alignment of domestic policies with EU competition policy and internal market regulation, without the corresponding benefits of access to decision-making and EU funds available to full members. In addition, such an approach may result in a loss of bargaining power in subsequent negotiations on full accession as important areas of membership would have already been agreed.

The experience of EU moves to establish region-to-region cooperation underlines a) sensitivities and suspicion amongst the CEE states about EU motives; b) the weakness of initiatives whose implementation remains at the discretion of the EU Presidency (responsible for CFSP); and c) the importance of developing measures to monitor and implement agreed EU decisions. In considering enlargement, therefore, the full implementation of existing agreements and decisions must be assured.

For Poland and Hungary, full membership is the essential guarantee of security - alternatives will not suffice. The security dimension refers not just to instability in the Balkans and uncertainty about Russian foreign policy but to perceptions about a political order in Europe based on cooperation rather than coercion or fear. In addition, the failure of NATO to provide adequate security guarantees hastened CEE moves to join an EU which is itself developing a security profile (through the WEU). This is of particular concern to Germany for which:

'The deepening and simultaneous expansion of the European Union are decisive for securing peace and freedom. In this sense, the issue of European unification is a question of war and peace in the next century... We cannot forget that the prospect of membership has a direct influence on security policy'.[30]

Sweden, set to join the EU, attaches priority to the security of the Nordic region which, it argues, can be addressed through political and economic cooperation with the Baltic States and Russia.[31] A second consideration for the EU in moving towards an Eastern enlargement concerns policy towards its Mediterranean neighbours where France, Spain and Italy share major security interests. It must maintain balance in its relations with the East and South - to this end, its Mediterranean policy is undergoing review.

The altered state of Europe in the 1990s forced the question of a defence and security policy for the European Union onto its agenda.[32] In response, the WEU, the defence arm-in-waiting of the EU, took steps to both 'deepen and widen' itself.[33] The degree to which it develops a defence capacity will influence outside perceptions of the role of the Union in the European and international order, in particular that of the creation of a Western sphere of influence. In this context, the attitude of Russia, whose foreign policy has acquired a distinctly assertive, nationalist tone in 1994, cannot be ignored. Its reaction to any enlargement of the Union to include the Baltic States must also be taken into consideration: would this be considered to be opposed to its interests in the 'near abroad'? Would a EU with a specific defence policy significantly alter that perception? Alternatively, can the Union address

Russian interests through simultaneous action?

In conclusion, there are strong integrating and disintegrating tendencies in EU relations with Central and Eastern Europe, just as there are within the development of the European Union. Germany, a reluctant leader, appears to hold the key to both: because of its strategic location at the centre of Europe, its inability to forge an independent *Ostpolitik* (for political and economic reasons), and the importance of the Germany to the EU, and in particular to France. The central role of Germany means that other EU (and indeed non-EU) states must take into account the utility of the EU as a framework for managing intra-European relations and a means of pursuing a specific European order when considering both its future development and eventual membership of the states of Central Europe.

*The author wishes to acknowledge the assistance of officials from the EU Commission, and Hungarian and Polish Representations to the EU interviewed in April-May 1994.

Notes

1. Kramer, Heinz (1993), 'The European Community's response to the 'New Eastern Europe', *Journal of Common Market Studies* vol. 31, no. 2, June, pp. 213-243; Murphy, Anna (1994), 'Securing Europe's Future: the Role of the European Community' in Williams, Andrew J, (ed.), *Reorganising Eastern Europe : European Institutions and the Refashioning of Europe's Security Architecture*, Dartmouth, Aldershot, pp. 17-40.
2. The European Council of Copenhagen 21-22 June 1993, *Europe Documents*, 24 June 1993.
3. Rummel, Reinhardt (1994), 'West European Cooperation in Foreign and Security Policy', *AAPSS Annals*, no. 531 January, p. 122. He notes that: 'The West Europeans who used to rely on the United States as their senior partner are now asked to carry the main responsibility for stability on the Continent. This role includes the resolution of conflict, the strengthening of democracy and market economy, the balancing of power, and the enforcement of basic norms', p. 122.
4. Hatschikjan, Magarditsch (1994), 'Foreign Policy Orientations in Eastern Central Europe', *Aussenpolitik*, no. 1, p. 53
5. This point is echoed in foreign policy statements and in interviews conducted by the author with senior policy-makers in the Czech Republic and Poland, September-October 1993. It is an important element of the political discourse about participation in the European Union and raises the question of where the borders of this civilization lie. See also Huntington, Samuel (1993), 'The Clash of Civilisations', *Foreign Affairs*,

vol. 73, no. 3, Summer, pp. 22-49.

6.   Speech by President Vaclav Havel to the European Parliament, 8 March 1994, *Europe Documents*, 16 March 1994, p. 2.

7.   Kolankiewicz, George (1993), 'The Other Europe: Different Roads to Modernity in Eastern and Central Europe' in Garcia, Soledad (ed.) *European Identity and the Search for Legitimacy*, Pinter Publishers for Eleni Nakou Foundation/RIIA, London, pp. 106-130.

8.   This linkage is may be strengthened by the differentiated regional impact of the transformation process. Szlachta, Jacek (1993), 'Poland's regional development under economic transformation' (paper presented to Friedrich Ebert Stiftung Conference on Regional Development in Poland, Warsaw 30 September-1 October, 1993) noted that the new regional geography is shaped by external factors such as the Association Agreements, foreign investment, the collapse of the CMEA and intra-regional cooperation.

9.   Kolankiewicz, *op.cit.* p. 112.

10. Conclusions of the European Council, *op. cit.* p. 5.

11. In 1992, the Visegrád States sought a 'general approach, framework and time perspective for the accession'. They argued that an evaluation of the economic transformation and economic policy goals in 1996 should be the 'moment both parties treat as a start of formal negotiations on full membership'. Prior to the Copenhagen Summit, they emphasized the importance of a signal regarding membership over a calendar for accession. Joint Memorandum of the Visegrád States, June 1994 (reported in *Europe*, 4 June 1994 and statements of Hungarian and Polish Ambassadors to the EU, *Europe*, 13 April 1994.

12. Author's interviews with policy-makers and politicians in Poland and the Czech Republic, September-October 1993. They emphasized the need for a more differentiated approach to the states of the region which would recognize the higher degree of progress registered by their states. Czech Prime Minister Klaus, since the division of Czechoslovakia, has resisted efforts to institutionalize and deepen cooperation amongst the Visegrád Group as he clearly saw a bilateral approach as leading to earlier EU membership. Altmann, Franz Lothar (1993) 'Chancen und Perspecktiven der regionalen Kooperation in Ostmitteleuropa' in Weidenfeld, Werner (ed.), *Demokratie und Marktwirtschaft in Osteuropa*, Bertelsmann, Gütersloh, pp. 417-431 argues that Western policy-makers must make it clear that regional approaches are building, not stumbling blocks, for all Europe.

13. Quoted in the *Financial Times*, 24 March 1994. He underlined the parallel process of integration into the EU and the development of contacts between the CEE states and NATO: 'Security and stability in Europe are indivisable', *Financial Times*, 27 January 1994.

14. See Deubner, Christian and Kramer, Heinz (1994) 'Die Erweiterung der

Europäischen Union nach Mittel- und Osteuropa: Wende oder Ende der Gemeinschaftsbildung' in *Aus Politik und Zeitgeschichte*, vol. 18/19, 6 May 1994, pp. 12-31.

15. European Council at Corfu, 24-25 June 1994, *Europe*, 26 June 1994.
16. Reif, Karl-Heinz (1993) notes that Eurobarometer surveys demonstrate a fall off in support from Spring 1991 which he argues took place against a background of controversy over the Maastricht Treaty but also 'clear signals of economic recession and increasingly "bad news" from Eastern Europe' in 'Cultural Convergence and Cultural Diversity as Factors in European Identity' in Garcia, Soledad, *op.cit.* p. 148.
17. Wallace, Helen (1993), 'Deepening and Widening: Problems of Legitimacy for the EC' in Garcia, Soledad, *op.cit.*, p. 101. Vaclav Havel, *op.cit.*, stated: 'it seems to me that the most important task facing the European Union today is coming up with a new and genuinely clear reflection of European identity, a new and genuinely clear articulation of European responsibility, an intensified interest in the very meaning of European integration' a task, he suggests, which could be addressed through a Charter for the Union which would 'define the ideas on which it is founded, its meaning and the values it intends to embody', p. 4.
18. Polish Government Memorandum on Accession to the EU, *Pro Memoria*, 11 April 1994, Warsaw.
19. CEPR (1992) *Is Bigger Better? The Economics of Enlargement*, CEPR, London. Their sum of Ecu 8 billion includes estimated CAP transfers; EC Commission (1994) European Economy, no. 53, p. 114, suggests a figure of Ecu 26 billion based on the assumption that each would receive per capita transfers of Ecu 400 per annum in 1999. Gros, Daniel and Brenton, Paul (1993) suggest transfers in the region of Ecu 21.2 billion in 1999 in 'The Budgetary Implications of Enlargement', *CEPS Working Document*, 78, p. 34. The discrepencies are due to different assumptions regarding the level of EU funds and agricultural output.
20. Gros, Daniel and Brenton, Paul (1993), *ibid.*, p. 36 (based on the assumption that agricultural yields rise to half of those of areas of similar climate in the EU).
21. See Tracy, Michael (ed.) (1994) *East-West European Agricultural Trade: the impact of the Association Agreements*, Agricultural Policy Studies, La Hutte.
22. EC Commission (1993) 'Towards a closer association with the countries of Central and Eastern Europe', *Sec (93) 648 final*, 18 May 1993, its report to the Edinburgh Council, 11-12 December 1992, *Europe Documents*, 9 December 1992.
23. General Affairs Council, 7 March 1994 reported in *Europe*, 9 March 1994. On 17 December 1993, UK Foreign Minister Douglas Hurd and his Italian counterpart Andreatta proposed closer links between the Associated States and the EU in the areas of CFSP and JHA to 'enable them align their

policies and practices more closely with those of the European Union and thus help to prepare them for eventual accession' and to redress the economic bias in the existing relationship, *Europe*, 22 November 1993.

24. Baldwin, Richard (1994), *Towards an Integrated Europe*, CEPR, London.

25. CEPR, *op. cit.*, pp. 86-90 argues that large migratory flows are unlikely provided that the EU encourages economic growth through more trade and the credible promise of EU membership. Basing its assumptions on income differentials, expectations and the limited data on migratory trends within the EC, it suggests that migratory flows of 5 per cent or 5.7 million from the six associated states, the Baltic States, Albania, Croatia and Slovenia. This is not a huge figure in the context of the EU population of 325 million but were such migration to concentrate on particular regions of the EU or coincide with recession in those regions, it could cause social tension and political difficulties.

26. Broader arrangements would facilitate intra-regional trade and investment within the Central European region where efforts to integrate have been limited to the Central European Free Trade Area (CEFTA).

27. European Council (1994), *ibid.*, p. 5.

28. Edited transcript of a speech given by Foreign Secretary Douglas Hurd to the Sejm Senate, Warsaw, 6 May 1994.

29. *Europe*, 9 March 1993.

30. Statement by Chancellor Helmut Kohl, 13 January 1994, quoted in *RFE/RL Research Report*, vol. 3. no. 12, 25 March 1994, p. 9.

31. Statement of Swedish Under-Secretary of State in the Ministry of Foreign Affairs, 27 April 1994 notes that 'the EU can become the glue which finally binds the various parts of our region together in a conclusive manner', p. 6.

32. Gastgeyber, Carl (1993), 'Optionen der Sicherheitspolitik: Ein gesamteuropäisches Sicherheitssytem?' in Weidenfeld, Werner, *op. cit.*, pp. 433-443.

33. St. Petersburg Declaration, 19 June 1992, *Europe Documents*, 23 June 1992; Council Communiqué, 20 November 1992; *Europe Documents*, 25 November 1992 and Kirchberg Declaration, 9 May 1994, which agreed to undertake work on the formulation of a common European defence policy.

Section C:
Rethinking Humanitarian Security

10 Can Ethnic Conflicts Ever Be Resolved? The Implications of Ethnic Conflicts in Eastern and Central Europe

GÁBOR KARDOS

Introduction*

According to the London European Security Working Group

> 'Europe will be secure when the whole idea of any cross-border attack by one European state on another is universally accepted as absurd, when, within states, different ethnic or religious groups tolerate each other, and minority rights are respected, and when there is no risk of any attack on a European state from outside Europe.'[1]

The first and third conditions set by the Working Group clearly belong to the military dimension of security, but the second leads further, to the idea of humanitarian security. Although the concept of humanitarian security came into existence as a consequence of the Third Basket of the Conference on Security and Cooperation in Europe (CSCE), the process started with a recognition of the protection of human rights as a major international concern by the UN Charter, which was equivalent to a recognition of the direct significance of individuals in international relations. As far as the rights of religious and ethnic communities are concerned, major steps had already been taken by the League of Nations.[2]

Humanitarian security implies the fulfillment of basic human needs, the internationally guaranteed realization of human rights, the protection of ethnic and national minorities, internationally controlled mass-migration and the preservation of the environment. Hence the concept of humanitarian security reflects different threats which have some common features:

- They are not related to military or economic aspects of security;
- The threats themselves are not necessarily imposed by states but also by non-

state actors;
- They cannot be deterred;
- The existing international security institutions are not capable of dealing with them.

During the years of the Cold War the humanitarian crises of the East affected Western Europe in a limited way because these conflicts were 'resolved' on the other side of the Iron Curtain. The exceptions obviously include the massive outflow of Hungarian refugees after the aggression of the Soviet Army in 1956 and the results of the Chernobyl nuclear disaster. With the CSCE humanitarian questions became part of the East-West agenda and remarkable changes occurred between the conferences of Helsinki I in 1975 and Helsinki II in 1992 in the management of these issues. As a consequence of the end of the Cold War order and the diminishing role of military security, a new security landscape emerged in Europe. As Carlo Maria Santoro concludes:

'The international political system - until now frozen in the worrisome stability of nuclear deterrence and the principle of European border untouchability - could give rise to a dynamic phase in which the unresolved controversies after 1918 and 1945 aggravated by the compression of decades, could open the path of tensions, crises, and maybe future conflicts for which existing international institutions from the EC to NATO, the CSCE and even the United Nations - would not know, despite their good intentions, how to offer any practical solution.'[3]

The threat of massive military attack from the Warsaw Treaty Organisation (WTO) has disappeared but instability and armed ethnic conflicts in the former East could continue to endanger Western Europe, although the countries of the ex-WTO are mainly a threat to each other. According to Charles L. Glaser, the wars in and between the smaller Central European states primarily threaten the humanitarian interests of the West but not their military security interests.[4] Dieter Mahncke articulates his view more carefully by saying that conflicts in Eastern and Central Europe do not pose an automatic threat to Western Europe as long as they can be isolated. But there is no assurance that a conflict can be isolated and the accompanying problems (nationalism, ethnic conflict, refugees) can spread to neighbouring countries. Beside this, such conflicts may be bad examples that gradually undermine the rules and the cohesion of the West European security community.[5] Stephen Iwan Griffiths emphasizes another highly important aspect, that

'(E)thnic conflicts raise problems difficult and uncomfortable problems, for practitioners of European security, especially in regard to the question of external interference in a particular state's affairs, as well as responsibilities of principal powers to aid countries or ethnic groups in distress. These are problems that many would still avoid thinking about, despite the necessity for new patterns of action in Europe.'6

As the Yugoslav crisis clearly demonstrates, the problem is not only the involvement of too many international organizations in the settlement process, but the way in which the leading Western powers use these institutions. As Pál Dunay states, the multi-level, multi-forum cooperation 'makes [it] possible for states to hide away from direct responsibility in the international arena when they deem it necessary.' 7

Why is Eastern and Central Europe different?

The issues of nationalism and minorities are dissimilar in Eastern and Central Europe from those in Western Europe since the social development of the former has been significantly different from that of the latter. According to András Balogh the most important historical differences are as follows:

- The nations living here enjoyed limited or no state sovereignty.
- The population was ethnically, religiously and culturally mixed.
- Significant differences manifested in the legal and social status and in the economic means of various national groups.
- The timing and intensity of the national awakening was different for the various peoples of the region.
- A national consciousness evolved which degraded or denied the historic role of rivals.
- The fulfillment of national aspirations was essentially at the expense of others and, moreover, in extreme cases, with the complete ignorance, neglect, or liquidation of the neighbouring community.
- In decisive periods outside powers played a crucial role.
- Compared to Western Europe this part of the continent was permanently characterized by economic backwardness.
- The limited use of one's mother tongue - due to the objective situation or to administrative restrictions - became a primary and immediate question of national awakening.8

Beside these factors, it is also important to underline the effects of communist rule in Eastern and Central Europe. Paradoxically this rule took place in the rigid context of nation states and excluded genuine integration, although the ideology was internationalist. This 'internationalism' meant loyalty to the Soviet Union, or more correctly to the interests of 'Mother Russia', as interpreted by the Kremlin. This was why Erich Honecker, the leader of the former German Democratic Republic, was frequently referred to as a German-speaking Russian nationalist in his home country. This 'internationalism' oppressed national feelings everywhere, so not surprisingly the fall of communism happened largely as a consequence of the revenge of nationalism.[9]

The essence of historical differences in the two parts of Europe is highly visible through the mirror of present day relationships to the nation state. These days Eastern and Central Europe is facing a rebirth of nationhood and sovereignty and due to the various historical dependencies and unresolved problems of the past an over-emphasis on sovereignty has become a characteristic feature throughout the region. The direction of development in Western Europe diverges from the nation-state identity into two directions: from 'above', towards the completion of the supra-nationalist integration of the European Union and from 'below', towards a path of regional cooperation cross-cutting state frontiers. This dispersion at least creates the opportunity for diminishing nationalism in Western Europe but fuels the flames of national sentiments in Eastern and Central Europe.

Due to the dissimilar historical development and different relationship to the nation state it is possible to identify another form of nationalism in Eastern and Central Europe than that which prevails in Western Europe. In Eastern and Central Europe the predominant form of nationalism is ethno-nationalism, whereas in Western Europe the leading (but not exclusive) pattern is one of state or civic nationalism. In the case of ethnic nationalism the centre of the phenomenon is an *ethnie* or ethnic community, by which is meant a named population with a 'myth of common ancestry, shared historical memories, elements of shared culture, an association with a specific "homeland" and a measure of solidarity.'[10] The foundation for membership of the *ethnie* is one of blood ties, the *ius sanguinis*. In the case of state or civic nationalism the community is the state and the decisive factor that determines membership is one of citizenship. These different forms of nationalism lead to important different consequences. State or civic nationalism is directly linked to territorial self-determination which 'seeks to achieve a particular political status for a defined territory and for all the people who reside in it'.[11] Ethnic self-determination is based on ethnic nationalism and involves a demand for the political status of self-government, and frequently independent statehood, but only for the members of the ethnic community.

Although nationalist intolerance always poisons the intercommunal relationship nationalists are only truly dangerous when they have access to governmental power. The best example is the hyper-nationalist Milosevic in Serbia or the not much better Tudjman of Croatia. But we might ask why the nationalists are in power in so many parts of Eastern and Central Europe or if they are not, why are such political forces influental, as with Zhirinovsky in Russia? Some of the explanation comes from the differences between Eastern and Central Europe and the Western part of the continent listed above but other reasons are common with the causes of ethnic conflicts in the broad sense.

The causes of ethnic conflict in Eastern and Central Europe

As it has been demonstrated by the war on the territory of the former Yugoslavia and of the Soviet Union, ethnic nationalism and conflict has tremendous destructive potential. Ethnic conflict is directly interconnected with the violation of human rights, civil wars, the mass flow of refugees, ethno-terrorism, interstate disputes and tensions over minority rights and borders. As a Canadian scholar states:

> '(E)thnic conflict presents a wide range of challenges for foreign policy and interstate cooperation. Human rights issues and refugee situations represent one level in which nations are closely interlinked by ethnic conflict; conflict management, conflict resolution and intervention in civil wars another.'[12]

In consequence, the resolution of ethnic conflicts can be seen as the key to an understanding of humanitarian security, and also of the complex notion of security in Eastern and Central Europe. Ethnic conflicts therefore deserve special attention and it seems completely justified to do more than simply state that nationalism is the underlying factor behind ethnic conflicts.

As a correct point of departure, it is important to emphasize that it is not that ethnic groups and national minorities destabilize the states of Eastern and Central Europe, because these countries are already destabilized.[13] The main reasons for destabilization are economic (foreign and domestic debt, decline in production, inflation, the collapse of the Russian market, etc.) social (old and new poverty, unemployment, a sharp rise in criminality, etc.) and political (authoritarian tendencies, right and left wing populism, political apathy in the population, etc.). At the same time it is also quite apposite to echo Jan Zielonka's observation that it is the same politicians who speak about domestic anarchy and foreign aggression to security experts who describe their country as a stable and peaceful island to foreign investors.[14] Be that as it may, the complexity of problems in Eastern and Central Europe are a cause of permanent frustration and make the situation ripe for all manner of intolerance, including ethnic hatreds.

Beside the general destabilization in Eastern and Central Europe a lot of other problems generate ethnic conflicts. Among these are:

- The dissolution of the *Zwangsordnung*. The fall of the communist political system and the withdrawal of the Russian imperial policemen from Eastern and Central Europe led to the resurrection of the buried but unresolved problems of the past, atavistic fears and historical pain and glory.
- The traditions of violent conflict resolution in intercommunal disputes, which include aggressive action against persons whose only fault is that they belong to the rival ethnic group. Their identification is not an obstacle

in such actions, for:

'(D)eadly mobs in one country after another have devised ghoulishly reliable methods of ascertaining ethnic identity in their effort to accomplish simultaneously two goals: to kill members of a target group and to avoid killing members of one's own group or of a third group. If they cannot rely on visual cues to identity, they find others.'[15]

- The fights and conflicts between different ethnic groups are frequently manifestations of the power struggle between former communist leaders. Even the collapse of the Soviet Union and Yugoslavia can be interpreted this way.[16]
- A leading source of fear and insecurity is the collapse of the multi-ethnic 'socialist' federations. A lot of ethnic groups feel insecure because they believe that they should belong to new states with new dominant ethnic groups: Abkhazs and Ossetians in Georgia, Albanians in Macedonia, Serbs in Croatia, etc.[17] As an American scholar concludes: 'The persecution of minorities by newly liberated nations may be a form of aggressive compensation for prior oppression at the hand of foreign elites.'[18]
- The radicalization of the ethnic revival could lead or fuel intercommunal disputes. Anthony D. Smith distinguishes three different forms of 'ethnonational transformation.' The first is one of 'vernacular mobilization', which involves a rediscovery by the intellectuals of traditions, costumes, memories, and especially languages, etc. and their dissemination to the ethnic population. The second is the 'cultural politicization' of the vernacular heritage. Traditions then become weapons in the cultural war, especially against outsiders. The third phase is the consequence of other two: 'ethnic purification', including segregation, expulsion, deportation and even extermination of the members of other groups.[19] The final aim of this purification is the ethnically homogenous state. The next step is the demand for an ethnic state which unites all individuals of the *ethnie*.
- The process of the creation of a new nation state itself involves a lot of issue areas that can lead to conflict. Beside the frequent element of disputed borders, two other factors are highly significant. The first can be described by using Charles Tilly's frequently quoted observation: 'war made the state, and the state made war'[20] - to stabilize statehood external and internal enemies are needed, and sometimes wars with them. The second could be summed up by Massimo d'Azeglio's statement from the period of Italian unification in the last century: 'We have made Italy, now we must make Italians!'[21] In a new state, unity is a top priority, and in Eastern and Central Europe there is a tendency to view multilingual useage or different religious practices as factors endangering this national unity. This understanding of unity leads to the constitutional principle of a 'unitary nation-state' in what were multi-

ethnic, multi-cultural countries and an aggressive homogenization.
- The ruling interpretation of democracy in Eastern and Central Europe is majoritarian. 'Winners take all' and pay no significant attention to minority wishes without heed as to whether these groups belong to a political or ethnic minority. This practice is exceedingly dangerous to interethnic relationships and to political pluralism. As Vojin Dimitrijevic observed:

> 'The tendency to base the political order on the ethnos and not the demos does not only result in the marginalization of "alien" ethnic groups but warps the pluralistic process, where the member of a minority does not act as a citizen, [but as one] who chooses the political party closest to his or her social interests.'[22]

- The privatization and capitalist restoration in general causes a fear for some majority populations of a loss of influence and power that had existed when the majority dominated a situation of total state ownership.[23] This process reinforces the role of interpersonal relationships and traditions in social management - a basis for nationalism - in opposition to the impersonal forces of the market.
- Psychological factors of uncertainty are also closely related to the new political freedoms. According to President Vaclav Havel the people were shocked by freedom, because they were not used to living in liberty. These individuals had some guarantees in the past, although unpleasant ones and now they are looking for replacement guarantees. To belong to a tribe seems to be the most satisfactory solution.[24]
- One of the consequences of the fall of the centralized communist political system was the revival of local ethnic communities. Immediately after the political change the problem emerged as to which community should dominate the modest local infrastructure and resources. If the high school originally belonged to the minority community and was then confiscated by the state and given to the majority who is now the owner, whose language should now be taught? And if the school is to be in the hands of a minority again what will be the fate of majority students and teachers who did their job there for many years?
- The change in the social role of law represents a unique problem. In most countries of the region in the past the rights of minorities could represent no more than mere declarations which had very little to do with reality. Therefore, it did not represent a major risk if in certain instances they were broadly phrased, as they would remain rights only on paper. As a result of the change in the political system the law is beginning to fulfil its social function. Today, the content of minority legislation is no longer immaterial. As a consequence of this, it can happen that in the area of native language education, for example, the old regulation, at least in

concept, guaranteed a wider opportunity for minorities than the new.
- The lack of a human rights culture represents a further problem. During the communist dictatorship human rights did not represent more than constitutional declarations by the power élite. At the same time, the democratic opposition construed them as political demands, or tried to act as though they truly existed. Today, when the guarantee of general human rights takes place within a framework of more appropriate laws, the problem is in its practice. People are not accustomed to turning to legal defence for their human rights, something natural to them if faced with, say, a conflict over inheritance. There is an absence of legal precedent and the multi-party system absorbed, even partly factionalized, a large segment of the human rights movement. In the midst of the disintegration of civil societies, all these manifestations can be taken as a matter of course. They are in any case extremely detrimental from the point of view of protecting the rights of someone who belongs to an ethnic community. Moreover, the role and the independence of the judiciary both from political power and ethnic bias are problematic. As Gáspár Biró observes:

> '(I)n much of the region no one has yet seriously raised a demand for an independent judiciary, which might steady the state amid political and constitutional turmoil, judges in all countries remain employees of justice ministers, and the practice of judicial arbitration of the constitutionality of government actions is still in an embryonic phase.'[25]

- Ethnic conflicts are exacerbated by nationalist propaganda and when 'nationalists have a near monopoly on public discourse, there exists no counterbalance to this myth-making.'[26] This statement proved to be definitely true in Serbia, where the propaganda generated such strong national sentiments that Milosevic won the general elections three times in a row. This myth-making gives the illusion to the people, that nationalism - in the absence of other alternatives in public debate - provides a natural order of things. This 'natural order' also includes étatism, authoritarianism and privileges.[27]
- Ethnic conflicts become even worse when extreme nationalists try to 'resolve', in reality, to prolong them. Their 'resolution' frequently involves a violent shift in the ethnic balance by expulsion. The situation evolves into tragedy because it rapidly descends into barbarity. As Janusz Bugajski observes: 'I would argue that militants in Bosnia-Hercegovina have deliberately conducted a slow and brutal campaign against civilians to provoke and heighten communal hatreds so that Serbs, Muslims and Croats will be unable and unwilling to live together for the next generation.'[28]

Ethnic conflict and the revision of borders

The Cold War order in Europe was equivalent to a preservation of the territorial status quo. This fact itself proved that order meant no more than negative peace - signifying merely the absence of open violence - because negative peace '. . . is tantamount to a stabilization of the status quo especially as regards national boundaries, while positive peace should give a chance to peaceful change.'[29] On a theoretical level it is easy to state that positive peace should provide the possibility of peaceful change, including the revision of borders but for the most of the practitioners this question is still taboo.[30] Even the revolutionary events of the end of the Cold War in Europe have not changed interstate borders. New states were born on the territory of the former Soviet Union and Yugoslavia without touching the outside (interstate) borders. The unification of Germany has produced a lot of international legal commitments reinforcing the outside borders of the new *Deutschland*.

In the case of ethnic conflicts in Eastern and Central Europe the potential territorial changes can be seen either as a part of the problem or as a part of the solution. Almost everybody, both in practice and in theory, excludes territorial changes, but as C. G. Jacobsen observes:

'You can not propagate democracy while condemning captive peoples'. There are all-too-many borders that were delineated by dictators and authoritarian regimes, imposed by war or fiat, and sometimes specifically designed to contain ethnic mixes that would preclude viable independence. To "recognize" these is a prescription for war, not peace.'[31]

The original version of the Balladur plan (the *Projet de Pacte sur la stabilité en Europe*) also hints that minor border rectifications are necessary.[32] This idea within the original Balladur plan provokes all of those questions which are generally raised if the issue of territorial change is disputed. Does this possibility encourage the escalation of the conflict as states and non-states improve their bargaining position? How should the Western European states react if certain states support recessionist groups in neighbouring states? What will be the case if the open border disputes cannot be settled by negotiation? What constitutes, 'minor' territorial change?[33] There are no easy answers to these questions. Pál Dunay states:

'There is a great potential for problems if countries try to revise current territorial settlements, as vast geographical areas were part of other countries in the past. One could artificially differentiate between countries which would be on the "defensive"or the "offensive". Most countries of the region could demand some parts of the territory of other countries, at the same time being subjected to demands of others.'[34]

An examination of the problem of territorial change can easily lead to a conclusion of *veritas duplex*. The inviolability of borders could keep ethnic conflict alive, as it is the case in Nagorno-Karabakh which belongs to Azerbaidjan. Although more than 90 per cent of the population is Armenian, this province historically was a part of Armenia and was given to Azerbaidjan by Stalin. But the possibility of the revision of borders - as for example in the case of the Krajina, where the Krajinian Serb Republic was established and, according to certain authors, frontier change would be justified[35] - could lead to a domino effect, and to the international reinforcement of the ethnically unified state, rewarding secessionism and irredentism. Consequently, *the territorial dimension is both part of the problem and part of the solution in ethnic conflicts.* Because of the risks of territorial change this cannot be a preferred solution but can not be excluded completely either, if all of the parties and international institutions involved in the negotiations see it as a workable way of coming to a settlement. This is a narrow path for exceptional situations, and only under massive international guarantees.[36] It is necessary to add that to have the consensus of all parties involved on a negotiated border change seems to be illusory, especially in Eastern and Central Europe where the national consciousness mythicizes the territory of the state so that its size serves as a compensation for its general backwardness.[37]

Common sense and conflict resolution: principles for consideration

In conflicts generally, but especially in ethnic conflicts, common sense is one of the first casualties. Hence it is important to underline that the simple, practical principles of common sense are frequently more capable of providing an input for resolution, than sophisticated theories. The following principles are not necessarily universal, they are valid mainly in Eastern and Central Europe, because they are based on the experiences of social development in this part of the continent.

Beware of the 'lessons' of history

The reason why the student of ethnic conflicts has to be careful with history is not interconnected with the problem of how we should learn from the past. In this respect Cicero was probably wrong when he stated that history is the schoolmaster of life, and it is easier to share Hegel's opinion that peoples and governments have never learnt anything from it, or at least not more than a minimum. The reason for being cautious with the past comes from the frequent misuse of history. The misapplication of history means two things. Firstly, the parties involved in ethnic conflict (and generally in any conflict) always highlight those events of the past which seem to prove their version of the truth. Secondly, the parties use selected events as justification for their present behaviour and this could have an impact even on a neutral observer. For example, C. G. Jacobsen correctly criticizes the bias of the international press towards the Serbs in the present war on the territory of the former Yugoslavia but his argumentation mixes up the horrors of the past and the present as was exactly the intention of the Belgrade leadership:

> 'Western TV crews have not visited the Genocide Against the Serbs exhibition at Belgrade's Museum of Applied Arts, with its pictures of eyeless and axed heads - Ustasha trademarks, today as during the World War II -, or filmed the headless corpses that float down the Danube with signs saying "to the meat markets of Belgrade".'38

The terrible events of the past can provide a kind of explanation as to why horrible things are repeated but they can never serve as a justification for present actions. The Ustasha's massacres in the Second World War do not provide an excuse for the Serbian killings of today.

Democracy itself does not resolve ethnic conflict

Democracy, especially if it is simply interpreted as the rule of the majority, is not a solution to the problems of different ethnic minorities preserving their self-identity. One of the founding fathers of the US Constitution, Madison, observed that 'In all cases where a majority are united by a common interest or passion, the rights of the minority are in danger.'39 In the specific case of ethnic and religious minorities,

> 'a majority may set aside the rights of an ethnic or religious minority under the way of what one might call a *standing passion*. In earlier centuries, religious fanaticism has been the mainspring of this form of majoritarian domination. Today, ethnic hatred, sometimes combined with religious differences, is proving a horribly potent source of oppression.'40 (italics in the original)

The way out is the protection of minority rights, declared and guaranteed both on a national and on an international level. On the domestic scene the institutions of the rule of law (an independent judiciary, constitutional court, ombudsman, etc.) could play a decisive role in the realization of those rights.

Do not put too much trust in the state

Eastern and Central Europe always had 'too much state' in the everyday life of their societies. The strong, omnipotent state is a ruling political tradition there. Ethnic and religious minorities are in an ambivalent relationship with the majoritarian state. On one hand the minorities are afraid of the state, because the state has been far from impartial in the conflicts between different ethnic communities within the same country and has never attempted to create the delicate balance between the interests of the majority and minorities, so that the principle of compromise has never been practiced. Equally the state regards ethnic minorities as a national security risk and sees this as a justification of a curtailment of their rights.

On the other hand, as far as the financing of cultural and educational institutions are concerned, minorities expect everything from the state. This is the case not only as a consequence of the concept of an omnipotent state but also because of the poverty of the minorities. This approach has the result of conserving a strong dependency on the central will, and a benevolent understanding by the state budget. The real solution comes from the development of civil societies of minorities and a tax policy which enables members of different ethnic groups to finance their own institutions.

Alternative models of a solution

It seems obvious that there is no general solution to ethnic conflict. Institutional arrangements to serve the peaceful coexistence of different ethnic communities should reflect local circumstances. Consequently, model building should be done carefully so as not to exclude a blend of different variant solutions. Probably the most decisive factor is whether it is possible to arrive at a solution if the population is ethnically mixed or the different ethnic communities live on separate territories. Other elements that must be considered include the size and the level of organization of ethnic communities, the traditions of state administration, the quantity of mutual trust and a lot of other factors that determine the characteristic features of the institutional arrangement. Thus it is not by chance that the autonomist state came to existence in Spain, in a historically divided country, evoked by José Ortega y Gasset in his famous essay as *España invertebrada* (Spain without a backbone)[41].

A possible interpretation of the different solutions might be as follows:

Territorial decentralization may be useful in the service of a good intercommunal relationship because this solution can provide assurances both to the majority and to the ethnic minorities. In the eyes of the majority territorial decentralization is much less of a danger to the unity of the country than political autonomy for those territories where the minority communities live, because territorial decentralization can be seen much less as a step towards secession. For the minority communities territorial decentralization can provide a possibility of forming the local majority. This solution can work only if the boundaries of the existing territorial units have not been changed in favour of the majority and no recent settlers have arrived to alter the ethnic balance. Furthermore, specific rules are necessary to protect schooling rights and the official use both of the languages of the local majority and minorities.

This solution has some disadvantages as well as, for example, territorial decentralization may lead to the reinforcement of ethnic divisions ('your village - our village'). A further problem is that, if minorities are not able to form the local majority, territorial decentralization cannot help them much. This is the reason why a long list of minority rights is needed.

Minority rights. The most important internationally recognized minority rights are derived from ;

- The International Covenant on Civil and Political Rights;
- The Convention on the Prevention of the Crime of Genocide;
- The International Convention on the Elimination of All Forms of Racial Discrimination;
- The UN Declaration on the Rights of Persons Belonging to National or Ethnic, Religious and Linguistic Minorities (UNGA-Res. 47/135 of 18 December 1992);
- The Document of the Copenhagen Meeting of the Conference on the Human Dimension of the CSCE;
- Recommendation 1134 (1990) on the Rights of Minorities adopted by the Parliamentary Assembly of the Council of Europe; and
- Recommendation 1201 (1993) on an Additional Protocol on the Rights of National Minorities to the European Convention on Human Rights adopted by the Parliamentary Assembly of the Council of Europe.

The attention of the reader should be drawn to the fact that, beside the right to belong to a minority, and the right to non-discrimination, the following rights are also enshrined in this international legislation:

- linguistic freedoms (the right of recognition of their mother tongue, the right to use their mother tongue, including its use before public institutions and in penal procedure, the right to use their own name, the right to the installation of place name signs in the minority language); education rights (the right to learn the minority language in the educational system, the right to establish their own educational institutions);
- the right to establish and maintain their own associations, the right to participate in public affairs and the right to establish and maintain unimpeded contacts across frontiers with citizens of other states with whom they share a common ethnic or national origin, cultural hesitage or religious beliefs.

Territorial autonomy provides comprehensive self-government to those regions where minorities live. As far as the competence of the autonomy is concerned two possible ways for its regulation can be found, for example in the Spanish Constitution. Article 148 enlists the different fields of territorial autonomy, such as urbanization, local roads and railways, the financing of cultural institutions, local economic policy in the context of the national economic system, etc. Consequently, Article 148 confines the power of autonomy to these specific items. According to Article 149 - which is the other option - all powers which are not reserved to the central state are conferred on the autonomous communities, but those powers which are not referred to the autonomous communities by their own charter remain in the jurisdiction of the central state. In the case of any conflict the legal norms of the central state prevail. The recognition of the autonomous status and the extent of its powers take place in the context of a special procedure, which includes representatives of both the central parliament and government.[42]

Territorial autonomy, especially if its competence is wide, could easily lead to a complicated state administration.

Personal and cultural autonomy. The idea of personal autonomy comes from Otto Bauer, an Austrian social democrat, whose starting point was the mixed population on the major part of the territory of the Austro-Hungarian Empire.[43] The essence of personal autonomy is analogous with a church. Everybody can decide freely whether he would like to be a member of a church and to participate in the administration of the affairs of the religious community. A person living anywhere within a country could register himself as member of an ethnic community and through this he could participate in the self-government of that community. To have a workable personal autonomy it is necessary to provide registration guarantees because in Eastern and Central Europe, a lot of people suffered for having admitted their ethnic identity. Besides this it is highly important to have democratic practices within the self-governing ethnic community as well as being granted real competence. This competence can be related to cultural autonomy, which means a complete power to make all decisions concerning the educational and cultural institutions of the community, financed by the state.

Territorially based consociational democracy. Consociational democracy is characterized by a grand coalition of the political leaders of all significant elements of the plural society, a mutual veto in the making of vital decisions, a representation of all major subcultures in the Cabinet with other important bodies roughly respecting the same rules of proportionality. Proportionality could also exist in civil service appointment procedures and all of the subcultures should enjoy an autonomy in dealing with their own affairs.[44] Territorially based consociational democracy exists in Belgium, between the Flemish, the French and the German speaking communities.

Personally based consociational democracy works in the Netherlands and does not reflect ethnic division, but rather religious and ideological cleavages (the Catholic, Calvinist, Liberal, and Socialist blocks in the society). If the enlisted conditions of a consociational democracy are fulfilled between the different ethnic groups in a country with an ethnically mixed population, this system can facilitate a better interethnic relationship.

Consociational democracy has its drawbacks. This system separates the ethnic communities and it is expensive because it doubles or triples administrative costs. Beside this, consociational democracy is frequently not flexible enough to accommodate the changing demographic and political realities, it gives too much power to the élite of the ethnic communities and it limits the electoral system by insisting on a system of proportionality.[45]

If one looks at how this model works in reality in Western Europe, a disappointing conclusion can easily be arrived at. Frequently, the most liberal decentralization is not enough for certain communities, majority intolerance does not die out, and violent incidents still occur. However - as Béla Faragó has pointed out - this pessimistic vision does not mean that Eastern and Central Europe could not draw positive conclusions from the examples of decentralization and autonomy in Western Europe, because there are no other solutions available.[46]

* This paper was prepared in the context of the NATO Fellowship Programme.

Notes

1. London European Security Working Group (1992), *European security Discussion document*, November, The British American Security Information Council, London, p. 1.
2. See for example Kardos, Gábor (1994), 'Facing a New Reality: The Humanitarian Dimension of the CSCE', in: Williams, Andrew J. (ed.), *Reorganizing Eastern Europe: European Institutions and the Refashioning of Europe's Security Architecture*, Dartmouth, Aldershot, pp. 145-157.
3. Santoro, Carlo Maria (1992), 'Nationalism in Europe: Trends and Threats', in: László Valki (ed.), *Changing Threat Perceptions and Military Doctrines*. Macmillan, London, pp. 168-169.
4. Glaser, Charles L. (1993), 'Why NATO is Still the Best: Future Security Arrangements for Europe', *International Security*, vol. 18, no. 1, pp. 7-8.
5. Mahncke, Dieter (1993), *Parameters of European Security*, Chaillott Papers 10, September, Institute for Security Studies, Paris, p. 10.
6. Griffiths, Stephen Iwan (1993), *Nationalism and Ethnic Conflict. Threats to European Security*, SIPRI Research Report, No. 5, Oxford University Press, Oxford, p. 125.
7. Dunay, Pál (1994), *Institutional Aspects of the Yugoslav Settlement*, Unpublished manuscript, Budapest, p. 1.

8. Balogh, András (1993), *Conventional Wisdoms on National Minorities and International Security*, Budapest, A European House Publication, November, pp. 17-18.
9. Carrère d'Encausse, Hélène (1993), *The End of the Soviet Empire*, New York, Basic Books, p. 270.
10. Smith, Anthony D. (1993), 'A Europe of Nations - or the Nations of Europe', *Journal of Peace Research*, vol. 30, no. 2. p. 130.
11. Shehadi, Kamal S. (1993), *Ethnic Self-determination and the Break-up of States*, Adelphi Paper 283, London, IISS/Brassey's, December, pp. 4-5.
12. Carment, David (1993), 'The International Dimensions of Ethnic Conflict: Concepts, Indicators, and Theory', *Journal of Peace Research*, vol. 30, no. 2, p. 137.
13. Törzsök, Erika (1994), 'Miért gyanú·sak az autonómiatörekvések?' (Why are we suspicious of efforts at autonomy?), *Magyar Hírlap*, 24 January.
14. Zielonka, Jan (1992), *Security in Central-Europe*, Adelphi Paper 272, London, IISS/Brassey's, Autumn, pp. 33-34.
15. Horowitz, Donald L. (1993), *A Harvest of Hostility: Ethnic Conflict and Self-Determination after the Cold War*, Durham, Duke University, Manuscript, p. 6.
16. Sajó, András (1994), Nemzeti kisebbségek védelmének gondjai egy nacionalista államban (The difficulties of the protection of national minorities in a nationalist state), *Világosság*, January, p. 4, p. 8.
17. Shehadi, Kamal S., *op. cit.*, p. 7.
18. Bugajski, Janusz (1993), 'Balkan Futures: Understanding Ethnic Conflicts', in *International Conference on Armed Conflicts in the Balkans and European Security*, Ljubljana, 20-22 April, 1993, Ministry of Defence, Center for Strategic Studies, June, Ljubljana, p. 280.
19. Smith, Anthony D. (1993), 'The Ethnic Sources of Nationalism', *Survival*, vol. 35, no. 1, Spring, pp. 56-57.
20. Tilly, Charles (1975), (ed.), *The Formation of National States in Western Europe*, Princeton, Princeton University Press, p. 42. quoted by Snyder, Jack (1993), 'Nationalism and the Crises of the Post-Soviet State', *Survival*, vol. 35, no. 1, Spring, p. 13.
21. Quoted by Welsh, David (1993), 'Domestic Politics and Ethnic Conflict', *Survival*, vol. 35/no. 1, Spring, p. 64.
22. Dimitrijevic, Vojin (1991), 'The Human Dimension of Post-Totalitarianism', In: Eide, Asbjørn and Helgesen, Jan (eds), *The Future of Human Rights Protection in a Changing World*, Norwegian University Press, Oslo, p. 39.
23. Bugajski, Janusz, *op. cit.*, p. 282.
24. *Time*, August 17, 1992 pp. 25-26, quoted by Kipp, Jacob W. and Thomas, Timothy L. with Spero, Joshua B. (1993), 'International Ramifications of Yugoslavia's Serial Wars: The Challenge of Ethno-National Conflicts for a Post Cold War European Order', in *International Conference on Armed*

Conflicts in the Balkans and European Security, Ljubljana, 20-22 April, 1993, Ministry of Defence, Center for Strategic Studies, June, Ljubljana, p. 106.

25. Biró, Gáspár (1994), 'Minority Rights in Eastern and Central Europe and the Role of International Institutions', in: Laurenti, Jeffrey (ed.), *Searching for moorings. East Central Europe in the International System,* UNA-USA, New York, p. 104.
26. Snyder, Jack, *op. cit.,* p. 18.
27. Sajó, András (1994), 'Nemzetérzület és alkotmányosság', (Nationalism and Constitutionality), *2000,* vol. 6, no. IV, April, p. 5, p. 6.
28. Bugajski, Janusz, *op. cit.* , p. 288.
29. Rumpf, Helmut (1984), 'The Concepts of Peace and War in International Relations', *German Yearbook of International Law,* vol. 27, p. 437.
30. Shedadi, Kamal S., *op. cit.,* p. 72, p. 89
31. Jacobsen, C. G. (1993), 'Myths, Politics and the Not-So-New World Order', *Journal of Peace Research,* vol. 30, no. 3, p. 249.
32. See Shedadi, Kamal S., *op. cit.,* p. 78.
33. *Op. cit.,* p. 79.
34. Dunay, Pál (1994), *Adversaries All Around? (Re)-Nationalization of Security and Defence Policies in Central and Eastern Europe,* The Hague, Netherlands Institute of International Relations, Clingendael Paper, Clingendael, January, p. 17.
35. Jacobsen, C. G., *op. cit.* , p. 248.
36. For a discussion of the mechanisms for border change, see Shedadi, Kamal S., *op. cit.,* pp. 76-80.
37. Tabajdi, Csaba (1994), *A nemzeti tényezö funkciói s diszfunkciói Közép-és Kelet-Európában* (The functions and disfunctions of the national factor in Central and Eastern Europe), Európa Ház, Budapest, pp. 8-9.
38. Jacobsen, C. G., *op. cit.,* p. 245.
39. As quoted by Elster, Jon (1992), 'On Majoritarianism and Rights', *East European Constitutional Review,* vol. 1, no. 3, Fall, p. 20.
40. *Ibid.*
41. Gasset, José Ortega y (1963), *España invertebrada.*(13th ed.), Madrid, Revista de Occidenta.
42. Faragó, Béla (1993), Onrendelkezés és önkormányzat Nyugat-Európában (Self-determination and self-government in Western Europe) *Magyar Szemle,* 5, pp. 538-539.
43. Hanák, Péter (1993), *Ragaszkodás az utópiához,* (Adherence to Utopia), Budapest, Liget, pp. 198-199.
44. Lipjhart, Arend (1977), *Democracy in Plural Societies,* New Haven, Yale University Press, pp. 25-44.
45. Shedadi, Kamal S., *op. cit.,* p. 69.
46. Faragó, Béla, *op. cit.,* p. 541.

11 Humanitarian Security and Involuntary Migration in Europe

JUDIT TÓTH

Graeci, qui alios barbaros nominabant,
se tantum humanos et doctos putabant
[The Greeks, who considered themselves educated and humane,
thought of all other races as barbarians]

Barbarians at the gate? A map of European migration

The above quote was a very first, but eternally remembered, sentence from my Latin text book. But although it is easy to sit in a cosy armchair near the fire place, and see asylum-seekers and forced migrants in need of protection as a modern formulation for these ancient 'barbarians', this still is to select too easy an escape route from the current realities of European migration.

Apart from migratory movements by EC citizens, there are two major tendencies that can be noted in contemporary Europe. Firstly, the states of Central Europe have become important transit, as well as new host countries while still preserving their own 'sending' role, at least to some extent. Secondly, ethnic conflicts and the vulnerable position of minorities have produced large-scale migratory movements from certain Eastern and Balkan European states. In some cases this has led to millions of persons becoming displaced, as in Yugoslavia, or migrating in considerable numbers, as with gypsies and Hungarians from Romania. Ethnic migrants (especially Germans, Greeks, Armenians, Poles and Turks) were the first to make use of the new emigration opportunities provided by the political changes of 1989-90. They migrated overseas and to Israel as well as to EC states. However, instead of the expected large-scale movements from the former Soviet Union, there has been significant internal migration and an extended short-term migratory outflow of a commercial and tourist nature.

The number of asylum-seekers from the Central-Eastern European states

(Bulgaria, Czechoslovakia, Hungary, Poland, Romania) to the EC practically doubled in 1991-92.[1]

Country of origin	1991	1992
Bulgaria	15 094	33 203
Czechoslovakia	1 873	3 109
Hungary	646	1 163
Poland	5 899	5 979
Romania	50 872	111 346
Total	76 375	156 792

This region has undergone a period of political, social and economic transition, so that while it has kept up its sending role it has simultaneously registered extensive transit and receiving migratory movements. Available surveys and statistics indicate that Poland, Bulgaria, Hungary and the Czech Republic have become the cross-roads between South-Eastern and Western Europe. Seventy per cent of migrants that pass through Bulgaria from the traditional migrant producing countries have the ultimate intention of settling in Western European industrialized states. Two substantial migration flows to Western Europe cross Bulgaria. Although 42 per cent of the migrants enter the country with tourist visas, only half of them declare they have left their homeland for the purpose of tourism, and 98 per cent of interviewed aliens who entered legally intend to leave Bulgaria illegally.[2] Among the real motives of transit migrants, temporary work and 'suitcase trade' are more frequent than a fear of ongoing conflicts in the country of origin. A first category of migrant is made up of those who leave the Middle East and desire to migrate to Central and Western Europe (above all to Germany and Austria). The flow that previously passed through the former Yugoslavia has now been largely re-oriented through Romania. A second flow comes from the CIS and Romania, crossing Bulgaria and entering Greece, a preferred destination for 22 per cent of all surveyed migrants. A considerable number of migrants are able to find work in Greece and seem to be a preferred labour force in that country.

A large group of transit migrants (their minimum estimated number is about 100,000) either have their own resources and networks for their short stay or rely on contacts in Poland or in the West to reach their goals. Another group includes Africans, and persons from the Baltic states and the Middle East who use Poland for a relatively comfortable 'waiting room' where they may find temporary jobs or channels to the West. This additional labour potential has seriously affected the labour market in Poland as well as in other states mentioned above.[3]

For the above mentioned reasons a comparatively limited number apply for refugee status in Poland, the Czech Republic or Bulgaria, and a large proportion

of prior applicants disappear during the proceedings.   This fact may be
illustrated by the growing number of illegal border crossings to the West.[4]

Illegal border crossings (aliens)	1991	1992	1993
at the Polish borders	13 589	33 581	15 248 (1 Oct.)
at the Bulgarian borders	3 166	2 170	1 227 (1 July)
at the Czech(oslovak) borders	18 000	32 000	43 000
at the Hungarian borders	18 882	13 486	4 876

War in the former Yugoslavia and ethnic clashes have produced the most
dramatic European migratory movement.   By March 1993 the number of
displaced persons and victims in need of protection had increased to 3.8
million according to the United Nations High Commission for Refugees
(UNHCR).   A relatively small number of countries have received the largest
share of displaced persons from the former-Yugoslavia although they have
found refuge in numerous states.   EC countries have provided temporary
protection for about 400,000 persons, but other states like the USA, Australia,
Canada, Pakistan and Malaysia have also offered admission for them in certain
numbers.[5] Neighbouring countries have also received displaced persons and
asylum-seekers from this region, despite the fact that Croatia and Hungary face
economic difficulties.   About 300,000 Muslims from Bosnia-Herzegovina have
been sheltered in Croatia, while Croats and Muslims are engaged in fighting
against each other in Bosnia-Herzegovina - so putting their fate in doubt.
Hungary has received about 80,000 displaced persons from the former
Yugoslavia.[6] A certain proportion of these sheltered people may already have
stayed for such a long time in the host country that they have become
integrated and do not intend to return to their homeland.   The policies of
receiving countries will determine whether a prolonged stay will be permitted -
for example for humanitarian reasons. In this case the massive migratory
movements will lead to a diaspora of a large part of the population of former
Yugoslavia.
    Migration from Northern Africa and Turkey to the EC region is of a quite
different character from the intra-European movements.   Whereas the
migratory movements in new democracies may be considered a relatively new
phenomenon, their 'waiting room' function may induce a transformation into
countries of immigration - immigration from Northern Africa into the EC
also has long-established roots, dating from the colonial past or from
recruitment programmes.   Although regular migration from the mentioned

regions can be expected to decline in the near future, there is a reason to believe that irregular and illegal migration from there may still increase, where it will challenge the humanitarian principles of the native population.

Migratory movements from the farther sending countries are based more on asylum-related flows than on traditional, colonial ties.

Main sending countries toward the EC region have been as follows: Afghanistan, Angola, Ethiopia, Ghana, India, Iran, Pakistan, Nigeria, Sri Lanka, Zaire, Somalia, Iraq,[8] and toward the Central European region, too: Albania, Romania, Bulgaria, the former Yugoslavia and the Soviet Union.[9]

In 1992, as against the situation that prevailed in 1991, there was a certain increase in the number of asylum applications, basically due to the situation in Yugoslavia. In 1993 - apart from Yugoslavs there was a significant decrease registered in other categories in some states. The 1993 figures relative to the number of asylum requests reflect different tendencies in other receiving countries. Instead of a universal pattern, there is a growing correlation between the refugee and admission policies of European governments that can be noted.

It is difficult to make any reliable predictions of possible refugee flows on the basis of recent figures. An initial problem is the absence of comparable statistical sources on asylum-seekers and refugees.[10] The second difficulty is that there is no satisfactory model that analyses forced migration. There are numerous descriptions of 'push and full factors', a 'labour force equilibrium' model, discussion of 'root causes', or 'topographic and demographic invitations', all of which may capture some elements, but do not provide an adequate explanation of the totality of migratory movements. The third mental, or even politically manipulated, obstacle is one of an overestimation of the range of asylum-seekers in comparison with total number of aliens lawfully residing in European states. For example, the proportion of asylum-seekers in the total foreign population (excluding EC citizens) in the EC countries was about 5 per cent in 1991.

Controversies in current migration policies

Within the EC, thanks to political liberalism and memories of inter-state conflict, joint efforts have been made to create a border-free Community with a large, unified market. At the same time, the inward-looking, statist traditions are pulling the member states in the opposite direction, inducing them to close their doors, firmly protect their borders and declare anti-immigrant sentiments for the consumption of public opinion. Strong adherence to the concept of sovereignty makes the member states reluctant to reform a nation-state or to pool them together within a regional framework in the common interest. These inner conflicts may be considered an obstacle in formulating a coherent migration policy and, within its context, a humanitarian policy, in the

Community.

The Maastricht Treaty on European Union was a compromise between the statist and the integrationist approach to migration issues.[11] It marked a modest advance over statist trends by establishing the (now) European Union's (EU) competence in the determination of which third countries' nationals will in future require visas when crossing the external borders of the EU, and the establishment of a uniform format for visas by 1996. However, with the exception of the visa question (and measures to cope in an emergency situation occasioned by a sudden influx of non-EU citizens), issues of migration remain outside the EU's competence. The appended lists to the Treaty enumerate the areas of common interest: asylum policy, rules governing the crossing of external borders, and immigration policy (on conditions of entry and movement of third country nationals, residence, family reunion and access to employment of third country nationals and unauthorized migration). Under these rubrics humanitarian issues cannot be found directly but rather indirectly. EU institutes have started the preparation of harmonized rules, common actions in these fields within the Community and in some external, associated Eastern or regional partners, for example through the inter-governmental mechanism established to combat illegal migration by the Conference on East-West Migration, held in Budapest during February 1993 and in the working group on falsified, or altered, travel documents held in Brussels during April 1994.

Such institutions to consider migration and asylum policies can be considered as stop gap measures rather than as long-term solutions. Their main purpose is to reduce migratory pressure by preventing the causes and conditions that cause large-scale migratory movements. This goal is accompanied by a firm desire to control the whole machinery of non-EU migration by administrative measures. It is intended at a future date to harmonize legislation relating to the admission and integration, as well as the repatriation of, asylum-seekers and lawfully residing migrants. These efforts are leading not only to restrictions but also to a broadening European régime of cooperation, while few West European states want to adopt a preferential immigration regime for East Europeans which could be openly discriminatory, or be perceived as discriminatory. East Europeans would like to replace the Southern migrants that now reside and have obtained jobs in the industrialized countries of Western Europe. These opposing interests could well result in a stronger preference for short-term measures related to control and, in practice, more selective admission by EU states.

The above mentioned internal conflicts may encourage a short-term and 'police-oriented' admission policy in Eastern and Central Europe too. In this region there is still a strong feeling of social solidarity which serves to balance the administrative and legislative restrictions against asylum-seekers, refugees and displaced persons with necessary humanitarian support for them. But this societal capacity is limited by the frustrations felt in the region as a result of great economic, security and institutional transition. The other factor missing from a long-term admission policy is the absence of a proper infrastructure, and a lack of expertise, statistical knowledge and experience relating to the management of migration. A key driving force of actual migration flows has been that of ethnicity in Central and Eastern Europe. This fact will inevitably influence future legislative, administrative and foreign policy preferences. In this way the region may become engaged in trans-European cooperative measures related to the admission, integration, and voluntary repatriation of refugees or other humanitarian activities in a limited way, while having to become more active in combating infringements of public order, and in fighting against irregular migration (with exceptions being made for their own ethnic minorities). The question remains as to when and how this region will be able to successfully strike such a balance, given these migration pressures, as well as economic imbalances and long-term trade deficits, for the development and investment co-operation and contact with a fully integrated Europe that it so desires and needs.

For Central and Eastern European countries such a joint approach would imply arriving at common 'seasonal' immigration regulations, and administrative cooperation amongst themselves and with the West European states. It remains to be seen how and to what extent such cooperation between Central and East European countries can develop at policy and operational levels in relation to harmonized immigration and principles of asylum, and how they can arrive at common, regional positions in international fora. The Visegrád Group has established a mechanism for economic cooperation[12] whose effective function is to make itself and its member states more attractive as a destination region. For this reason it will also naturally develop preventative and self-protecting policies on migration cooperation within the Group.

Certain documents that have been adopted by different institutes of the Council of Europe have endorsed a revision and improvement of the legal framework concerning migration among the Visegrád states and agreed that they must be based on well-defined, comprehensive policies sustained by a broad political consent in order to ensure social peace. The restrictions adopted by some of the West European countries, as under the Schengen Agreement, the Dublin Convention, and the Border Crossing Convention, inevitably lead to a concentration of a large number of migrants from the neighbouring and more distant regions, and to recurring political and economic crises. In the light of contemporary migratory movements it has been recommended that negotiations and agreements are designed to increase cooperation with the new immigration countries in order to develop their administrative infrastructure and capacity for dealing with migration.[13]

Main issues related to humanitarian principles

Refugees

Three main issues are to be advocated in the EU in the near future in the areas of common interest. The first is a harmonized application of the definition of refugee, in accordance with the 1951 Geneva Convention. This effort aims to concentrate mainly on exclusion clauses by introducing some indirect limitation on admissibility. Simultaneously, among the governments of Central and East European administration a more extended definition has developed due to the introduction of relevant regulations to deal with the issues of temporary protection and mass flows. However, these countries have not as yet developed either pre-screening methods to assess the admissibility of applications nor have they yet developed the sophisticated training for their staff in such proceedings. These facts influence the direction and route of flows of asylum-seekers and the scale of irregular or illegal migration toward the liberal, less restrictive countries where the opportunity for social integration and housing conditions are poor, thus putting at risk some humanitarian principles.

The second priority is to develop and implement minimum standards for a fair as well as an effective asylum procedure. The 'European Consultation on Refugees and Exiles' of 1990 summarized the main requirements of a fair and effective procedure for determining refugee status, as ones which ensured standards derived from a fundamental respect for dignity and humanitarian obligations, as understood by the relevant international instruments.[14] A range of restrictive measures adopted since the late 1980s[15] has attempted to justify a consideration of each asylum request on its particular merits. In the European Union 1993 framework for action, aimed at developing asylum policy, there appears a proposal to elaborate a Convention on manifestly unfounded asylum applications and an implementation of the third host country principle, in the context of a harmonization of substantive asylum law. The Dublin Convention (1990), not yet ratified by all EU member states, is designed to prevent the submission of multiple or successive applications by an asylum-seeker in more than one state, and to determine the rules of state responsibility for procedure. These examples of harmonized asylum proceedings have tended to promote policies of *refoulement* and led to mechanical decisions being taken about asylum seekers, frequently at the border. Another result has been to make a burden-sharing system impossible not only for certain EU states, but also for Central and East European countries in general.

The third pillar of common asylum policy is that the social integration and legal status of recognized refugees has been partly neglected in comparison with restrictive measures directed against them. Refugees may enjoy certain advantages derived from free circulation in an integrated Europe and their status is moving closer to that of nationals. In the new host countries this convergence between nationals' and immigrants' status has not been adopted. Due to a reestablishment of laws on citizenship, national passport laws, minority and social rights, legal status and supporting programmes will not provide the necessary integrative conditions for really segregated and vulnerable groups.

Temporary protection

More and more persons are falling outside the established definition of a refugee who nonetheless need international protection. Civil wars, and ethnic or religious clashes generate massive outflows of refugees. According to the Edinburgh Declaration of 1993, in such cases action by the European Union will have to be directed to the restoration and preservation of peace. In addition, humanitarian assistance may contribute to alleviating the plight of displaced persons in the region of origin, because war refugees and uprooted people should be accommodated as closely as possible to their original homes, in order to allow a speedy return. Such assistance should, in particular, enable them to stay in the nearest 'safe havens' to their home. At first sight this appears a rational solution, but upon closer examination this proposal can be considered a cynical and selfish one. How are the refugees from a civil war to survive so close to the scene of their recent tragedy?

The history of suffering and persecution teaches us that the neighbours of a refugee's country of origin often experience the same poverty or have been rendered poorer due to the crisis in the region by, for example, a frozen transit trade and foreign investment. This 'next door' principle determines the fate of displaced persons and the burdens of host countries by their geographical position.

The 1991 Communication of the European Commission contains suggestions on a harmonization of rules and practices regarding *de facto* refugees but immigration ministers have not adopted specific proposals. Mass flows from Yugoslavia speeded up the process of considering what protection was to be offered to particularly vulnerable groups (at the Copenhagen Ministerial Meeting in June 1993). Temporary protection was to be provided for a sudden mass influx of persons in need of international protection. Although a resolution was adopted, the harmonized terms of temporary protection were not put on the agenda, and the measure remained within the competence of national legal frameworks.

An ad hoc committee on refugee law of the Council of Europe (CAHAR) did not go much further when it issued a report in 1993 on mass flows of refugees from Yugoslavia, merely recalling the importance of UNHCR EXCOM conclusions on minimal standards which should be provided for displaced persons and temporarily protected refugees in a mass inflow into a host country.[16]

A really welcome development would be to adopt a binding international instrument on temporary protection, on the basis of the above-mentioned EXCOM conclusions or of other human right instruments[17] as a harmonized legal solution. In the light of intra-European migratory movements, minimal standards of temporary reception for displaced persons are more urgent and important than a convention on manifestly unfounded asylum requests or on which should be the host third country.

The *non-refoulement* and safe country principle

For different political reasons, many European states have made their previous liberal asylum laws more restrictive. Multilateral treaties like the Schengen Agreements of 1985 and 1990, and the Convention that determines the state responsible for examining applications for asylum lodged in one of the member states of the EU (the Dublin Convention), the prepared Convention on the crossing of external borders and the Treaty on European Union reinforce these trends endangering the respect of the *non-refoulement* principle. These legal instruments represent a policy by the EU countries to minimize their exposure to refugee inflows from East and South, and to divert them to 'safe' or 'host third' countries away from the target country or even out of the EU area.

Since the 1970s the 'safe country principle' has also spread in Europe. It operates as a practice without a clear, detailed theoretical basis, due to the absence of a commonly accepted, clear definition. The harmonized interpretation and practical reciprocity of this principle have not yet been established. According to different national legal provisions, the 'safe country' principle functions, firstly, as a screening method to determine the admissibility of asylum requests, thus preventing a process of individual screening or, alternatively, as a clause to exclude a claimant being granted refugee status. This principle is preferred by administrative authorities because the competent administrators can avoid a lot of new asylum proceedings and prevent further backlogs. On the other hand, this principle is said to be a possible instrument of selection between applicants who need protection in the country where they have submitted the asylum request and applicants with manifestly unfounded asylum requests (for example, those who have enjoyed or can enjoy protection in a third host country). This probable selection is claimed to therefore contribute to a focusing on well-founded asylum application and genuine asylum-seekers.

In practice, there have been certain difficulties with the 'safe country' and 'host third country' principles.[18] According to international requirements, a country may be considered a safe one if, firstly, it is a state party to the 1951 Geneva Convention and/or the 1967 New York Protocol, and it provides legal opportunity for asylum procedure. Secondly, it must respect human rights in general and especially the right of return and family unity, and security must be ensured on its territory. Thirdly, protection must be provided against torture, inhumane and degrading treatment or punishment and against the activity of the security services of the country of origin. Fourthly, the applicant must be able to return and stay in that country without a risk of *refoulement*. Lastly, the recognition rate of asylum-applicants coming from that country must have remained under a certain level. No safety standards are established, because these preconditions are based on formal distinctions. For example, although some sending countries are state parties to the 1951 Geneva Convention and the 1967 New York Protocol, and they have ratified different human right instruments, they still ignore human rights standards either in general or in special fields. There are some other countries which acceded to the 1951 Geneva Convention with a geographical limitation. In this way these countries (for example Hungary) cannot be considered safe countries for applicants falling under this limitation. Finally, countries undergoing social and economic transition need a longer period to establish democratic and constitutional institutions under a rule of law.

The 'safe country' or 'host third country' principle is accompanied with the 'direct route requirement' which requires direct travel from the country of origin to the country of destination. This latter principle is transgressed if the applicant spends more than a determined (in the European provisions fourteen days to three months) period in a third country before his or her arrival at the intended destination state for submission of the asylum-request. These determined residence periods in a third country vary in national provisions. The residence duration has been neither standardized nor well-published. This exclusion clause does not make substantial distinction among individual motives, or reasons of residence in a transit country, such as unwanted or unpredictable technical, health or family circumstances.

A longer residence in a third, transit country may be connected with family, labour or cultural reasons in the most frequent cases. One of these prior connections to a third country is accepted by states (for example family reunification, a former job, studies, or the cultural proximity of minorities across the border) but without any standardization of these connections. In this way, there is a big variety of tolerated relations to third states and of their evidence based on more subjective justification.

There are available selected, up-to-date, relevant files on countries of origin. This fact does not mean that all other countries in the files may be automatically qualified as safe. Due to the absence of a safe country definition, it is necessary to collect legal and practical administrative data on:

- the *refoulement* and *non-refoulement* of asylum-seekers by administrative authorities in different states;
- readmission agreements in Europe;
- a standard meaning of 'non serious risk of persecution', frequently used as a

reason for refusal;
- evidence of transit and residence in a third country;
- a detailed itemization of the respect for human rights and their implementation towards certain social groups and minorities by countries in transition.

In addition, information and proof on safe countries are not only difficult to access, but lists of safe countries are not regularly published, or brought up-to-date in a proper way.

It is impossible to apply the 'safe country principle' in an isolated way. There are close interrelations between this principle and the other preventative and screening instruments toward asylum-seekers, for example the readmission agreements. Readmission agreements are an umbrella term that may cover the fate of migrants to a state which is responsible for their admission on the basis of an undertaken obligation (for example, between Hungary and the Ukraine, Romania, Slovenia, Austria and Croatia), or the travel and repatriation of rejected asylum-seekers, and on certain financial aid for readmission (for example, between Germany and Romania, and Bulgaria and Poland). Asylum-seekers who come illegally from a safe country or through a host transit country may be refused entry and subjected to readmission agreements more or less automatically without reference to any procedure on the merits or justification of any individual case. This may lead to the exclusion of even temporary protection for displaced persons in need.

Family unity

Although there exists a wide selection of international instruments that refer to the principles of family unity,[19] European countries allow a limited and different degree of family reunification. The first question attaches to the personal scope of lawfully admitted aliens. The Conference of Plenipotentiaries that adopted the 1951 Geneva Convention referred to this principle, but it was not embodied in the text itself. The reasons for this reluctance could be based on the fact that an improvement of family unification has created an opposition of interests in the sending, transit and receiving countries. Thus there is no chance of a universal, harmonized meaning and definition of this principle being accepted in the near future. The resolution adopted by the EU immigration ministers at Copenhagen in 1993 pays attention to certain categories of family members but not to a classification of convention refugees, temporaily protected and other lawfully resident immigrants' rights on family unity in practice.

The second question that needs to be discussed concentrates on family members (spouses, children, parents, grandparents, dependants, and siblings) and the preconditions for reunification (for example, the waiting period, and the maximum age of children entitled to be admitted for family reunification). Due to restrictive admission measures, family reunification, and immigration of family members will remain the main source, as well as the main channel for, migratory flows into and within Europe. A harmonization could be influenced by not only internationally legally binding instruments (in the UN, CE and EU) but even by cross-cultural factors (for example, polygamy, concubinage, and homosexual relationships). The Council of Europe has started discussions on this topic and data collection on legal provisions and practices concerning refugees and temporarily protected persons.[20]

A third, extensive and unresolved problem is connected to the assistance of family reunification in the authorization procedures (entry to a state, and the issue of visas and residence permits) and to social integration (in housing conditions, in the labour market or even by a family-oriented naturalization law). In the restrictive admission process the importance of an independent residence right, and the certification of family members after a qualifying period will be increased. On the other hand, if family reunification is limited in the West, a remigration flow will be provoked toward the transit states in Central and Eastern Europe, causing additional burdens on the families concerned as well as on the receivers.

Finally there is a serious need to urge the ratification of the UN Convention on Migrant Workers and their Families (1990) by more and more European states. This lesser known convention lays down the human rights of migrant workers, including those who are in an irregular situation. It makes clear a frequently ignored maxim that human rights should be applied irrespective of the legal status of the migrant concerned.

Repatriation

The best and the most cost-effective form of repatriation has remained voluntary repatriation, in close co-operation with international mediative organizations (for example, IOM and the UNHCR). The EU has expressed its concerns about the unintended migration attraction of promoting voluntary return, and thus no effort has been made to harmonize such schemes among member states. Only the Council of Europe has endorsed a certain preparation of co-operation in this field.[21] The key questions of voluntary repatriation are as follows: what might be the target groups (asylum-seekers during proceedings, asylum seekers ordered to leave, provisionally admitted aliens, former asylum seekers with a humanitarian permit, refugees); monitoring during and after arrival, safeguarding the rights, and protection of returnees and how these can be provided (by international organizations and NGOs); the re-integration and preventing re-emigration (on the basis of burden-sharing between the donors and country of origin). There are, however, more proposals in this field than there are results.

Burden-sharing

In the context of the flows from the former Yugoslavia, the host third countries are most likely to be those closest to the conflicts, such as Croatia, Slovenia, Hungary, the Czech Republic and Poland. Due to the safe country principle and the largest receiving country (Germany's) constitutional amendment, the pressures on the Eastern region may be particularly heavy. But none of these states has the necessary infrastructure, resources or experience to deal with large numbers of refugees.

The other weak point of the missing burden-sharing system is a clear classification of sharable burdens. For example, political tensions, growing intolerance and prejudice towards refugees can be reduced by humanitarian assistance in kind only in part. A less developed and experienced administration is not able to control and distribute the necessary information on accommodation needs, integration and cooperation in the most effective way. Deficits and wastage simultaneously characterize the new host countries.

Transit and newly receiving countries on the bumpy road toward a more effective European cooperation and burden-sharing model, could feel tempted to follow the EU lead by introducing some similar rules on the consignment of refugees to a 'safe first country' (such as the rough rules on manifestly unfounded application and safe country principle adopted in 1993 by the Czech Parliament through the amendment of its Act on Asylum in 1990). This policy may stimulate a conceivably endless exchange of different groups of asylum-seekers among the European states or a breakdown of law and order in the vulnerable Eastern host states because of refugee pressure.

Some conclusions

Experience indicates that restrictive policy measures, even if seemingly useful in the short-term, are of limited enduring use and have well-extended unpredictable effects on migratory movements. The more restrictive an admission policy is pushed, the larger and better organized are the illegal migration flows that can be caused. Instead of control-oriented measures, a human dimension-oriented migration management, a 'regulated openness', should be favoured. This suggested new approach may help to lessen the long-term impact of the totality of migratory movements on all actors. New doors should be opened for trans-European cooperation, thus reducing the burdens of geographically and socially vulnerable receivers and the pressure for massive emigration by dealing with root causes as well as humanitarian injustice.

Notes

1. Communication from the Commission to the Council and the European Parliament on Immigration and Asylum Policies (COM (94) Brussels, 1994).
2. IOM Migration Information Programme: Transit migration in Bulgaria, Poland and Czech Republic (April, 1994, Budapest).
3. Transit migration in Central and Eastern Europe (UN ECE Population Activity Unit) country reports related to two workshops (21-22 June 1993, Geneva and 16-17 December, 1993, Warsaw).
4. Legal cooperation between the Council of Europe and countries of Central and Eastern Europe - The conditions of aliens (Seminar by the CE, Barcelona, 8-10 March, 1994), state reports.
5. See Note 1 above.
6. See Note 4 above.
7. Secretariat of Informal Co-operation on Refugee Policy (January, 1994, Geneva).
8. See Note 1 above.
9. See Note 4 above.
10. See Note 3 above.
11. Ghosh, Bimal (1993), *The Future of East-West Migration* (manuscript)
12. Free Trade Agreement among the Central-Eastern European States (Poland, Czechland, Slovakia, Hungary) in 1993.
13. Recommendation 1188 (1992) by The Parliamentary Assembly, Council of Europe, on migratory flows in Czechoslovakia, Hungary and Poland.
14. ECRE Document (1990) on *Fair and Efficient Procedures for Determining Refugee Status*, October, London.
15. For example, see UNHCR EXCOM 1983/30. Conclusion on abuse of asylum or Resolution on manifestly unfounded application by Immigration Ministers, EC, November, 1992.
16. From *Selected Meeting Reports* by Council of Europe, CAHAR (1993-1994). The cited passage recalls UNHCR EXCOM Conclusion of 1979/15, 1980/19, 1981/22.
17. Council of Europe (1993), *Parliamentary Assembly Report on Right to Asylum* (by M.Frank) proposed a European Convention on territorial asylum or on right to *de facto* asylum or a new Protocol on asylum to the European Convention of Human Rights (1950).
18. 'Safe country principle' - CAHAR document issued by the Hungarian delegation (1993).
19. For example the (1948) Universal Declaration of Human Rights; the (1950) European Human Rights Convention, the (1975) Helsinki Process, Final Act.
20. 'Family unification' - CAHAR document issued by the Finnish delegation (1994).

21. 'Voluntary repatriation' - CAHAR document issued by the Swiss delegation (1993).

Annex 1

Asylum-seekers in Europe (1991-1993)

Receiving countries	1991	1992	1993
Belgium	15 354	17 647	22 039
Germany	256 112	438 191	322 599
Denmark	4 609	13 883	6 121
Spain	8 138	11 708	5 778
France	47 380	27 000	26 507
Greece	5 944	4 000	827
Ireland	31	250	65
Italy	28 000	2 500	1 075
Luxembourg	238	2 000	381
Netherlands	21 615	20 346	35 399
Portugal	163	200	2 091
UK	57 700	32 000	22 350
Austria	27 300	16 200	3 571*
Switzerland	41 600	18 100	15 808*
Norway	4 600	5 200	12 876
Sweden	27 300	83 200	37 700
Finland	2 100	3 600	1 930*
Subtotal	**548 184**	**696 025**	**517 117**
Hungary[a]	53 359	16 204	5 366
Poland	1 000*	1 350*	830
Czechoslovakia	2 944	762	0
Czech Republic	0	0	817*
Slovakia[a]	0	0	2 046
Total	**604 512**	**714 341**	**526 176**
[a]with Yugoslavians			
Bulgaria	n.d.	n.d.	219

* partial data

Sources: see notes 1, 4 and 5.